LONERGAN
AND
SPIRITUALITY

Towards a Spiritual Integration

Tad Dunne, S.J.

A Campion Book

LOYOLA UNIVERSITY PRESS

Chicago

© 1985 Tad Dunne, S.J.
Printed in the United States of America

Loyola University Press
3441 North Ashland Avenue
Chicago, Illinois 60657

Design by C. L. Tornatore

Library of Congress Cataloging in Publication Data

Dunne, Tad, 1938-
  Lonergan and spirituality.

  Bibliography: p. 229
  1. Lonergan, Bernard J. F.—Criticism and interpretation. 2. Spirituality—History of doctrines—20th
century. I. Title.
BX4705.L7133D86 1985   230'.2'0924   85-10148
ISBN 0 8294-0495-3

To Margaret

Contents

Preface

This book is addressed first of all to men and women who hold the following beliefs:

1. that the best life is a spiritual life;
2. that the only adequate social solutions to the world's problems must have a spiritual foundation;
3. that a spirituality for today needs to integrate these personal and social dimensions into a harmonious whole.

Hence the subtitle, "Towards a Spiritual Integration."

Secondly, this book is addressed to those who realize how necessary it is to reflect on method as well as content in science and scholarship today. Thus our aim will be the same as Bernard Lonergan's. His major works, *Insight* and *Method in Theology*[1], aim towards integrating scientific, scholarly, philosophic, and pastoral endeavors to bring the world back to its senses. This integration is not some doctrine about spirituality. Nor does it start from any theory in the ordinary sense of that term. Instead it begins with the presence or absence of conversion in those of us who hope to do something practical for the betterment of the world. It spells out the spiritual processes by which we

---

1. *Insight: A Study of Human Understanding* (London: Longmans, Green and Co., 1957); *Method in Theology* (New York: Herder & Herder, 1972).

produce and criticize all doctrines and theories. And it specifies the strategies needed to organize a wide variety of disciplines so that we may cooperate with God's redemption intelligently.

So this book may be thought of as an introduction to Bernard Lonergan for those who know little about his work. But it is also an extension of his thought into the area of spirituality for those who know his work well.

Lonergan's own writing style is quite compendious. Many students find his works difficult to read because they are unfamiliar with the specific philosophic myths and contemporary ideologies which Lonergan wants to expose. Therefore I have included many concrete examples throughout the text. I have also added questions at the end of chapters two through five to facilitate classroom discussions of the contents of those chapters. I hope to bridge the gap between abstract methodological reflections and the familiar questions that arise from our everyday experiences.

Thirdly, this book is meant to contribute to the ecumenical movement in the widest sense. Therefore it is not meant exclusively for Catholics or Protestants. It is not even written exclusively for Christians. Now I happen to be white, male, a Roman Catholic, a Jesuit, a priest, and an American with Irish and Canadian roots. So some of my examples will surely reveal the limitations and blind spots that go with any person's biography.

Nevertheless, there is a great deal that can be said about "God" and about the redemption of the world without starting from doctrines formulated in particular historical circumstances. We will begin with the human person as full of wonder, as questioner, as feeling drawn towards what makes sense, what is truly worthwhile, what is worthy of love. It is this experience of being drawn beyond ourselves that gathers men and women of any culture and any religion into those movements that might be called ecumenical.

Behind every book stands not only an author, who must take criticism alone, but a community, with whom he or she must share any credit. So let me acknowledge my community of reflection.

Credit is surely due to the faculty and students of Regis College of the Toronto School of Theology. Their enthusiasm for my interests and their kind correctives have been an indispensable support. In particular I want to mention Margaret Brennan, IHM, to whom this book is dedicated. During my eight years of teaching at Regis, Margaret and I have worked together in the Integration for Ministry Program. Her dedication to the church and her vision for ministry have enabled me to experience that special kind of love that springs from loving the good together.

Then there is Bernard Lonergan, SJ, a man who knew more about love and has sacrificed more self-interest for love's sake than nearly anyone I know.

Heartfelt gratitude also to those who labored over the manuscripts with me: Brendan Carmody, SJ, Dianne Heinrich, CSP, Richard Bautch, NSJ, and Robert Flack, SJ. Finally, if gratitude can be called a debt, then when I think of what I owe to the brotherhood of the Society of Jesus I can only declare myself bankrupt.

CHAPTER ONE

An Integrating Spirituality

Since our overall aim is to outline a strategy for changing the social order through a "spiritual integration," let us begin by looking at how the social order and spirituality are related. We will first propose a thesis that locates a common core in both. Then we will examine how poorly we in the twentieth century have worked out that relationship. From there our strategy ought to be fairly clear.

1. Order

When we look at the disorder of our world, we cannot help but have some prior notion of order. Every thinker—philosopher, historian, literary critic, or scientist—thinks of being human as a quest for order. We expect to find the struggle for order whether we are looking at the history of an entire civilization, at classical literature, or at a psychological neurosis. Obviously we do not expect to find peaceful order everywhere, but neither do we expect to find total chaos. No matter where we look, we find seekers and wonderers suffering an unquenchable desire for order.

This does not mean that every man and woman is a pure seeker. An arrogant ruthlessness lives in each of us. We see it in the totalitarian dictator as well as in the militant capitalist. And yet, our most malicious brothers and sisters have something in common with the most altruistic. Both are responsible for the actual social order or disorder that exists. In other words, we can trace the outer breakdown of social order to some inner breakdown in the personal order, just as we can trace social progress to its sources in an inner personal achievement of the soul.

1

Where society does break down, whether it is due to malice or weakness and ignorance, the locus of the breakdown is not City Hall or Moscow or Wall Street. It lies in the inner processes of real persons, in men and women with names and addresses. They may be linked together in common cause, but never without the inner acts of belief and consent. So the quest for order which constitutes the meaning of being human appears simultaneously as a quest for an ordered soul within an ordered civilization. We cannot have one without the other. The thesis upon which this book stands can now be stated forthrightly: The foundations for order in the soul and for order in society are the same thing.

What does this expression mean, "foundations for order in the soul"? The word *foundation* can evoke a picture of the cement blocks supporting a house, but that image is too static for our purposes. *Foundation* can also evoke a picture of civic leaders organizing a city, as in the "foundation of Rome," and this gets a little closer to what we want because it includes the more dynamic origin and interchange of ideas and values. Still, our thesis is meant to evoke a third and more basic picture of a foundation within the soul that itself is the recurrent cause of buildings being built and cities being founded.[1] Strictly speaking, the soul should not be conceived as a process that is ordered but rather as a process that does the ordering. Furthermore, the soul is designed not only to put buildings and cities in order, drawing from its own ordered ideas; it must also order itself. So the foundations for order in the soul already belong in some way to the soul. What our thesis means is this: There are norms built into the soul that we can discover, and these norms have the power to put order not only into our communities but also to put order into the soul itself.

This sounds very optimistic. History urges us to add immediately that the achievement of the ordered soul and an ordered society is a constant struggle, and it is subject to failure. Within most failures, whether accidental or deliberate, we can discern a mistaken view of how the soul stands in relation to the social order. The mistake of the social activist is that he or she thinks that, given enough hard work and dedication and self-sacrifice, a social order will emerge which will replace the need to struggle for spiritual integrity. Such activists have been so impressed by the arguments put forth by Marxists and liberal sociologists — arguments that human thinking is largely shaped by the economic and social systems—that they seize on these systems as the real source of disorder in the commonweal. Their mistake leads to a twin disaster.

In the public sphere they fail to understand the inner roots of what their Christian counterparts call the "social structure of sin" and, lacking this requisite understanding, they apply all their remedies to the symptoms rather than to the causes of social decay. Their efforts may temporarily hold in check this or that group driven by the heart's desire for power or money or revenge, but success is short-lived. Not only are there other oppressive groups lining up for employment, but the recently liberated oppressed use their new power to drive the same oppressive machines over other people.

There is also a disaster going on here in the private sphere. Activists generally do not attend to matters of the inner heart in their own lives, and consequently they have no real experience of quality living. They fail to live on a level of interiority which, ironically, they strive to make possible for everyone else. If they never allow themselves the enjoyment of the values of silence, of beauty, of solitude, of celebration, then they are never in a position to help others appreciate them. Burn-out is inevitable. So their efforts do not last, and it is a pity that good hearts have been charred beyond recognition.

2. *The Split Soul*

Ordinarily we do not create meaning anew. We accept or reject a tradition, a set of cultural mores, an inherited religion. We test the practicality of theories that have been handed down to us, usually in a form abbreviated by commentators. But we usually do not examine theories about personhood or community in any systematic fashion. Yet this is not to say that ordinary people do not think about these things. We think about them all the time. The trouble is, our thinking always seems to get confused as soon as we ask about root causes of social disorder and about needed correctives. While we may be very perceptive about how this week's news developed out of last week's, few people, including economic theorists and political scientists, ever attempt explanations of a more general nature. The usual result is unenlightened action that looks good in the short run but, in the long run, proves to complicate the problem further. No doubt, then, there is something wrong with our thinking about social problems.

3

Why have we not proved equal to this intellectual challenge? The answer given by most Christians is that intellectual work is not only difficult but also impractical and, in too many cases, productive of more harm than good. So we are caught on the horns of a dilemma. Shall we trust our common sense, our generosity, our practicality and avoid theorizing altogether, or shall we attempt yet another theory about human persons in community in the hope that it might give us the direction we so desperately need?

This dilemma has been with us for a long time, and we have already tried to deal with it in several ways. There have always been, and probably always will be, good-hearted but weak-minded people willing to sacrifice all their time and energy in social projects. This is the activist solution. It eschews theory and embraces instead the stirring image of a self-sacrificing Christ, the "one for others," as if Christ could have been untouched by the world of theory had he lived in our own times.

At the opposite pole, there is the spiritualist solution, which eschews both commonsense practicality and all theory in favor of interior union with God and constant prayer for others. I do not mean to imply that this position is afraid of involvement with the world. Holy men and women have always been courageous in their struggles against the forces of evil. But many a holy person has been tainted with a form of unthinking obedience which, although they are willing to be an instrument of God's salvation in the world, they despair of understanding how that salvation works itself out concretely in history. They do not care to understand why cities rise and why they crumble, why arts and letters make for a better life, or why Ireland or the Middle East are engaged in protracted civil wars. They see little hope in studying economics or psychology or history from a Christian point of view.

For most of us, however, activism and unthinking obedience represent extreme positions. We fancy ourselves able to live in the secular world in an active, meaningful way and still be able to move easily into a religious world where we dedicate ourselves to loving God and neighbor in genuine charity. After all, what else can we do in the face of a secular culture but learn to get along with it at times, but get along without it also? This is the preferred solution and, for that reason, it is the more damaging to the soul and to the human order. At least mindless activism and mindless religious devotion are easily recognized

4

and easily accused of mindlessness. But is anyone bothered by the fact that he or she lives in two worlds? Look at what this requires of us. It obviously tends to make religion a Sunday-only reality. But on a deeper level, it splits our very souls into two different worlds, each with its own language, its own view of human struggle, and its own purposes. In one language we may speak of economic booms, tax reform, emotional problems, juvenile delinquency, advertising campaigns, and so on. In the other language we speak of the Lord, of the Cross, of grace and providence, of discerning spirits, and of prayer. But there is no way to speak both languages in the same sentence. Nor is there a sharing of languages between two groups. We have one group of secular friends and one group of religious friends. If we are fortunate and have the same friends in both groups, we may be able to move from one language to another, but our friends must move when we do. Let one not talk about social progress while the other talks about divine providence.

The fact that we must speak two languages, secular and religious, should make us suspect that we also have two minds about the world. For example, with our secular mind we accept the adversarial style of interpreting world events that characterizes our news corporations. Even when we disagree with the interpretations themselves, we still think in this Who-Is-the-Enemy-Now? fashion. On the other hand, in our religious mind we are expected to imagine God as loving the sinner while hating the sin. In other words, while our secular mind pits one group against another, our religious mind pits all human beings against the malice in their own hearts. The real enemy, we say, is within. But we rarely find a religious sister, a priest or bishop, or a layperson, who is truly free from an adversarial view of human conflicts, whether international or the conflicts at their own dinner tables. And just as rarely do we find politicians who are truly concerned about the inner integrity of the people whose minds they want to change. Only with great difficulty does Christianity speak for social justice in ways that make practical sense to a secular world, while at the same time showing some of God's infinite love for every last human being. We are of two minds and we cannot easily put them together.

Living in two worlds, with two languages and two minds, it is no surprise to find that we are bewildered about the purpose of life, so bewildered that the expression *purpose of life* itself has become meaningless. To most people, it evokes an image of life as it ought to be ("The purpose of life is community!"), or, for the less sanguine, life as it most likely will remain ("Life is dog-eat-dog"). To some others (Ayn Rand and liberal democracy in general), "purpose in life" refers only to individual goals. There is no "purpose" other than what people in fact desire. The religious view is that God has "purposes"—that these are truly the "purpose of life" and that any other conception should be connected to this basic meaning. But who among us can easily speak about God's will to the terminally ill, the jobless, the tortured, to say nothing of corporate executives, politicians, and the extremely wealthy? Who, indeed, make it their regular effort to integrate their personal goals with the purpose for which God made them?

3. Understanding Change

How has this schizophrenia come about? Certainly there are plenty of historical figures connected with the split between the religious and the secular spheres—Voltaire, Machiavelli, Marx, Freud. But no historical explanation can overlook a fundamental shift that has taken place in the West. It is a shift in what we mean by the word *knowledge*.

During the past 700 years, Christians have been able to achieve some measure of intellectual integration of the soul with the order of the universe. The effectiveness of this integration usually depended on the fortunes of the Thomistic synthesis. But while the schools seemed to carry on a love-hate relationship with Thomas, there was another set of changes taking place that Thomas never dreamt possible and that Thomists largely ignored: the emergence of empirical method in science and historiography.

What these disciplines brought to the Western mind was the question, How did change occur? It was a new kind of question because the Aristotelian/Thomistic synthesis, as well as its Platonic/Augustinian rival, thought that a true science, as opposed to mere common sense, could make statements only about what is fixed as true. Science could not deal with what changes. Today we are satisfied with a science that gives us explanations that are merely likely. We do not need certitudes. We need only enough understanding to be able to cooperate with material reality and with one another in a functional way, and so we may find the more ancient notion of science rather strange.

Where knowledge used to mean certitude about facts, it now means understanding how things work.[2]

We ought to reflect, however, on what a massive difference this new question has made to our spiritual integration. In our religious living, we still largely depend on what we hold as certain, or at least on those beliefs we have committed ourselves to, even though we might not understand what effect these beliefs have in our culture. At the same time, in our secular living, it is normal to want to understand, and to be modest about certitudes. Thus we cling to the classical ideal of science in our spirituality while we embrace the empirical ideal in our daily lives.

Let me give a few examples. In the Gospels we are urged to turn the other cheek, walk the second mile, refrain from asking for our property back from a robber. Or, in the Spiritual Exercises of St. Ignatius, the retreatant is led to prefer poverty, contempt, and humility out of a desire to imitate Christ. These texts bother us. We say to ourselves that they represent extreme ideals because the pure case never seems to arise for us. But there is another explanation of why we are bothered, one that pivots on our need for understanding how change functions. We have been given these ideals to believe in, and, because of our need to ask the empirical question, "How does this change occur?" we need to see what such non-retaliatory practice does to our selves, our communities, and to the larger social order.

Gandhi saw it. His commitment to non-violence was not merely obedience to an injunction or an ideal. He understood how passive resistance worked to turn the hearts of enemies and to break down the us-against-them view of human conflicts. But we Christians have little "understanding" of self-sacrifice, in the sense of an empirical theory that explains how things function. We believe in redemption; we believe that redemption somehow comes through love and self-giving; but there simply is no generally accepted grasp of how the values emerging from faith actually work to turn around a declining culture. Before the scientific revolution, our ancestors lived in a hierarchical universe, and so Christian values were legitimated by looking to see who was offering them, and by asking whether this line of tradition lay within the hierarchical pyramid at whose apex was Jesus, the Apostles, and the canonical Scriptures. But now we need to legitimate spiritual values further by understanding how they function in

7

the psychological and social orders. And the trouble is that few people are aware of this need. We trudge on in our double-mindedness, convinced of God's authority and love, but confused about how they enter the human order.

We can expect that if we have artificially divided our minds into two parts, then something will go wrong in each part. The evidence is overwhelming that this is the case. In our secular minds, we have become expert in dealing with quantifiable processes, but we fail when it comes to understanding and enhancing the quality of life. So the natural sciences are successful while the human sciences lag behind. We can build a technology, but we still cannot build an orderly economy, let alone a just political and cultural order.

Meanwhile, in our religious minds, we gradually learn to refine our prayer; we learn to distinguish the more important doctrines of the church from the less important ones; we become familiar with degrees of authority in official pronouncements and degrees of assent in ourselves; we have begun to investigate the relations between spirituality and psychology and the arts. But only sporadic efforts have been made to relate spirituality to social justice, to economics, and to the fundamental problem of understanding historical process.

From the point of view of the religious mind, the secular mind appears materialist. Even though it is rooted in highly analytical techniques, it is not satisfied with ideas. The secular mind wants tangible results and it wants them now. It relies on quantitative measures rather than qualitative. It regards the material surroundings of living rather than the spiritual core. It regards human conflicts as them-over-there against us-over-here. But the religous mind can equally be criticized by the secular mind. The religous meaning of *knowledge*, rooted as it is in a penchant for absolutes, tends to be idealist. So the religious mind speculates on what could be, and it overlooks what is. It gets lost in grand theories in the sky while ignoring the plight of real people on the ground. It may be more qualitative and spiritual than the materialist approach, but it is beseiged by material evidence that belies its lofty visions.

We must point out that we are not speaking of two groups of people, each with its own kind of singlemindedness. We are speaking of single individuals with two minds at odds with one another—a spiritual mind that clings to truths and a secular mind that seeks explanations for change. We are speaking of people who have to live in a culture that differentiates the secular and the sacred, but lacks the power to integrate them. We are speaking of ourselves.

4. *The Realist Mind*

Notice that as we reflect on our double-mindedness, we spontaneously take on a third mind: a realistic mind, a critical mind. We point to the limitations of materialism and idealism by appealing to a kind of realism. Our explanations had better fit our experience or we will look for a better explanation.

At first it may seem that this third mind, while it can criticize all performance and every ideal, fails completely when it comes to offering a method and a vision for action of its own. Just as good movie critics are not necessarily good movie directors, so the critical, realistic mind is not necessarily a creative, visionary mind.

But movie critics can educate directors about their own work. In a paradoxical fashion one critic can name the struggles going on within the director, of which even the director had been unaware. It is in exactly this sense that we want to use our realistic and critical mind to analyze the ordering processes that make up the soul. And so we will examine such processes as experience, understanding, judgment, decision, feelings, imagination, and love. We will follow the analyses given by Bernard Lonergan, but, like him, we do not intend to present the analyses as theories for everyone to believe. The whole point of this book is to understand and to verify for ourselves that our knowing, our acting, and our loving are of a certain character. This is a lab book, in other words, which contains a set of hypotheses about the soul for us to test.

By analyzing and verifying how each of our souls is an ordering process, we will be explicitly helping our souls to order themselves. We are trying to be realistic here, not about the social order directly, but rather about the order of the soul. We will first try to be as realistic as we can about the very nature of being realistic. What exactly goes on when we reach knowledge? How do these interior processes combine under the different tasks that confront psychologists, sociologists, historians? How do value judgments and friendships function in our ordering processes? How, indeed, do these same processes combine in the theologian and in the man or woman at prayer?

9

It should be clear where we are headed. If we can grasp the processes of the soul as functionally related to the creation of the social, historical order and to the love of God, then we will have spelled out for ourselves what our "foundations" really are. From there we will possess a single language about matters both sacred and secular. We will have a hold on a single mind—one that has integrated its own materialist and idealist routines into a coordinated, realistic whole. Our faith will not simply clutch at truths; it will also understand their meaning and functioning in the world we care about. By understanding our own interior processes, we will also understand the typical ways in which these ordering processes fail. In other words, we will understand what we call "sin" in terms that are intelligible to contemporary science.

I have been describing what Lonergan calls "intellectual conversion."[3] It is not a religous conversion in which we fall in love with God. I presume this has happened to you. Nor is it a moral conversion in which the objectively good means more than the subjectively comfortable. This too, I presume, has happened to you. But what very likely has not yet happened, or has only begun to happen, needs to be faced squarely. If you and I are to cooperate intelligently with God's redemption of our world, we need to understand for ourselves how the order of our souls functions as a source of the greatest of human achievements, likewise a source of the greatest disasters, and, thank God, as the means of the greatest divine graces.

In the following chapters we will examine the order of the soul in three steps. First we will examine how our knowing works. Some of the most basic differences between thinkers lie not in what they think about familiar topics but in what they think about thinking itself. So in chapter 2 we will examine the thinking processes that go on in each of us and try to spell out some rules on how to think more clearly and effectively. This will lead naturally to chapter 3, where we will look at how human thinking heads towards decision-making and action. There we will examine the role of feelings, memories, and conscience and explain how they function in creating a social order. Then, in chapter 4, we will look at the finest work of the soul, being in love. We will look at both human and religious loving and, again, we will see what differences loving makes to the social order.

From this high point of being in love, we will then turn to an examination of what it means to be a person in history. I have entitled chapter 5 "Storytelling" because only in telling stories do we really make history.

Finally, we will conclude with a summary chapter on what all this means for the spiritual integration of each of us and for the human community at large.

Notes to Chapter One

1. I am following Lonergan's notion of foundations as found in *Method in Theology*, pp. 130–132, 267–293.

2. See Bernard Lonergan, "Dimensions of Meaning" in F.E. Crowe, ed., *Collection* (Montreal: Palm Publishers, 1967), pp. 259–261. See also "Future of Thomism," "Theology in Its New Context," "Belief: Today's Issue," "Theology and Man's Future" in W.J.F. Ryan and B.J. Tyrrell, eds., *Second Collection* (London: Darton, Longman & Todd, 1974), pp. 47–48, 55–57, 94–95, and 139–140, respectively.

3. *Method in Theology*, pp. 238–240.

CHAPTER TWO

Knowing

The soul has been imagined by many philosophers as a kind of black box that takes in perceptions at one end and puts out words and actions at the other. To understand the order of the soul would appear to be a matter of grasping what goes on between that input and that output. But this picture is rather misleading. Once we begin to look at the perceptions that the soul presumably takes in, we realize that not all the input comes from the outside. Indeed, the soul first experiences interior inclinations, feelings, questions, wonderment; and, on account of these actions already going on within, it turns to the exterior world with its attention already channelled in specific directions.

It is because of these processes already going on in each of us that we inquire about the soul in the first place. But these processes *are* the soul, or at least the cognitive part of it. So, instead of imagining the soul as out there to be looked at, we will do better to start with our own experience of these interior inclinations, feelings, questions, and wonderment. Then, like detectives, we will look for clues within these experiences, trying to understand how they connect to one another. Then we will attempt to state our case on how knowing works, appealing to the evidence available to everybody within their own selves.

1. *Experience, Understanding, Judgment*

Our approach, then, following Lonergan's analysis,[1] will be to grasp the general relationship between human experience and human understanding, and then to relate both to human judgment. Why these terms are so important will become evident as we go along. First let us look at the relation between experience and understanding.

By *experience* we mean not only the external data that come through our five external senses, but also the interior data that come through innumerable internal senses that we have yet to name. By raising the question of the general relationship between experience and understanding, we presume that not all experience is always understood, but that experience can be understood. Indeed, experience does not become significant and is often not even noticed except insofar as we approach it with a view to understanding it.

We see this relationship between experience and understanding when we give names to things. Whenever we understand that one set of experiences is significantly different from others, we give it a name. And until we know the names associated with specific sets of experiences, those experiences just blend in with the background noise of our perceptual world. For example, unless I know such names as puce and mauve, I ordinarily do not perceive any difference in the colors they stand for. Similarly, the emotional development of youngsters growing up is roughly proportional to the number of distinct feelings they can name. An adult knows the subtle difference between resentment and jealousy, while a child knows only the elemental difference between feeling good and feeling bad.

Our understanding does more than simply *distinguish* experiences and *name* them. It also *correlates* one set of experiences with another, so that we associate smoke with fire and red sky at night with sailors' delight. This fundamental correlation is hardly scientific understanding. It is rather the practical matter of distinguishing and grouping large sets of experiences. In a word: familiarity.

Besides distinguishing, naming, grouping, and correlating experiences, our understanding can grasp precise relations between different sets of experiences. In other words, we can catch on to the idea of cause. For example, if I eat bacon and eggs every Saturday morning and suffer a headache every Saturday afternoon, I might make the connection and grasp a relation of causality between my diet and my throbbing head. Here, though, I use names of a second order—*cause, because,* and *on account of*—to express linked experiences. Without a fully developed second-order language that can express the wide variety of possible relations *between* experiences, we would not enjoy a fully developed grasp of the nature of the links.

In the New Testament, for example, we find Jesus making the ex-

14

traordinary announcement that he came not to bring peace but the sword, and to divide a family against itself (Mt 10:34). Exegetes assure us that Jesus did not *intend* to destroy peace, but that he simply *expected* his coming to destroy the peace. They point out that New Testament authors had not developed the second-order distinction between "purpose clauses" and "result clauses." Similarly, modern physics has had to define heat in contrast to temperature, and mass in contrast to weight, and so on, to be able to grasp the general relations governing data on physical things in the patterned forms in which they appear. I do not think it would be an exaggeration to say that every great advance in philosophical and scientific knowledge depended upon the creation of a second-order language that expressed the new understanding accurately.

To sum up what we have seen thus far, we can say that the act of understanding is a grasp of *why* data are related the way they are. Understanding grasps an intelligibility which is immanent in the data by posing and answering the question why or how. It moves first by distinguishing experiences (and so naming them) and then by getting an insight into the order that seems to keep one set of data in a specific relation to another set. This act of understanding, which we are also calling an *insight,* is a real event. I stress this because once we start examining it, we may be surprised to learn how silent the act is, how independent of physical movement, how difficult to represent in our imagination, and so we may wonder whether it exists at all. But insight is a real event; it is a real change in our understanding, not in our retinas.

We have been saying that what we experience is subject to understanding. But our experience is also subject to misunderstanding. Or we can come up with two different explanations of the same data. So there is a further process in thinking which we call *judgment.* Our minds are not content with an understanding that is merely orderly in itself; explanations should cohere with the full data of experience. So, by a judgment, we return to the experience to test our explanations. If one explanation leaves too many questions unanswered, we throw it out. If another explanation seems to account for all the data, we judge it to be correct. If no explanation fits the data, we can only judge ourselves to be uncertain and we will keep looking for other explanations. In all this we aim at reaching the truth, at understanding something as

15

it really is. We do not reach the truth of reality through experience alone. Nor do we accomplish it even through the most brilliant insight into that experience. We reach reality only when we pass judgment on the correctness of our insight. It is only when we check the data again to see whether our understanding leaves no relevant data unexplained that we can say whether or not we understand the reality in question correctly.

Notice that understanding and judgment are quite distinct operations. Understanding yields explanations; it answers the questions why and how. Ask me why or how, and I speak of causes, patterns, correlations. Judgment, in contrast, yields no explanations at all; it merely affirms or denies; it answers the question whether. Ask me whether or not something is so, and I will answer yes, or no, or perhaps, or probably. Even if you ask me whether some explanation is correct, I do not give the explanation again; I answer yes or no. But understanding and judgment are linked inasmuch as the explanations issuing from understanding are still subject to verification. A bright idea is not necessarily a right idea. It belongs to the very dynamics of our minds to want to know about reality, not just to become familiar with ideas.

For the sake of fixing our terms, let us associate experience with being attentive, understanding with being intelligent, and judgment with being reasonable or realistic.

Now experience, understanding, and judgment not only have different objects (respectively: data, intelligibility, and reality); they also feel different within ourselves. When we are merely attentive, we are observant, sensitive, and experiencing; but we are not asking questions about what we are experiencing. For example, when we are basking in the sun or suffering from an illness, we often deliberately put our minds to rest. When we do ask a question about what we experience, our consciousness of ourselves changes dramatically. We wonder why or how. We play with the data and, with luck, we will enjoy an insight that gives a plausible explanation. So the feeling of being intelligent is quite different from the feeling of merely being attentive. Likewise, when we move to the judgment that settles on which explanation best fits the experience, our consciousness again changes dramatically. It is the feeling of being reasonable or realistic. Next we wonder whether the workings of our mind really have met the realities about which we inquire, and sometimes we hit the nail on the head.

16

Because knowing is a combination of three distinct processes, we can easily see how some people use their heads ineffectively. Some people are very attentive, but not very intelligent. They can be extremely perceptive insofar as they notice subtle changes in details or in the mood of a situation, but they do not easily inquire *why* the changes have occurred. They are fascinated with experience but obtuse about understanding. Then there are people who are both attentive and intelligent, but not very reasonable. They notice changes and easily ask why, but they seize on the first bright idea that enters their heads, and they do not test it against the data. They live in their heads in the sense that they love explanations but hate the limits of reality as it actually appears in the stubborn data. In contrast, people who think effectively will use their powers of attention, intelligence, and reason in an integrated fashion.

Unfortunately, we are not born completely attentive, intelligent, and reasonable. As we grew up, we not only had to learn about the world around us, we also had to learn how to use our heads. In other words, besides learning about toys, trees, kitchens, and so on, we also learned the ranges, the limits, and the interconnections of experience, understanding, and judgment, even though few of us bothered to formulate the rules for thinking which we were actually following. Let me spell this out in more detail.

As children, we specialized in being attentive. We noticed at first far more data than we could ever understand. Then, gradually, as we understood practical ways of getting our desires met at home, and as we understood the formal rules of games, the social rules of fairness, and the mechanical workings of toys, we also understood something of how understanding could make sense out of experience. We understood, for example, that *playing* with the data of experience often gives an insight into how to be more practical, more inventive, more friendly, and more secure.

Later on, as teenagers, we learned the sobering truth that not all ideas are equally valid. The validity of an idea has to be tested by a reasonable return to the experiences that the idea is about. Still, like the child in us who learned to give experience as free a play as possible, we learned to give our understanding such a free play too, because we discovered that it improved the chances of hitting on explanations that were more probably correct. A person's high school years may be laced with fantastic explanations and wild dreams, but in normal intellectual growth, these dreams and visions are the midwives of reality as we subject them to the scrutiny of judgment.

But this learning to play with experience and to play with understanding takes time, support, and discipline; not everyone is so blessed. Those who are blessed find themselves in a good position for eventually becoming what everybody calls "realistic." Their intelligence is not lost in the clouds. It wants to understand the reality of this world. They are not only attentive to a wide variety of experiences, and not only intelligent about why things function the way they do, but ultimately realistic about which explanations best account for the data of experience.

So human knowing is not just looking from in here at what is out there. Looking gives only data. Human knowledge also involves understanding and judgment. The act of understanding is an interior, constructive assembly. Knowing may begin from looking, or hearing, or tasting, or feeling, but then it tries out various understandings until there are no data left unexplained. If you were a father trying to understand your teenage daughter, you would not spend all your time intently staring at her or trying to notice every last detail of her behavior. Looking is just experience. Rather, you would seek various explanations for the phenomena you experience. You would test out your interpretations to see if they make the obvious data intelligible. With any wisdom, you would not necessarily settle for the simplest explanation, but rather with the explanation that accounts for most of the questions you can think of. And even then, you might still be bothered by unformulatable questions, and so you humbly pronounce your judgment to be merely probable or conditional.

I hope the explanation thus far is clear enough. But let me add a warning about dangers ahead. It's extraordinary how frequently students of the human spirit find themselves talking as though knowing were nothing more than experience, long after they have verified its compound structure. So I would like to give some idea of (1) what understanding the structure involves and (2) what verifying the correctness of that understanding involves.

1. All you see on this page are black marks. By means of them, all I am offering is an explanation. I trust you have been trying to understand my explanation. You may have made a sketch of the structure of knowing, perhaps on paper, but almost certainly in your mind:

experience corresponds to data; understanding corresponds to intelligibility; judgment corresponds to reality. Notice that having the sketch in mind is not necessarily understanding. The sketch may be necessary, but you understand insofar as you grasped the relations between the three processes in consciousness, and between these processes and the realities you seek to know. A child, even a machine, could reproduce the sketch; but only an intelligent adult can grasp the intelligible relations involved. Indeed, if you have grasped the intelligibility, you can tear up any sketches you may have drawn on paper. Your insight, your understanding, is the source of all intelligible sketches and verbal explanations. Understanding the explanations which I am offering will not be too difficult as long as you realize that having a picture or a schematic diagram in mind is merely an aid to understanding and an aid to communicating that understanding to others. If all you can do is reproduce the pictures from memory, and not from intelligent understanding, then you have not understood why these black marks are patterned in the way you see them, nor, therefore, have you understood how knowing probably works.

2. What is more difficult is verification, particularly as we go further in our explanations. Understanding the explanations is not sufficient for us to reach knowledge of how in fact we know. There may be better explanations, so we have to make a judgment. To pass judgment on the correctness of this understanding, we have to return to the data to see if the explanation accounts for the whole of it. But the interior data on all the acts involved in knowing are complex, so we can expect to pass judgment with certainty on basic broad lines, but with some hesitancy about further details. And yet, the basic broad lines which we have already named—experience, understanding, judgment—are surprisingly easy to affirm. In fact, should anyone deny that knowing is a matter of experience, understanding, and judgment, such a person would be making a judgment on the correctness of an understanding of experience, and by that very performance he or she would be providing confirming evidence that knowing is structured as we say it is. However, as we go on to speak of conscience, love, religious experience, feelings, history, event, symbol, discernment of spirits, and so on, we will find that verification takes some time, dependent as it is on a conviction that the explanations must cover data whose relevance may not be immediately apparent.

2. *Belief*

Next we must speak of belief.[2] For while it may be very clear that knowing is a compound of experience, understanding, and judgment, very little of what you and I actually know has come from our own personal experience, understanding, and judgment. Most of our knowledge comes from believing others. Just think of everything we read in newspapers or watch on TV, or all the stories we know about family or friends. Likewise in schools, there is far more believing taking place than learning for ourselves firsthand. The experimental physicist takes as much on belief as the historian does.

And yet, is it not true that what we believe is somewhere rooted in somebody's immanently generated knowledge; that is, on the verified understanding of experience of some person or persons? Granted, a lot of what we take to be true may actually be mere fancy, but that makes a big difference to us. Either somebody is making up stories, as in the case of Orson Welles' "War of the Worlds" radio broadcast, or else people misunderstand their experience, as was the case when everyone thought that the earth was flat. So when we believe, we are depending upon somebody's real experience, real understanding, and real judgment. Even when we are skeptical, we are not skeptical about the value of belief in general. On the contrary, we are anxious to eliminate mistakes from our set of beliefs, because without belief each of us would know practically nothing.

It is important to notice that the knowledge that comes to us through belief does not necessarily begin from the immanently generated knowledge of one person. For example, we are fairly certain that cigarette smoking causes cancer. Now this is a statement of probabilities that holds for a large population, so the relevant data are not directly experienced by any one person. Individuals suffer disease; doctors submit reports; researchers believe the reports; theoreticians pursue insight into data that come to them in written form; and a tentative conclusion is reached that smoking causes cancer. We know this, but the knowledge was generated by the direct experience of a large group, a combination of beliefs and insights by a smaller group, and a judgment reached by a few, which they present for the belief of the largest possible group so that the rest of us may avoid the disease.

There is another important complexity to notice. Beliefs seem to move downwards from judgment through understanding to experience. Take the following statement from Erik Erikson, for example. He has asserted that after people meet the crises of intimacy they normally face crises of generativity. Now college students who read that will first believe it, then understand something of the mechanism whereby it works, and only later on experience the raw data in their own lives. It may be true that we cannot verify in personal experience everything that we take on belief, but there is certainly a readiness to do so. We dislike dogmatists telling us what to believe without any appeal either to our understanding or to our experience.

In spite of these complexities, however, the structure of belief has a relatively simple core. To understand how it works, we have to introduce the notion of a judgment of value.

A judgment of value concerns the worth of something that already exists or the worth of bringing something into existence. In contrast, a judgment of fact concerns merely whether something does exist, whether something has occurred, or whether some explanation is correct; it does not regard value or worth. I happen to think it is valuable to know how to cook, but whether or not I am able to cook is a question of fact. We will discuss judgments of value in more detail in our next chapter. We will see that they move us beyond experiencing, understanding, and judging to deciding and acting. They move us from the cognitive sphere to the moral sphere. But for now it is enough to note the ways in which value judgments enter into the cognitive sphere and enable us to believe what others have come to know, even though we have not had their direct experience, understanding, and judgment ourselves.

In the act of belief, there are three discernible value judgments. First, there is the general judgment that it is better to believe other people than to start from a Cartesian universal skepticism; only rationalists and paranoids seem to have difficulty making that value judgment. Second, we deliberate on the trustworthiness of our sources. We all know that the word of some people cannot be trusted, even though, we must admit, the foolish now and then have something to say. Third, we deliberate on the value of believing specific contents. These contents may be a proposition about reality (most of us *believe* that humans have walked on the surface of the moon) or a proposition about worth (Westerners *believe* in the value of free speech).

Someone might doubt whether we ever have to make a judgment

on the worth of believing a proposition about reality. If reputable sources were to report a major oil discovery in Russia, how could there be anything about oil being discovered which would make a person deliberate about believing it? Do we really ever doubt statements from reliable sources on the basis of what is stated? I believe we do it all the time, and we usually express our hesitation like this: "It's too good to be true" or "It's too terrible to be true." Recall the incredible reports of the Nazi Holocaust or the practically unbelievable trust of an Anne Frank in the midst of it. Think of the terminally ill, who normally go through a period of absolute disbelief and denial that their end is near; or think of yourself when someone says to you the preposterous words, "I love you." This is an extremely important area of human knowing because it does not involve the incidental pieces of knowledge that give us a view of nature and history but rather the awesome possibilities for malice or glory within the human reach.

There is more to say about belief, particularly about values we are offered for our consent, but for now we simply want to recognize that all human knowledge is a matter of experience, understanding, and judgment, even though the parts of this compound may be parcelled out among a large group of people through the mediation of value judgments.

3. *The Real World*

If knowing is a matter of experience, understanding, and judging, mediated largely through the value judgments that go with believing, then knowing is not a matter of just looking at what is "really" there. The "real" world, in other words, is reached through a combination of cognitive activities. Now it is one thing to acknowledge the truth of this assertion but quite another to grasp its implications. So let me speak for a moment about the extraordinarily common but nonetheless confusing notion of a "fact." It will help clarify how important it is to have a firm grasp of what we mean by the "real world."

What is a *fact*? The image we get is of a "thing" outside of us that does not change, no matter what we think of it. If it is a fact that a telephone pole stands on the street corner, then nobody's thought about it, no matter how mistaken, can change that. But this example of a telephone pole is misleading, and it is so for two reasons. First, the pole is so visible that knowing whether or not it is standing there seems to be identical to looking at it, though the knowing process is actually more complex than that.

We can get around this illusion which equates visibility with reality by taking a different example. Suppose your desk lamp does not work. You try a different bulb, you check the fuse box, you examine the switch and the plug. If all of these appear in good condition, you conclude there must be a break in the wire, somewhere between the plug and switch. You conclude this; you do not *see* the break, which in any case would be difficult to pinpoint. If you replace the wire and the lamp works, then you have no doubt that there is, in "fact," a gap in the discarded wire. You have verified, by *judgment*, an understanding of the evidence you experience.

In our example of looking at the telephone pole, we are so accustomed to our deft cognitional activities that they occur unnoticed. Beginning in infancy we constructed a world that is coherent and enduring, not merely by looking and seeing but by a whirlwind of hypothesizing and verifying that filled nearly every waking hour. It is this process of recurring experience, understanding, and judging that brings us everything we know and blends them into a unity so harmonious that we imagine we can "see" it.

The other reason why our example of the telephone pole is misleading is that, like the examples often given in metaphysics courses, it is insignificant. If we take examples closer to significant human living, we soon realize that facts do not stand on street corners to be looked at. They reside in minds—fallible minds. Here are some examples: Is it a fact that your brother loves you? Is it a fact that you were neglected by your parents when you were young? Is it a fact that the electric motor freed women from the drudgery of housework? Is it a fact that St. Paul wrote the Letter to the Colossians? Is it a fact that you have no commitment to socialist principles? No matter how you answer these questions, it is clear that you are judging the correctness of an interpretation. You are verifying an explanation. Four people spending an evening playing bridge often have different explanations of "what was really going on." And it is now commonly recognized that historians can know better what the "facts" were than the participants in historical events did.

Here is a good way to remember what a 'fact' really is. Look at the Latin root: *facta* means "constructed," as in "manufacture." In significant human living, the "facts" are verified explanations in fallible human minds. This is a disturbing realization. But is it not the case that we interpret our experiences for ourselves and that our interpretations can differ? This is not to say that there is no truth, that all we have is a welter of interpretations. No, we pass judgments, with more or less certitude, with the purpose of correcting misunderstanding. The point to recognize here, however, is simply that the 'real' world is grasped through human acts of meaning—through experience, understanding, judging, and believing—and that these acts are not one hundred percent infallible.

4. Community

Now this is only half the story. Not only do we *grasp* the real world through our acts of meaning. The major part of that world is itself *made up of* acts of meaning. That is, not only do our acts of meaning enable us to *know* the world around us; the most significant realities that we can know are themselves *constituted by* attention, intelligence, reason, and beliefs.[3] After all, what is a democracy, a culture, an economy, a polity; or what constitutes any real human community, any actually functioning set of relations between people, but a set of experiences, understandings, judgments, and commitments? Our imaginations may conjure up visual images of the socio-economic realities, but the significant part of these realities is entirely unimaginable. We may picture, for instance, Hitler's Third Reich as a phalanx of goose-stepping Nazis, but the reality is an operative set of interior processes. If the Allies had invented, instead of an atom bomb, an "amnesia" bomb that destroyed nothing but ideas and commitments, leaving all the uniforms, arms, banners, and buildings intact, the Third Reich could have vanished in a day. Even the texts of constitutions and laws have no force at all except in the measure that they fix ideas and guide commitments in the souls of living people.

I said that a community is made up of acts of meaning. The idea of *community* is perhaps the most pervasive moral notion in the twentieth century. Russian and Chinese Communism, existentialists, dramatists, anarchists, and the entire Christian world have symbolized the object of their hopes as "community" of some sort. But, again, what springs to mind when we see the word? A happy, cooperative group linked arm in arm? People who wear the same style of clothes, speak the same language, and share the same goods? If that is the notion which has guided our thought, then no wonder community has been so difficult to achieve. Unless we recognize that community is constituted by processes of the soul, and by nothing else, we will destroy community in our efforts to create it. The core reality within any community is invisible, intangible, inaudible—which is just another way of saying that community is not essentially composed of sights, surfaces, and sounds. It is composed of the acts of meaning by which we know and will. To put it very precisely, community is common experience, common understanding, common judgment, and common commitment. These are the necessary and sufficient components of any community. Where any of these breaks down, community breaks down. It becomes clear, then, that the more we know about the ranges and limits of human knowing and willing, the better position we will be in to understand concrete breakdowns in community and to set policy for its concrete development.

So for the time being we must set aside the question of how community breaks down. There is more to say on how reasonable people actually make judgments and what features they always anticipate in the real world.

5. Criterion for Judgment

Our hope here is that by understanding precisely how our acts of judgment work, we will be able to formulate a few key precepts that guide the ways in which we

a. make our own judgments,
b. persuade others to reconsider their judgments, and
c. accept on belief the judgments passed down to us through tradition.

The two kinds of judgments we will be considering here are the initial judgments on the occurrence of an event ("There is a forest fire raging in Michigan") and the follow-up judgments on the correctness of an explanation ("The forest fire was caused by lightning").

One of the most startling features about making judgments—and one of the most important—is the criterion we use. We pronounce something to have occurred or we pronounce an explanation as probably or certainly correct when we run out of questions relevant to conditions we set. The criterion for judgment, in other words, is the absence of relevant questions.[4]

25

The conditions that give rise to relevant questions take the form "if . . . then," referring to something in experience. For example, recall our broken desk lamp. "If I *see* a break in the wire, then I am certain the wire is at fault"; or, what amounts to the identical cognitive process, "If I replace the wire and *see* the lamp go on, then I am certain the wire was at fault." The questions relate the conditions directly to experience; and if the conditions appear met, then the questions vanish and the judgment follows.

We must belabor this point somewhat. Because we must *see* something about the lamp, we can easily overlook the inner activity of the mind that sets conditions on the seeing and relates it to the inner act of making a judgment.

Now we are not maintaining that this criterion of judgments prevents mistakes. We are simply saying that we become more subjectively certain as fewer relevant questions occur to us. Suppose, in our lamp example, that in fact the problem had been a loose connection between the wire and the switch, not a broken wire at all. Unknown to us, when we replaced the cord we provided a tighter connection and thus repaired the lamp by accident. In other words, we were certain about the wire, but dead wrong.

In this example, we happened to be too inexperienced to think of checking for loose connections. That particular relevant question never occurred to us. Perhaps humility might have tempered our judgment ("I think it might have been the cord"); but in that case, humility tempered the judgment because it raised a relevant question. Accordingly, we expressed our judgment as only probably or possibly correct.

Or take an example of a judgment that something occurred or is occurring. Imagine that you are startled out of your sleep at night by the sound of a telephone ringing. You sit up in bed and are perhaps unsure whether you merely dreamt you heard the phone or really heard it. You tell yourself, "If it's the phone, it will ring again," and you wait. Suppose you hear nothing. You conclude, "I must have been dreaming." Your hearing did not make that judgment; your mind did. You reached that judgment by framing a question in the form of a conditional statement: "If I do not hear it ring again, then I only dreamt it." The silence meets the conditions you put on your judgment, your relevant question is answered, and you go back to sleep.

Here again, you may have been mistaken. Perhaps you heard only

26

the last ring of a caller who was actually trying to reach you. But you will discover your mistake only if the caller raises a relevant question, such as, "Did you sleep through twenty rings last night?"

Do not be beguiled by these domestic examples. We are stating that all judgments on the occurrence of an event or on the correctness of understanding rely on the drying up of relevant questions. There may be relevant questions occurring to others, or to ourselves at a later date. Or there may be a better set of conditions we could have set. But to the degree that we are either ignorant of further questions and conditions, or are convinced that relevant questions could not arise, we become more firm in our certitudes.

This explanation of how we make judgments will likely raise the question of whether we can be certain of anything. For if the non-occurrence of relevant questions is the criterion of judgment then the very fact that we realize this raises a further relevant question about our certitudes regarding absolutely everything. How can we be certain of anything, once we admit the possibility that there may be relevant questions that have not yet occurred to us?

To meet this objection we have to make a distinction between the data of sense and the data of consciousness. For there is a surprising amount of certainty available through the data of consciousness which is not available through the data of sense.[5] The data of consciousness include our experiences of wonder, questions, insights, deliberation, imagination, feeling, judgment, commitment, and so on. The data of sense include simply whatever comes through the five senses: sights, sounds, touches, smells, and tastes.

Attend now to the data of your consciousness. Is it true or not that you make affirmations? Obviously a denial is self-contradictory; you would be claiming to make no claims, judging that you make no judgments, affirming that you make no affirmations.

We can also ask whether we perform the act of understanding. We can be absolutely certain that we do, since to doubt it presumes that we understood the question. In a similar fashion we can go on to ask further questions: Do we ask questions? Do these questions seek intelligibility in data? Are the data of consciousness which we name experience, understanding, and judgment related in specific manners? In all these questions, we settle on answers not because we can *see* anything inside ourselves but because a yes answer meets practically all the relevant questions and a no answer leaves nearly all of them unanswered.

So we do have some certitudes about processes in our own consciousness. To doubt them would amount to doubting that we could even doubt.

When it comes to the data of sense, things are different. Ordinarily speaking, we have far more certitude about *whether* something happened than we have about *why* or *how* it happened. I may be quite certain that I hear a hammering noise outside, but not certain why or how the noise is being made. And even in the case of being certain that something is going on, we may be imagining things, so we seldom say we are absolutely certain. In short, then, while we are often quite certain about occurrences, we rarely reach certitudes about explanations.

So there is a valid point in the question of whether we can be certain about anything: we cannot be absolutely certain about realities mediated to us by the data of sense. But we can be certain about some occurrences within mental process and about some explanations of how those occurrences relate to one another. We can be certain about what makes a statement only probably true, and we can be certain about the status of explanations regarding the data of sense. So it is certitude about inner processes that guides us in dealing with all other assertions and explanations.

We can now face the question, "So what?" The results of our analysis are quite practical. If all judgments that something occurred or that some explanation is correct depend upon the mind setting conditions that frame questions about experience, then

   a. we should not cling to our own certitudes in a way that prevents us from attending to experience; nor should we feel limited to only one way of questioning our experience;
   b. if we want to persuade others to reconsider their own certitudes, it will be more effective for us to present significant data or new questions than simply to present our own certitudes more insistently;
   c. if we want to do full justice to any judgment made by someone else and presented to us for belief—be it historical fact, philosophical proposition, scientific explanation, commonsense wisdom, or religious revelation—we ought to understand the conditions that were set and the questions that were posed in the minds of those who first proposed it.

As you can readily see, these precepts have wide-ranging applications. Eventually we will see how they apply in assessing historical facts and religious revelation. But for now we must finish our task of gleaning such precepts from our analysis of the mind's workings.

6. *Metaphysics*

Because we are able to reach some certitudes about the workings of the mind—that we experience, understand, judge, and believe— we can establish some absolutely basic certitudes about all the reality reachable by the mind. We must try to spell out what these features of reality are. As will be evident shortly, these basic certitudes guide all clear thinking, so again we will be able to formulate some key precepts that normally work in us only implicitly.[6]

These certitudes about the structure of the real are implicit, we say. Only metaphysicians bother to state them formally. But it is worth our while to state them formally—yes, it is worth our while to indulge in metaphysics—because a little time spent thinking about the acts of thinking will save a lot of time thinking about the objects of thinking. Sound thinkers generally ride by the seat of their pants. That is, they may know a great deal about certain topics, but they have difficulty explaining how their thinking works. To themselves, they seem to ex-perience mere "intuitions" that certain questions are more apt than others, and that other avenues will be blind alleys. While part of this intuition certainly comes from a familiarity with their fields, another part comes from an unformulated grasp of the meaning of data, of in-telligibility, and of reality—corresponding to experience, understand-ing, and judgment.

On the level of judgment, the very fact that we affirm our own knowing implies that we affirm a difference between real and not real, between existence and non-existence, between occurrence and non-occurrence, between is and is not.

Similarly on the level of understanding, the very fact that we ar-ticulate the specific intelligible ordering of our knowing as experience, understanding, and judgment implies that we are certain of at least some intelligibility in the universe. It is the conviction that things are intelligible which impels us to test and refine all explanations in science, scholarship, philosophy, and everyday common sense.

And on the level of experience, the very fact that we attend to data for the purpose of sifting important data from the unimportant implies that we expect some data to be merely coincidental accumulations and other data to be ordered by the laws we are out to discover.

Let us investigate these three certitudes in more detail, beginning at the level of experience. Corresponding to experience, sound thinkers know that ultimately the givens of the data are intelligible; it can all be questioned. With respect to specific questions, certain data may be relevant and other data may not be, and their job is to find out which is which and why.

Furthermore, sound thinkers are convinced of the need to stay close to data. If they fail to follow you at the beginning of a conversation, they ask you "What are you talking about?" If they lose you in the middle, they say "Give me an example." And if they lose you at the end, they ask "So what?" They know that *explanations should make sense of data*, and they care little about big words or purely logical deductions that distract them from this central concern.

When clear thinkers are in creative moods, they know that "playing" with data is the most likely path to invention. Take the violin, for example. Its rather strange shape emerged long before acoustical engineering became a science. It evolved to its present shape because artisans "played around" with wood, bows, and strings.

Our point is this. In the activity of intelligent thinkers we find an implicit metaphysics that sees data as that part of reality which limits each thing to its specific form of being. The possibilities inherent in reality lie ultimately in its data. To put it in Aristotelian terms, reality has 'potency' and we discover it in data.

Corresponding to understanding, we find that sound thinkers possess one remarkable ability: they know the difference between getting the point and missing it. We have all enjoyed insights, of course. But insights always work with images, and there is the danger that we will mistake the image for the insight. We see this in people who laugh at the wrong place in a joke. They are so eager to enjoy laughing together that they fail to see the precise incongruity that makes the joke's point. We see it also in poor teachers. They can be so hypnotized by the image of themselves imparting knowledge to empty minds that they talk as if they understand things, when all they understand is how to use words and cause reactions.

The list of examples of intellectual bluffing could go on. What we want to stress here is that intellectually honest men and women are convinced that reality has an intelligibility within it, that this intelligibility is reached not by imagining or describing or feeling but by an insight, that an insight is communicated not by a description of data but by an explanation of how the data hang together. In Aristotelian terms, reality has "form" and we discover it through insight.

And corresponding to judgment, our sound thinkers are convinced that if wishes were horses beggars would ride. In other words, reality is stubbornly independent of our hopes, desires, visions, or wishes. Willy Loman, in Arthur Miller's *Death of a Salesman*, refused to face the reality that traveling salesmen had become useless in his line of business. He pretended to himself to be important and successful, turned a blind eye to the failure of his two boys and to the devotion of his wife, and created an aura of reality by hoping where there was no hope.

There is a profoundly important principle here, relevant to the daily lives of every ordinary person as well as to every great philosopher. We can put it like this: Reality is what it is. Things either happened or they did not happen. In Aristotelian terms, there is a component in reality called 'act' and we reach it through judgment.

So, from an affirmation about the structure of knowing, we realize that we implicitly affirm a kind of parallel structure in anything we could call *real*. This structure has no content in this discussion; it is merely heuristic. But it does represent features about reality that we simply never deny. Corresponding to our judgment we affirm a difference between occurrence and non-occurrence. Corresponding to our understanding, we affirm a difference between the intelligible and the unintelligible. And corresponding to our experience, we affirm a difference between related and unrelated data given by reality. While this may seem like an excessively formal view of the 'real', it gives us a view that is comprehensive and enables us to make sound fundamental distinctions upon which further distinctions will be based.

What precepts can we formulate that will make this metaphysics of practical use? To put it quite generally, we could simply say "Respect data, intelligibility, and reality in the way clear thinkers do." Or we could put it very precisely as three separate precepts:

Be attentive (respect all data as possibly intelligible)

Be intelligent (know the difference between getting a point and missing it)

Be reasonable (be realistic, not a dreamer).

These precepts apply to thinking about all reality whatsoever. It is because they are not restricted to any particular realities, and because they operate in clear thinkers whether or not they are formulated as such, that Lonergan calls them *transcendental precepts.*[7]

To sum up what we have examined so far, we acknowledged that human knowing must be, at least in its broad lines, a compound of experience, understanding, judgment, and belief. Then we saw how these same activities also constitute our social and cultural institutions; they are the fundamental building blocks of community. And finally, we discerned the basic structural features in all reality that human knowing could ever reach and formulated some of the key precepts that guide clear thinking.

Now it is one thing to say that clear thinkers respect data, intelligibility, and reality in specific, structured ways, and it is quite another to say that the realities themselves are so structured. For if we can say even a few verifiable things about the structure of reality, we ought to be able to give scientific and scholarly investigators a framework within which to work. Scientists and scholars, after all, need to understand exactly what different types of intelligibility they can expect to find in, say, planetary motion, hurricanes, cell reproduction, and civil wars. Very few of them can explain the differences. They simply follow the procedures they were taught in graduate school. And these are the people who advise politicians on pollution control, nuclear energy, foreign policy, economics, and national defense.

Lonergan has in fact worked out an account of the basic intelligibility to be found in all reality. A "design of the universe," in other words. In his study of how understanding works, he has outlined two basic and interlocking kinds of explanation which mirror two basic and interlocking ways in which reality is in process. It will be immensely helpful to those involved in empirical studies of any sort to understand these two complementary ways in which we understand. Only by articulating the kinds, the ranges, and the limits of our understanding can we render an account of the methodological commitments that underlie all our studies.

32

So in the following four sections we will review Lonergan's notions of intelligibility, of intrinsic intelligibility and "things," of classical and statistical intelligibilities, and, finally, the fundamental design of the universe of our experience.

7. *Intelligibility*

We begin with a few basic clarifications of the meaning of intelligibility and of the warrant we have for thinking that the world has a fundamental design.

Just as 'real' is the object of judgment, so 'intelligibility' is the object of understanding. In everyday speech we might say "I understand how this insurance policy works," but we mean that we understand *correctly*. By itself, the act of understanding is distinct from the act of judgment. Understanding answers how or why; judgment answers whether. Perhaps it would be more accurate to say that the object of understanding is "possible intelligibility," so that we cover not only cases of understanding, and not only cases of *mis*understanding what already exists, but also cases of understanding leading to invention, creation, and sheer play.

We should also be careful not to confuse *intelligible* with *intelligent*. The intelligible is what intelligent persons are looking for when they ask how or why. Again, we must be careful not to think therefore that the intelligible is "out there" and intelligence "in here." Intelligence happens to be intelligible also. It is safer to adhere to an implicit definition that calls the intelligible the object of intelligence, and then fixes intelligence by referring to the data of consciousness we named "understanding" or "insight." So the intelligible can be defined as everything about which we intelligently ask how or why.

Does intelligibility really exist? That is, is intelligibility a property of reality, or might it be never anything more than a mental scheme? Since our insights into nature and history are so often fallible, the argument can be made that the actual object of insights is not some intelligibility in reality but just mental concepts, and that this subjectivism is what accounts for the phenomenon of one interpretation succeeding another *ad infinitum*.

In response to this objection, we can look not to outer nature and history, where interpretations do indeed suffer revisions, but to inner intelligence itself. In section five, we saw that there is one *judgment* that we can make with absolute certitude—the fact that we make judgments. Similarly, there is a core set of insights that no scientific revolution will ever overturn—the insight that explains how experience, understanding, and judgments are related to one another. The reason we will never overturn this insight is that it has to do with the very method by which any insight is generated and tested, revised or overturned, corrected or affirmed.

From this central core of verifiable insights into insight, we can move on to all the realities affected by insight. We understand the core cognitive processes to be constitutive in a variety of ways of whatever makes sense in art, invention, economics, politics, and culture. Just exactly how insight functions in each of these realms may be subject to some revision, but few people would doubt that they possess a real intelligibility flowing from real insights.

Moving out further to the realm of the natural sciences, we find much more revisability in scientific insights. But this is no warrant for believing that the realities under investigation possess no intelligibility in themselves. On the contrary, even though scientists have never enjoyed perfect certitude about what that intelligibility is, they go forward on the presumption that should their hypotheses not account for all the data, it is precisely because those data are intelligibly related in a way they have yet to discover.

With these basic clarifications out of the way, we can get down to the business of outlining the various kinds of intelligibility within the universe of our experience. Notice that last phrase, *of our experience*—meaning if not my personal experience, at least the experience of somebody. It is crucial to this approach. By it we exclude any sorts of intelligibility that we have no data on; we aim at understanding everything we can ask questions about and nothing more. But that is plenty, and, indeed, it may be everything.

Surely a philosophy of knowledge could give many cogent reasons for expecting the universe not only to have pieces of intelligibility within it, but to be itself an intelligible whole. Yet most of us need no convincing. From our childhoods we asked how and why about everything. Our modest successes in gaining understanding confirmed the legitimacy of our expectations that the reasons for some things tend to link up with the reasons for other things. And, as if to cap off this conviction, we believe in a God who is an intelligent creator of everything.

Within our belief that God knows everything lies the affirmation not only that each single thing makes sense, but that the whole of creation makes one overall sense. Well, perhaps not absolutely everything. We acknowledge mistakes, stupidities, disasters, and outright malice. But while we have not yet attempted to include anomalies within a metaphysics of the universe, we still expect God to make sense out of everything eventually. The overall intelligibility of the universe may not be complete, but it is surely on its way; and if not in this life, then in a next.

In order to investigate this overall intelligibility, however, we ought first to have a clear idea of just exactly what *intelligibility* is. Our common sense is rather biased about this question because it specializes in understanding the usefulness of things and tends to ignore questions about how things work except insofar as that understanding has immediate practical advantages. But when we consider the act of insight itself, we see that its own proper goal is not to make practical changes but simply to understand the intelligibility intrinsic to things. So to approach the question of what the intelligibility of all things might be, we need to see what the intelligibility of any "thing" is.

8. *Intrinsic Intelligibility and 'Things'*

When we were young, our intelligences specialized in the fundamental routines of cause and effect. As infants we learned the various effects of our crying, sucking, and so on. In childhood we learned the effects of language and gesture. Although we could hardly have been aware of it at the time, we experienced the differences between *efficient*, *material*, and *final* causality. Efficient cause is a matter of grasping the if-then relations of physical action: if I push this wastebasket, it falls over. Material cause is a matter of grasping what materials are necessary for specific activities: if I want to paint a picture, I must have the paint. Final causality requires grasping the relation between human intention and human action: if I don't want to eat the vegetables on my plate, I'm not going to. Final causality surely is a nuanced version of an 'if-then' relation, since not all our desires become fulfilled — often because of the opposed intentions of others: "If you don't eat those vegetables, I will not let you have dessert!"

Perhaps the most important specialization of our early youth was learning that there are further 'if-then' relations that reside in things themselves; they have nothing to do with our personal hopes and needs. We learned, for example, that clocks have mechanisms, games have rules, and pets have habits. We discovered that there are reasons why reality does not easily submit to our demands, and that these reasons lie somehow within the realities themselves.

It is with this entry into a world of 'if-then' relations independent of us that we, as youngsters, gradually caught on to the further idea of *formal* cause. That is, we became able to grasp that things function according to an intelligibility intrinsic to themselves, prescinding from efficient, material, and final causality. Similarly, in the youth of human philosophical history, Aristotle added the notion of formal cause to the already known efficient, material, and final causes. If I may be permitted a personal example, I can remember discovering that the automobile engine with all its pipes, wires, and strange bumps and indentations, was intelligible: everything in it had a reason, a function. No doubt I already knew of the other causes—which pedal makes it go and which makes it stop, the differences between metal, rubber, glass, and cloth, why my parents wanted to buy a car—but an entire new world of questions opened up to me once I saw that every bump had a reason, and that the reasons had sprouted in the minds of the engineers. This is not to say that I understood the engine thoroughly; I understood very little. But I understood what the form, the how, the function of the machine means. Whether or not each of us remembers getting such an insight is beside the point. Somewhere in our youth, all of nature opened up to us in this new fashion. We realized that trees are processes that follow laws, that falling objects follow laws, that the sounds of a piano follow laws. We grasped the meaning of intrinsic intelligibility.

This breakthrough into the world of intrinsic intelligibility is an intellectual release from a self-centered world. Previously, our intellectual developments specialized in those 'if-then' relations which condition our personal lives. What we experienced about efficient, material, and final causality was an undifferentiated grasp of how we might act in our homes and neighborhoods with our parents, siblings, and friends. But intrinsic intelligibility disregards our personal role, and, for as long as the periods of our intellectual curiosity last, we forget about our own comfort and pride. We tap the spring of a pure desire to know. We become able to analyze even our experiences of efficient, material, and final causality, and we understand them as such. We thematize the

36

processes involved in physical dynamics, material and capital formation, human purpose and commitment.

Now this universe in which we find intelligibility intrinsic to reality is a set of 'things'. As you can see, by 'things', we mean something rather technical. So before we go any further, we must work out a definition of a 'thing' that will be useful in the chapters that follow.[8]

Because knowing is a compound of experience, understanding, and judgment, any 'thing' which can be known has the three metaphysical components of potency, form, and act. Earlier we saw what these components mean in terms of mental processes. By potency, a 'thing' has data that we can experience; although not by data alone do we recognize things. By form, a thing has understandable causes for being in its present form; although not by experience and understanding alone do we recognize which among many possible causes are the correct ones. By act, a thing exists as a unity distinct from other things; and only by the conjunction of experience, understanding, and judgment do we affirm the intrinsic intelligibility that keeps the thing a unity.

To put this in more useful terms, let us say that 'things' exist because of events. That is, the realities that make up the universe are contingent upon events, actions. The apparently inert stone imbedded in a field of grass is a massive aggregate of atoms in various states of excitement; it settled into that particular field because of geological processes that we consider intelligible. Likewise a committee exists through the events of commitment, remembering, judgment, and insight in its members. Every time they meet they depend on events that successfully organize the necessary materials, energy, space, and time.

So 'things' are not necessarily physical and visible. Our brains are physical but our minds are not; our hearts are physical but our loves are not; our groups are visible but our communities are not. Yet all are real things. So, in what follows, whenever we investigate the intrinsic intelligibility of things, you can expect that we will ask about the events that condition their existence. In short, 'things' are event-conditioned.

Next we should notice that some events on whose occurrence 'things' depend occur regularly while others occur at random. So there is a need to distinguish two kinds of intelligibility intrinsic to 'things'. Both kinds occur in the universe of our experience, and in most cases, both kinds have roles to play in the emergence of any specific 'thing'.

In the next two sections we will discuss Lonergan's notion of two kinds of intelligibility and how they combine to make up a single design of the universe. It will be an explanation of the same evolutionary character of reality as studied by Teilhard de Chardin. Now, as it happens, many readers have no great interest in understanding what the design of the universe might be. Their faith in God has brought them to the affirmation that the universe does have a design, and they feel no great personal need nor any great academic need to understand it for themselves. If you are such a reader, then I suggest that you skip immediately to section eleven of this chapter. For the rest of the book, it is sufficient that you have understood that all 'things' are event-conditioned.

9. Classical and Statistical Intelligibility

We said above that there are two basic kinds of intrinsic intelligibility in the universe of our experience.[9] The first kind is made up of the functional relations we grasp by a direct insight. Lonergan has named this 'classical' intelligibility to associate it with the insights reached by the classical founders of modern science: Bacon, Newton, and Galileo. The second kind of intrinsic intelligibility is the probability we grasp initially by an 'inverse' insight that realizes that there is no classical intelligibility available and then by a direct insight that sets an ideal frequency around which a set of events cluster. Lonergan has named this 'statistical' intelligibility.

Remember that by 'things' we mean not what is *out there* to be looked at, or even *in here* to be experienced. We mean what can also be reasonably affirmed to exist and intelligently understood as event-conditioned. From the point of view of intrinsic intelligibility, everything we know, from rocks to committees, depends for its existence on the occurrence of events.

Now when we are trying to understand specific event-conditioned things, we normally expect to find both classical and statistical regularities at work. One part of a thing's existence is conditioned by *functional relations* always found in things of its type and another part by merely *random* factors. Let me illustrate this by an example. Imagine one brick dropped from about forty-eight feet. We know that it will take approximately two seconds to hit the ground. Now imagine a ton of bricks bundled together dropped from the same height. Do you expect the bundle to fall more quickly because it's heavier? Actual measurements show that the increased weight makes no difference in time. And we might have expected this. The ton of bricks is just an aggregate of single bricks, each of which falls forty-eight feet in two seconds. Did you get the insight? If so, you grasped a functional relation between distance and time, and you understood why weight plays no significant role in falling objects. This example, as it happens, is nearly identical to a thought-experiment devised by Galileo to grasp the nature of free fall.[10] Direct insight into the functional relations reveals that falling time depends only on distance, not on weight, other things being equal.

Notice that we have to say "other things being equal," knowing very well that they seldom are. We neglected air density, surface texture, and frontal area. We neglected the difficulties of precise timing. These are the random factors; no two bricks are exactly alike, and the same brick cannot be dropped in exactly the same manner twice. And this amounts to saying that we cannot get a direct insight into these random factors. It is no mean feat to realize this. Scientists spend a great deal of energy trying to sort out which portions of events are directly intelligible and which are not. But they do have a technique for grasping an intrinsic intelligibility in these random factors anyway. Once they get the inverse insight that there is no functional relation to be grasped in certain aspects of things, then they think of averages, ideal frequencies, chance, and probability. Let us look more closely at the sort of intelligibility we find in random events—the sort of intelligibility we call 'statistical'.

In each single instance of an event-conditioned thing, the conditionings may have either an intrinsic or a merely coincidental relationship to the thing under consideration. In either case, we can take the statistical approach. For an example of the intrinsic conditionings upon our falling brick, we can see that besides the laws of falling bodies, there will be laws of aerodynamics that apply to an actual falling brick in a unique way. But the number of possible unique ways actual bricks fall is beyond our capacity to investigate, so we drop bricks of different weights, shapes, and sizes in different densities of air; we record the data and look for average effects. There will also be merely coincidental factors, however, factors that are not covered by any functional relations whatsoever, and these are usually the kinds of events we are keenly interested in predicting. For example, rainfall in New York, or a gambler's chances of rolling a seven when the stakes are high. In these cases, we are defining a set of occurrences by limits of space and time, thereby introducing empirical factors that exclude all events occurring elsewhere and yet are not part of the intrinsic intelligibility of the set of events before us. There is no intrinsic connection between New York City and rain. Gamblers are interested in what dice will do during the time their money is at stake, but only the superstitious think that dice will behave differently when others try their luck.

In such random events, we are not interested in understanding intrinsic functional relations that reveal *how* things work; we simply want an answer to the question, "How often?" This question occurs to us whenever we inquire about the "state" of things—the state of one's health, of a nation's economy, of an educational system. We expect such answers as "usually," "seldom," or "nine times out of ten." We are not after an exact explanation of how our economy functions; we want an exact number that represents, say, average interest rates or the odds against a recession. We want to know what percentage of students from this school graduate with honors or go on to gainful employment.

A grasp of "How often?" is just as much a grasp of intrinsic intelligibility as a grasp of functional relations is. Where we investigate events gathered into a set by purely geographic and temporal boundaries (usually of cultural importance), we introduce purely coincidental, not functional, relations among them. So we try to set some ideal frequency and a standard deviation from the ideal. We know perfectly well that actual frequencies and deviations will not match the ideal, but we also know that the mismatch will never be regular. That is, because we understand, through an 'inverse' insight, that there is no functional relation to be determined, we can expect that irregularities must vary from the ideal only in random ways.

Let me give an example. A recent accounting of 200 games of cribbage played by different pairs of experienced players found that the person who deals first tends to win 55 out of 100 games. The question is, do we understand anything about the intrinsic intelligibility of cribbage in knowing this ideal probability? Yes: we know that the functional relations set by the rules of the game combine with the randomizing effects of shuffling, over a large number of games, to produce a very specific result—a 55% probability of winning in favor of the initial dealer. And we know that if there should be any *regular* deviance from this norm, then there is a functional relation at work we haven't accounted for—such as an ace up a sleeve.

We are so used to asking about the state of things that we regard the question "How often?" as part of human nature. And yet, for the greater part of human history, we have had no exact understanding of what statistical understanding is all about. For that we needed to see the precise difference between probability and chance. The difference is crucial. By 'probability' we mean an ideal frequency of occurrence of a specific class of events within specific spatio-temporal boundaries: in Akron, Ohio, nine days out of ten are cloudy. Probability gives us a positive understanding of events *taken as a set*. By 'chance', we mean the kind of variations from the probable—namely, random. This last week in Akron has been unusually sunny. So chance refers to the negative understanding of *each event within a set*. Probability and chance always go together; they define one another. And because they do, the chance element in individual events does not eliminate positive intelligibility in those events taken as a set.

Let me stress how important it is to allow an intrinsic intelligibility to sets of random events without denying a purely random factor in them. There are theological fundamentalists who expect God's providence to work either through efficient causality or through the formal causality defined by functional relations, but not through the formal causality defined by probability. We can understand their reasoning. They want to insure that every event in creation is under providence, so they imagine that the world is either directly but invisibly "pushed" by God or is part of a chain of events under the sort of laws found in Newton's physics. Enamored of classical insight, they are horrified at the idea of randomness. They have a terrible time trying to understand coincidences, evolution, and the surprising creativity of the human mind, except by some notion of divine intervention interrupting its own divine plan. They fail to see that an affirmation of sheer coincidence is not a denial of functional relations governing each event, nor is it even a denial of an intelligible regularity in the set of events taken as a whole. It is simply a denial of intelligibility where we intelligently grasp that there is none. And on the positive side, it is an affirmation of an intelligibility in an entire set of randomly conditioned events of

41

a specific type. The fundamentalist mind would have little to lose by affirming mere coincidence—it would lose only a simplistic picture of a clockwinder God—and it would gain a profound appreciation of God's subtle but continuous creation of the new out of the old through probabilities.

10. World Design

We can now get an intelligible worldview by seeing the universe of our experience as ordered by a compound of classical and statistical intelligibility.[11] In other words, within this universe of event-conditioned things, we can not only discern a difference between directly intelligible events and random events, we can get a single insight into the complementary ways in which they combine. In this single insight we will grasp the unity of world-design.

Of all the insights of the classical type available to the investigation of scientists, by far the most fruitful are those that grasp intelligibility in events that repeat themselves. The circulation of water over the globe, for example, follows a small set of laws dealing with falling bodies, surface tension, evaporation, and saturation. But we can get a single insight into the circulation itself by grasping the circle of situations water finds itself in. The same is true for the nitrogen cycle, on which living things depend. Or take, for example, this cycle of processes that make up the feeding system found in animals: foraging, digestive, vascular, muscular, foraging, and so on. These four processes form a self-supporting circle: the food from foraging enters the digestive system; the digestive system enriches the blood; the vascular system strengthens the muscles; and the muscles are used to forage, and so on. Should any one of these processes break down, the whole circle breaks down; though in most animals there are also supportive circles of processes that allow for some adaptation.

We usually call these self-supporting circles of processes a 'system'; but, more accurately, they should be called 'schemes of recurrence'. Thus, our earth 'system' of four seasons is really a scheme of recurrence dependent on the regular variation of the earth's tilt with respect to the sun. Likewise, human society contains a scheme of recurrence on which it depends, and without which it would collapse. In this scheme, the circle of events runs: situation, insight, apt action, better situation, further insight, more apt action, and so on. Obviously, human society contains a lot of other factors that seem forever to get in the way, but at least we have rather easily located the fundamental 'system' behind all human progress.

Now these self-supporting schemes of recurrence have both horizontal and vertical links to other schemes. The feeding system in animals which we spoke of above becomes an element within a wider ecological system—which is nothing more than a horizontally related set of schemes of recurrence. So, for example, bees gathering honey also pollinate flowers and, to their chagrin, provide a sweet meal to a foraging bear. But this entire ecological system itself has vertical links to other schemes of recurrence. There are physical and chemical schemes "beneath" it, so that if the meadow where bees, flowers, and bears cohabited were to be contaminated by toxic materials, the ecological system itself would be destroyed. Similarly there are psychological, economic, and social schemes "above" it. The meadow may be the subject of an artist's painting, the source of a farmer's honey business, or a meeting place for a camping club. These depend on the ecological schemes of recurrence of a meadow just as the meadow itself depends on physical and chemical schemes.

It is the range of vertical links that gives us an insight into how higher schemes of recurrence give an intelligible ordering to lower ones. Let us look at several schemes of recurrence that we are familiar with. In atoms, electrons orbit their nuclei. In compounds, atoms share their outer-orbit electrons with compatible outer-orbit electrons of other atoms. In living cells, long-chain proteins linked in helix form by amino acids unlink, gather aggregates of molecules into their own pre-coded order, and thereby reproduce themselves. In animals, cortical organizations of cells process electro-chemical signals in what we call hearing and seeing; they set routines of waking and sleeping, eating and eliminating, coming to birth and giving birth. In humans, the recurring processes of insight, judgment, and commitment create and sustain what we call the person, the home, the economy, the polity, the culture, the technology, and the world community, such as it is.

All these things—atoms, molecules, cells, animals, and humans— have one feature in common: their existence depends very concretely on the recurrence of a set of events. And our knowledge of these things is a matter of grasping the circle of events, the recurring scheme, that constitutes its intrinsic intelligibility. Perhaps you have noticed that our examples moved from what we commonly call the physical to the spiritual. And we moved up without any jump in categories. There was no reason to, because the difference between the physical and the spiritual is not essentially a matter of visibility; it is rather a matter of a difference in recurring schemes. What those schemes may be is up to specialists in the various fields to discover. But we can at least grasp the nature of what those specialists are after. The physicist, the chemist, the botanist, the biologist, the psychologist, the sociologist all aim to grasp the recurring events that condition the things in their respective fields.

You may also have noticed that as our examples moved from physics "upward" to the fully human scene, it was not a smooth glide but a step-by-step movement. This is because the recurring schemes that define the various genera are relatively rigid. But this rigidity does not keep the genera distinct in the concrete. The recurring schemes condition not only the things proper to their sphere, they also condition lower recurring schemes, so that human schemes organize biological, biological schemes organize cells, cellular schemes organize molecules, and molecular schemes organize atoms. Obviously, not all the lower things enter into the organization of higher things, but all the higher things in our list depend on the successful functioning of the lower schemes they govern. Chemicals will break down if the atoms fission; cells will break down if chemicals change; life breaks down if cells decompose; knowing and willing break down if life dies.

Now while this is not by any means the whole story, we can say this much, that the universe is at least partly organized into a *conditioned series* of schemes of recurrence. In other words, where there is regularity, we can expect to find higher recurring schemes dependent on the successful functioning of lower recurring schemes. We grasp each scheme by a direct insight into its functional relations, and we grasp the whole conditioned series of schemes by a direct insight into how each higher scheme is functionally related to its lower ones.

Next, we have to ask the question, "How do the higher schemes emerge, once the lower schemes are in place?" And for this part of the story, we turn to the notion of statistical intelligibility—that is, to probability. The very fact that higher schemes exist says that the spatio-temporal situations from whence they sprung possessed a probability that the set of events that constitute the higher scheme would occur.

The higher scheme, in other words, had a probability of emergence. We must also assign a probability of survival to the higher scheme, since its constituent events may also grind to a halt.

To get an idea of these two probabilities—of emergence and/or survival—consider the difference between the dinosaur and the turtle, and between a human and a vacuum-tube radio. The dinosaur and the turtle, both being of ancient lineage, are each a conditioned series of schemes of recurrence with a high probability of emergence. But it appears that the turtle has outdone the dinosaur in probability of survival. Humans and vacuum-tube radios, relatively recent arrivals on the universal scene, have had a lower probability of emergence. Humans, however, enjoy a rather high probability of survival, while the lowly old vacuum-tube radio will not have lasted a century.

We can now state in a very few words a surprisingly comprehensive understanding of world-design: *The universe of our experience is a conditioned series of schemes of recurrence that emerge and survive according to probability.* The view originated with Bernard Lonergan: he calls this world-design 'emergent probability' for short.

Please do not let your imagination carry you away; stay with insight. It is dangerously easy to imagine the universe as wanting to get somewhere. This is a classic problem of teleology. How do we explain why cells replicate, why beavers build dams, and why the sun shines? In our world-design of emergent probability, we are not saying, for example, that the universe is as large and as old as it is *in order that* human life may appear. That would give the universe a personality and a will of its own, making it an autonomous source of final causality. We are merely saying that schemes of recurrence with a low probability of emergence, but which have actually emerged, will correlate with large initial spaces and long intervals of time. It means a grasp of formal, not final, causality. But once we have understood those schemes of recurrence linked in conditioned series which make up the concrete things of our universe—that is, once we have grasped an intrinsic intelligibility—then is there any need to project an anthropomorphic will and intention on subhuman reality? I thoroughly doubt it. True, there is a final causality in the universe, rooted in God's kind purposes, and we have yet to examine that. But we need not restrict God either to efficient causality or to the classical type of formal causality if we are trying to explain chance and evolution.

Emergent probability by itself has sufficient power to account for the teleological character of the universe. In the first place, it gives a picture of the universe that is neither a mechanical determinism nor an absolute relativism. Later possible schemes of recurrence may or may not emerge from earlier ones. Even a possible scheme of recurrence with a lower probability of emergence than some other possible scheme may chance to emerge earlier, and, by binding up materials needed by the more probable scheme, may practically eliminate its possibility. But in any case, the very fact that schemes of recurrence possess both a probability of emergence and a probability of survival says that the universe possesses a dynamism towards increasing systematization. We must say "a dynamism towards" because, God knows, events of chance and of malice can, because of their lack of intelligibility, destroy cells, organisms, ecosystems, economies, psyches, and so on. So emergent probability admits breakdowns and blind alleys. Surely today with nuclear weapons we must admit that even the human race has suddenly faced a lowered probability of survival. But for all that, world-design is an intelligible process with an increasingly systematic character. That is what we mean by its teleological character. It includes the actually functioning routines, but it is not restricted to them, for it also possesses an open dynamism towards further ordering.

The notion of emergent probability is applicable in absolutely every science, at least as a background structure if not a direct object of attention. For scientists study intrinsic intelligibility, and unless they possess an *a priori* expectation that 'things' are event-conditioned and that event-conditioning processes will be a compound of classical and statistical intelligibility, they will fail to understand what makes for a genuine explanation. Emergent probability is particularly important in theology today because it enables us to reinstate the notion of divine providence in terms compatible to hard-headed scientific thought. In 1932, J.B. Bury published *The Idea of Progress*, in which he expressed this disturbing idea: "It was just the theory of an active Providence that the theory of Progress was to replace; and it was not till men felt independent of Providence that they would organize a theory of Progress."[12] Bury convinced a great number of people, scientists and non-scientists alike, that the idea of providence blocked scientific progress. But with the notion of emergent probability we can explain the intrinsic intelligibility of human progress, find it coherent with world-design, and accept the idea that a divine designer works through a "conditioned series of schemes of recurrence that emerge and survive according to probability." There is more to be said about emergent probability, particularly in chapter 5, when we will talk about the nature of history; but for now it will be enough to have grasped the main lines of the notion.

11. The Problem of Integration

We have tilled acres of intellectual soil. And, while we have tried to be as concrete as possible by giving familiar examples, there remains an air of the "intellectual" about this account of knowing. Ordinarily our days are spent on practical and immediate matters. We meet bodily needs; we play; we pray. In everyday living, the real is there to be seen and touched. The floor is solid wood, not a conglomerate of atoms made up mostly of empty space. We see stars above exactly as they are at our present moment, not as they were hundreds of years ago when their arriving light began its journey across space. In our prayer, God is nearby, albeit invisible. Any other meaning of God's "presence" seems an impenetrable mystery.

No doubt, theoretical reflection on ordinary living has enhanced our lives to some extent. Without science, philosophy, and theology we would remain uncomprehending victims of nature's whims. Today, it is practically impossible to live an integrated life of common sense without the faithful services of theory. But the realm of common sense and the realm of theory each has its own principles of integration. Common sense demands a dramatic integration, usually accompanied by the appropriate set of feelings and images. Theory, as we saw, demands the absence of relevant questions about intrinsic intelligibility. This is what sets our problem of an overall integration of both realms.

I am not speaking here about tendencies in commonsense people to belittle theory, nor of tendencies in scientists to get lost in theories irrelevant to human life. I am talking rather about people who are familiar with both realms but expect commonsense principles of integration to apply in the theoretical realm. I am speaking, for example, of colleagues of Einstein who, because they could not *imagine* the speed of light staying constant no matter how fast its source was traveling, remained unconvinced by his rather simple calculations that explained all the relevant data. I am speaking of the popular scientist

47

on TV who talks as though molecules "wanted" to become cells, and cells "wanted" to come alive. There is no need to imagine material reality as having human desires once we grasp the increasingly systematic character of world-design functioning according to emergent probability. I am speaking of theologians who are not content unless they can *imagine* the Son of God existing as far back in time as we can feature, and then, at the appointed time, entering the womb of Mary to begin a human life along that same time line. There is no need to arrive at an imaginative reconstruction of events to explain the data of Scripture or the interior data of one's religious faith. These otherwise brilliant theoreticians may know their subjects, but they do not fully understand their methods.

The problem of integration, then, must be met by the rigorous kind of work we have attempted in this chapter. It means going outside both the realms of common sense and of theory and into the realm of method. Here, by *method* we mean the dynamic range of methods innate to human knowing, not some fixed recipe *produced by* knowing to meet recurring problems. Lonergan has named this realm 'interiority'. And he has named this work 'intellectual conversion'. For, I hope you have already become aware, it requires a conversion to see that knowing is an intellectual construction and to let go of the common-sense notion that knowing is just looking. We did not deduce this from basic principles; deductions do not precipitate conversions. We induced it from personal experience. Once we made the breakthrough–knowing that we know through a compound of experience, understanding, and judgment–then we entered upon the real world comprising a compound of data (potency), intelligibility (form), and existence (act), and we formulated the intrinsic intelligibility of the real world as emergent probability.

But do we totally abandon the old myth that the world is simply out there to be looked at? Not exactly, for that would mean a repudiation of commonsense procedures that are vital to everyday life. Instead, we ought to understand the procedures of common sense and theory so that we can move from one realm to the other without confusion. For real spiritual integration does not take place within one realm of meaning alone. Rather it should allow us to integrate the realm of common sense with the realm of theory and any of these realms with the further realms of religious transcendence, art, and scholarship.

12. *Intellectual Conversion*

To finish off the initial work of intellectual conversion—I say "initial" because the work never ceases—let us compare and contrast the procedures of common sense with the procedures of theory. These procedures originate in different patterns of experience and they each use descriptions and explanations in their own fashion.

We begin first with 'patterns of experience'—a notion which Lonergan developed to account for different orientations found in human attentiveness.[13] We have said that experience alone gives us nothing but data, that knowing also demands understanding and judgment. However, data does not pass in front of our eyes like ducks in a shooting gallery. We are already oriented in our attention towards certain purposes, and so we filter and select data long before we get any answers to questions. We can discern six basic orientations in how we pay attention: biological, aesthetic, practical, mystical, dramatic, and intellectual.

The *biological* pattern of experience is oriented towards eating, mating, sleeping, and self-defense. The *aesthetic* pattern is oriented towards making our inner affectivity outwardly visible, audible, palpable; it seeks to stimulate and represent the flow of our feelings. The *practical* pattern, of course, aims at getting things done, making things work, bringing forth the shelters and instruments we need in daily life. In the *mystical* pattern, we shut out all other patterns in order to commune silently with the divine object of our longing. In the *dramatic* pattern, in which we spend most of our lives, we aim at dignifying human life. We focus on style, deportment, character, and the flair that is proper to the human spirit. We try to dress, to walk, to eat, to work, and to make love in honorable ways, because we know we are more than mere animals. But in all these patterns, the insights required to live them out aim at understanding how things or persons are related to us personally. We do not ask how things are related to one another; that is, we do not ask about formal causality, intrinsic intelligibility.

Only the *intellectual* pattern of experience attends to data with a view to understanding the relations of things to one another. We may enter the intellectual pattern for purposes that are ultimately practical or dramatic or mystical, but as long as we are in the intellectual pattern, we try to stave off questions of usefulness, dignity, or holiness.

These concerns, worthy though they be, can interfere with the pursuit of truth and understanding. It is quite difficult, as we well know, to remain in the intellectual pattern for long periods. We are easily distracted by hunger, by practical needs, by poetic expression, by the image of ourselves teaching others, and even by the urge to pray.

However, these problems of intellectual concentration can be met by self-discipline. The more serious problem is to see clearly what the criteria are for grasping intrinsic intelligibility. This problem can be met only by an intellectual conversion. And even when we have made the initial breakthrough, there remains the ongoing and enormous task of catching ourselves slipping out of the intellectual pattern and into the dramatic pattern, in particular, and using dramatic criteria for grasping intrinsic intelligibility. For integration in the dramatic pattern of experience demands imaginative representations and the ability to charge a situation with emotion; it aims directly at value judgments on situations at hand. In the intellectual pattern, integration must resist these urges and aim coolly at negotiating questions of intrinsic intelligibility. For example, in much of today's literature on psychological stages in the life of a man or woman we find clear pictures drawn of what each stage tends to look like, and the pictures have an integrative power. But very few writers appeal to our insight; they appeal to the integrative power of imagination, not understanding. For an excellent contrasting example of a psychologist explaining the intrinsic intelligibility of human development, see Piaget's *The Development of Intelligence in Children*.[14] Even if you are not interested in the topic, you will get some idea of the rewarding clarity that results from clinging to the intellectual pattern of experience.

It is important to learn to identify in our selves the difference between the intellectual pattern and the dramatic pattern. It will certainly be valuable in guiding our own thinking. No matter how firmly we remain in the intellectual pattern, our thought eventually seeks expression in talk and writing, and, when it comes to convincing others, the dramatic criteria tend to weasel their way into our explanations. There may be very good reasons for using those dramatic criteria, but if we use them unknowingly, we effectively teach others to discount insight in favor of imagination.

Also, knowing the difference between the intellectual and dramatic patterns will help our reading. Have you ever noticed that certain parts of books seem unusually difficult? When we are young, we naturally think of ourselves as not intelligent enough to get the point, but after having met an author or two, and finding them quite like ourselves, we realize that in many cases it was not our own minds that grew tired, it was theirs. There are few authors writing about theoretical matters who have mastered in themselves the difference between the intellectual and dramatic patterns. Knowing that difference in ourselves gives us a sharp razor for distinguishing it in others, a razor that grows sharper with use.

Basically, the difference between the intellectual and the dramatic patterns lies in their respective aims. The intellectual pattern aims at explaining the relations of things to one another, while the dramatic aims at establishing, maintaining, or enhancing relations between ourselves and others. In the intellectual pattern we attend to a set of data regardless of our personal affection or distaste for it. We want to understand objective things in their intrinsic functioning, not in their potentiality to advance our own reputation, bring comfort to our personal lives, or secure our individual or collective futures. Obviously, the intellectual pattern heads for results that eventually serve human needs, but the direct pursuit of those needs belongs to the dramatic pattern.

In the dramatic pattern we attend to data with a view to passing value judgments or to let our selves and our feelings be known to others. The dramatic pattern of my life becomes integrated when my external actions, internal feelings, and expressive words form a consistent whole. And others recognize this integration in me not primarily by their intellectually patterned experience of me but by their dramatically patterned experience—which they understand by grasping the relations of things to themselves were they in my place. It is difficult, therefore, for us to pass judgment on the dramatic integration of foreigners because their common sense relates things to themselves in quite a different manner from our own. But once we grasp the difference between these two patterns of experience, it becomes somewhat easier to pass judgment on at least the intellectual integration of practically anybody.

A second distinction we must grasp if we are to carry out our intellectual conversion is the difference between *describing* and *explaining*.[15] It corresponds somewhat to the difference between the dramatic and the intellectual patterns of experience inasmuch as descriptions relate things to ourselves while explanations relate things to one another. But we use descriptions also in the aesthetic, biological, mystical, and practical patterns, as well as in the intellectual pattern itself. Indeed, one of the many reasons why we lose our bearings in the intellectual pattern is that we must deal regularly with descriptions and yet go beyond them to explanations. So let us look at how descriptions fit into explanations. We can find three distinct and important connections.

First of all, description brings data to the threshold of understanding. Recall our example of the falling bricks. We saw that a single brick and a bundle of bricks accelerate at the same rate in free fall. I say we "saw," but while almost anybody can imagine this, not everyone grasps the nature of free fall, that it is independent of weight. And yet, everyone who does grasp it had to begin by imagining it or seeing it. In other words, insights need descriptions, images, pictures, perhaps even sounds or textures or smells. But the insight is none of these. Until the insight comes, the description serves only to represent the understanding we hope eventually to enjoy.

Second, once we have expressed our insight, we need to return to the data—to the descriptive contents—to pass judgment on the correctness of our understanding. In the case of our bricks, you might want to run a test by dropping a house key and a large book together to see if they land simultaneously. (But remember, do not be fooled by what you see. You do not lay eyes on the nature of free fall. You are verifying your understanding by eliminating leftover questions.)

Third, the things we want to explain may be of vital importance to our personal lives but also be so profound that we know very well our explanations will fail to plumb the depths. But we must act and take responsibility for our actions. It is a rare luxury to be able to act on full understanding. So we deal with these partially understood realities through the descriptive elements that constitute symbols. I am thinking of such realities as friendship, commitment, one's own birth or death, heaven and hell, eternity, and so on. For example, we describe heaven as a place of light and comfort, and hell as a place of darkness and torment, even though we say they are not "places." We imagine friendship as an association of two bodily persons, even though life keeps reminding us that something far more invisible is involved. This kind of description may have an important place in homilies because it incites hope in the face of life's mysteries. But it should be presented as a humble admission of our lack of understanding rather than, as too often happens, a glowing claim that we have achieved new insight.

In brief, then, description brings us to the threshold of explanation; it makes possible a judgment on the correctness of explanation; and it stands for the realities we cannot explain but must deal with anyway. But description does not explain. Explanations, as we have already seen, answer the questions how and why. Either they grasp a scheme of recurrence or they grasp that there is no scheme of recurrence at work in particular situations. Explanations can gather piecemeal explanations into larger wholes and thereby arrive at successively higher viewpoints which may combine classical with statistical intelligibility. A definition of *explanation* could be given here—in terms of "intrinsic intelligibility" for example—but it is far more effective to ask you, the reader, to attend to your own experience of the difference between visualizing the free fall of bricks and understanding "why" weight makes no difference. Indeed, even if you have *not* understood what this paragraph is about, but *know* that you do not understand, it is because you *do* know the difference between seeing the print and getting the point.

Let me illustrate the difference between description and explanation with two examples. For a long time, when people suffered the accumulation of pockets of watery liquid under the skin, they were said to have "dropsy." But now we know that dropsy is not a disease; it is a *condition* that can be brought about by any of several different diseases originating in the heart, kidneys, or liver. Whoever first saw the difference between a condition and a disease knew the difference between a description and an explanation. A condition we describe, but a disease begs explanation. The same basic question can be asked about nervous breakdowns, allergies, and backaches. The descriptive viewpoint knows a lot about these ailments, particularly about what they look like and what to do when they strike. But the explanatory viewpoint does not rush to name these "diseases," for they may be symptoms of any of a variety of distinct problems. Indeed, they may be the body's natural cures for schemes of recurrence we do not understand but which would eventually destroy us.

Or take the theological notion of "eternity." The descriptive viewpoint sees it as an endless time line. We imagine life after death as going on in time. We think of God's eternity as duration without beginning or end—in time. And we have difficulty imagining the beginning of time on earth because we can still wonder what happened five minutes before time started. But the explanatory viewpoint grasps that "eternity" signifies merely the negation of time (usually to emphasize the excellence of God); it does not give any positive meaning. We are deliberately left without a solid picture, because the whole point of discussions about eternity is usually to deny that we can talk about certain realities in verbs with tenses of past, present, and future. To say that God is eternal is simply a statement that divinity is not by nature conditioned by time. What divinity is, God only knows.

We could give many more examples, and we will. In the pages to follow we will try to understand the intrinsic intelligibility of such realities as faith, hope, love, grace, and discernment. Notice, if you please, that you already have a picture, a descriptive viewpoint, of each of these. But if you have followed our analysis of human knowing this far, then you have the beginnings of an explanatory viewpoint as well. You can expect, therefore, that we will treat these religious realities as schemes of recurrence, functioning in a universe of emergent probability. We will define our terms not by giving genus and species but by pointing to our personal experience of conscious processes and by relating the event-conditioned 'things' we find there to the external schemes of recurrence we call a social order, a culture, a polity, a technology, social progress, social decline, and the actually functioning redemptive schemes originating in divine love.

But first we have to finish our analysis of the order of the human soul. We not only know; we also act. And beyond knowing and acting, giving them direction, there is loving. Were our study taking place within the dramatic pattern of experience, we would be directly interested in knowing how to act and whom to love. But we intend to stay in the intellectual pattern and ask how acting and loving function in the soul and how spiritual integration in the soul is absolutely necessary for spiritual integration in society.

Discussion Questions: CHAPTER TWO

Here are five questions that ask you to apply some of the materials of this chapter to various problems in science and theology. They are designed either for writing out answers or for discussing in a class. My own replies to the questions can be found in the appendix (p. 201), but please test your own understanding first before reading my responses.

Question 1

Read the following passage from Augustine on how God is present to us everywhere:

> Thus did I think of you, O Life of my life, as great throughout infinite space in all directions, penetrating the entire mass of the world and beyond it in every direction through unbounded magnitude—as if the earth possessed you, the heavens, too, and all things were bounded within you, but you were nowhere bounded. Just as the body of the air—the air that is above the earth—does not hinder the light of the sun from passing through it and permeating it, not by breaking it up or cutting it, but by filling it up completely, so I considered not only the mass of the heavens and the air and the sea, but also that of the earth to be permeated by you, to be capable of being permeated in all its greatest and smallest parts in order to receive your presence, governing all things which you have made by a hidden inspiration from within and from without. Thus did I conjecture, for I could not think otherwise. It was false of course.

"It was false, of course!" Why exactly is this picture of God's presence a false one? Is God not really everywhere?

Question 2

Carl Sagan, author of the book *Cosmos,* and star of the televised series by the same name, has described the universe in wonderful, exciting terms. But read the following excerpts. Is there something about them that makes you uneasy? Is he really following scientific canons?

> ". . . one day, quite by accident, a molecule arose that was able to make crude copies of itself."
>
> "It is only by the most extraordinary coincidence that the cosmic slot machine has this time come up with a universe consistent with us."
>
> "Somehow the distant planets sensed the sun's presence."
>
> "For myself, I find it elevating that our universe permits the evolution of molecular machines as intricate and subtle as we."
>
> "Evolution, however, has had billions of years to practice. DNA knows."
>
> "By definition, nothing we can ever know about *was* outside [the physical universe]."
>
> "The Cosmos is all that is or ever was or ever will be."

Question 3

In chapter 2 we contrasted three fundamental approaches to reality, the materialist, the idealist, and the critical realist. Compare the following passages. First, the idealist. This is a representation by William James of what the idealist position (which he formerly held) appears to be for him:

> Most of us . . . are mere syllables in the mouth of Allah. And as Allah comes first in the order of being, so comes first the entire sentence, the Logos that forms the eternal absolute thought. Students of language tell us that speech began with men's efforts to make *statements*. The rude synthetic vocal utterances first used for this effect slowly got stereotyped, and then much later got decomposed into grammatical parts. It is not as if men had first invented letters and made syllables and sentences of the words; − they actually followed the reverse order. So, the transcendentalists affirm, the complete absolute thought is the pre-condition of our thoughts, and we finite creatures *are* only insofar as it owns us as its verbal fragments.
>
> We see that no smallest raindrop can come into being without a whole shower, no single feather without a whole bird, neck and crop, beak and tail, coming into being simultaneously; so we unhesitatingly lay down the law that no part of anything can be except so far as the whole also is. . . . We think of ourselves as being only a few of the feathers, so to speak, which help to constitute that absolute bird.

Next, in contrast, the materialist view (James' own position):

> The bird metaphor is physical, but we see on reflection that in the physical world there is no real compounding. "Wholes", are not realities there; parts only are realities. "Bird" is only our *name* for the physical fact of a certain grouping of organs, just as "Charles's Wain" is our name for a certain grouping of stars. The "whole", be it bird or constellation, is nothing but our vision, nothing but an effect on our sensorium when a lot of things act on it together. It is not realized by any organ or any star, or experienced apart from the consciousness of an onlooker. In the physical world taken by itself there *is* no "all", there are only the "eaches" − at least that is the "scientific view".

And finally the critical realist view of Lonergan:

> Again, the acknowledgment that the real is the verified makes it possible to affirm the reality no less of the higher system than of the underlying manifold. The chemical is as real as the physical; the biological as real as the chemical; the psychic as real as the biological; and insight as real as the psychic. At once the psychogenic ceases to be merely a name, for the psychic becomes a real source of organization that controls underlying manifolds in a manner beyond the reach of their laws.

What criteria do each of these positions use in determining whether something can be real or not? That is, to what processes in consciousness do each of them refer when they decide something may or may not be real?

Question 4

What would you do if they found the bones of Jesus? Suppose some archeologist found the bones of a thirty-year-old male, obviously crucified, with the INRI inscription on wood thrown in among the remains. What would your reaction be? Would you cling to skepticism until better scientific proof could be offered? Or might you resign yourself to watching the foundation of your faith be shattered? Or would you rejoice that even further data on the Jesus whom you love has been unearthed?

Question 5

Lonergan has articulated the design of the world as 'emergent probability' — the emergence of recurring schemes (which underlie regularities) according to probabilities. How does such a notion square with Providence? Isn't divine Providence much more personal and loving? Doesn't God have kind purposes for this world? Or at least doesn't any analysis of "world design" tend to downplay God's direct interventions into history?

Notes to Chapter Two

1. In this entire analysis I am paraphrasing and abbreviating a massive amount of material in Lonergan's thought. For Lonergan's own compendious treatment of these materials, I suggest "Cognitional Structure" and "Dimensions of Meaning," in *Collection*, pp. 221–239 and 252–267.

2. See *Method in Theology*, pp. 41–47.

3. Ibid., pp. 78–79.

4. See *Understanding and Being: An Introduction and Companion to "Insight"*: *Halifax Lectures by Bernard Lonergan*, ed. Elizabeth A. Morelli and Mark D. Morelli (Toronto: Edwin Mellen Press, 1980), pp. 133–155; *Insight*, pp. 280–281, and the leads given in its index under "virtually unconditioned."

5. *Insight*, pp. 333–335.

6. See *Understanding and Being*, pp. 240–245.

7. *Method in Theology*, pp. 20, 53.

8. See *Insight*, pp. 245–254; *Understanding and Being*, pp. 125–131.

9. *Insight*, pp. 33–69, 105–121.

10. See Herbert Butterfield, *Origins of Modern Science, 1300–1800* (London: G. Bell, 1958), pp. 82–83.

11. *Insight*, pp. 121–128.

12. J.B. Bury, *The Idea of Progress* (New York: Dover Publications, 1955; first published in 1932), pp. 21–22.

13. *Insight*, pp. 181–189.

14. *The Origins of Intelligence in Children* (New York: International Universities Press, 1952).

15. *Insight*, pp. 291–292, 295–296.

CHAPTER THREE

Acting

When we speak about acting, we enter that further dimension of the human soul which we commonly call the moral order.[1] Here we should speak of the human drive towards the good and of the role of judgments of value, feelings, conscience, and moral conversion. From the descriptive viewpoint, these aspects of the moral order seem to belong strictly to the individual person, but when we move to the explanatory viewpoint, we will see each of them as irreducible elements in the social structures of good and evil which link individuals together in community. From there we will be able to speak of historical progress and decline.

Still, we find the relevant data on the moral order primarily within ourselves, and so we will continue to analyze the structure of consciousness in order to grasp the intrinsic intelligibility of moral action. We have already seen that the cognitive order of the soul has three levels—experience, understanding, and judgment. With the moral order we come to a fourth level. Like each of the first three levels it has many processes within it. Prior to a decision, there are the movements of feelings, the assent of value judgments, and the voices of conscience. After a decision come commitment and action and change. So, since deciding seems to be the pivot of freedom between interior moral movements and objective commitments, let us refer to this entire fourth level of consciousness as "deciding."

Deciding does not merely go beyond experience, understanding, and judging. It completes them. Knowledge alone does not change the way we live; it does not make us better persons. Decisive action does. And decisive action depends on experience, understanding, and judgment to present a sound view of real situations. In the opposite direction, the three cognitive levels depend on the moral level to give their respective cognitive objectives a higher integration in some moral objective. A scientist's knowledge of nuclear physics ought to have some useful purpose. There are some very intelligent people who are also moral derelicts. Hedonistic moral objectives have, in a sense, ruined the ultimate goals of otherwise fine minds.

When we say that the moral order completes the cognitive order, please do not get the idea that the moral order comes later in time, as though the mind must do its job before the heart can take over. We have already seen that experience is patterned according to objectives that require acting—biological, aesthetic, practical, dramatic, mystical, and even intellectual. If anything, the moral order precedes the cognitive both in time and in importance. So, in spite of everything we said about the cognitive order, we should think of it as massively conditioned by desires, purposes, feelings, and values.

1. Authenticity

Whenever we talk about the moral order, there is a tendency to focus on the problem of making choices. Discussions very quickly head for the ethical dilemmas familiar to us all, and then turn endless circles around the human inability to enjoy moral certitude. But let us back up for a moment and simply aim at understanding what the processes are that make up the moral order. Then we may be able to deal more intelligently with moral uncertainty.

We have already seen Lonergan's three transcendental precepts that regard knowing: Be attentive; Be intelligent; Be reasonable. On the moral level, there emerges a fourth transcendental precept: Be responsible. The four precepts make up the fundamental processes going on in us that make us authentic human beings. The precepts are dynamic processes, not written rules. Like all known processes, they work according to emergent probability. That is, these precepts are the principles that instigate the schemes of recurrence we have called experience, understanding, judgment, and decision, respectively. The precepts themselves are schemes of recurrence, because they seem to operate as long as humans are awake. But their success is under probability, for we are also subject to their failures. We can be inattentive, or obtuse. We can be unintelligent, or stupid. We can be unreasonable, or silly. And we can be irresponsible, or immoral.

We have seen that Lonergan calls these precepts 'transcendental'.

Again, the descriptive viewpoint might picture something eerie about the transcendental, but the explanatory viewpoint can make things quite clear. 'Transcendental' here means that the precepts transcend specific, descriptive contents and refer directly to the metaphysical elements of reality. Attention refers to data, or potency. Intelligence to intelligibility, or form. Judgment to reality, or act. And, to introduce a fourth metaphysical element, responsibility refers to worth, or goodness.

But there is a further connotation to 'transcendental'. We experience these transcendental precepts as questions. On the level of attention we notice where, when, and what. On the level of intelligence we ask how and why. On the level of judgment we ask whether. And on the level of decision we ask should or ought. Each of these four kinds of questions takes us beyond ourselves—we "transcend" ourselves—in a distinct manner.

Transcendental precepts are the living source of all other descriptive precepts, such as "Do not Kill" or "Do unto others as you would have them do unto you." And we do not accept such categorical precepts except insofar as we are attentive, intelligent, reasonable, and responsible ourselves. The most fundamental moral 'action', therefore, is to obey the transcendental precepts within us.

We can call this fundamental moral action 'authenticity'.[2] Concretely it remains difficult to tell whether or not we are being authentic. Bad will aside, the most authentic of persons struggles to discern whether habitual behavior is always responsible behavior in this or that specific situation. For example, suppose that every time you meet a certain friend you affect a gushy flow of delight. Are you not in danger of missing the unpredictable movements of more negative feelings on certain occasions? Actual feelings do not always correspond to habitual feelings. Or suppose you take a dim view of Democrats. Authenticity demands that you stay open to new questions for understanding rather than fixing your viewpoint on past insights alone. Or suppose your regular way of dealing with panhandlers on the street is to hand them a quarter and pass on without a word. May there not be times when the appropriate action requires some response quite out of character for you?

There is a tension, then, in authenticity. To really "be yourself" or to be truly "integrated" does not mean the absence of nagging questions. Nor does it mean always trying to calm unresolved feelings. Authentic persons have plenty of tension in their hearts. To put it in explanatory fashion, authenticity is a matter of being attentive, being intelligent, being reasonable, and being responsible. And that means facing questions. Modern psychologists have kept a lot of neurotics neurotic by suggesting that all tension in consciousness is unhealthy. But the real psychic illness is to ignore, deny, or avoid the tension of obeying the transcendental precepts that constitute authenticity.

When people are unauthentic (that is, inattentive, unintelligent, unreasonable, or irresponsible), we call them "unreal." They stand there bodily, but there's nobody home upstairs. They may be intelligent but unreasonable, or reasonable but inattentive, or any of the many other combinations. So we say that they're "not all there," or "not present to the situation," or "not dealing with a full deck." There is no end to the delightful metaphors for saying that something is missing that ought to be there. Hamlet's question, "To be or not to be," did not refer to his bodily existence; it referred to the presence or absence of an appropriate human response. To "exist" as a human, then, does not mean factual existence. It means moral existence. It means bringing forth a continuous stream of appropriate attention, intelligence, judgment, and decisions about situations at hand.

The 'existential question' is primarily a moral question, a question about worth, value, ought, should, goodness, responsibility. But it is not simply the ethical question of which path is right and which is wrong. There also lurks a deeper question about the long-range orientation of all our specific moral decisions. Moral decisions accumulate and take a general direction, giving our moral lives character and definition. But residual uncertainties and halting convictions accumulate too, leaving us uncertain whether we are becoming the moral persons we ought to be. Authenticity does not prevent mistakes in the short run, but it does tend to overcome mistakes in the long run, when our relevant questions find their quarry. Still, this "short run" may be the entire lifetime of an individual or a culture. Individuals can remain blind to the evil of their own selfishness just as cultures have remained blind to the evils of slavery.

We would love to know how we stand morally, but we do not know. In Hopkins' phrase, we are "time's eunuch" — impotent to know for sure what the passage of time and the wisdom of others may bring to light. Genesis portrays God as forbidding us to eat of the Tree of the Knowledge of Good and Evil, and how tasty that knowledge looks!

This discussion of existential questions sounds very philosophical. But the questions occur within everyday life, and we are not as convinced of our answers as we sometimes pretend to be. Take the following four ordinary experiences, for example: the experiences of waiting, of losing, of being our true selves, and of contemplating death.[3] In each of these we ought to notice how uncertain we really are about how moral our lives have been.

When we must wait—for a bus, a friend, a lottery, a rainfall, or sunshine—we hope for what we believe is good. Outcomes seldom match our hopes, of course, but not always because they do not reach hope's high aspirations. Often the outcomes turn out better. So experience tells us not to make our hopes too specific; we should leave room both for some measure less and some measure more than we hope for. And yet we do not want to leave too much room, for we know very well that certain possibilities would not be good for us in any sense. This "leaving some room" is the concrete way we acknowledge moral uncertainty about what we think is good for us. We do this not out of philosophical principle but out of a canny balance between the certainly bad and the uncertainly good. Is it not true that we must gingerly make our way through life with clear pictures of what revolts us, but with only foggy notions of what might please us?

Second, we wonder about losing. We lose all sorts of things: pens, photos, books. We lose opportunities; we lose direction traveling in a car; we lose our sense of humor; we lose friends. Life appears like a stream continuously passing us by. Some items may cling to us like eddies in a backwash, but eventually nothing stays. Even we ourselves will one day be washed down the same stream toward a meaningless oblivion. Is there anything permanent in what passes? What sense is there in going to this dinner party or in registering for that course? There is nothing left when it's over. All this sounds very pessimistic, I realize, but who is there that still does not raise the question? Is there not some act of faith, even in nonreligious people, that encourages us to believe that something permanent remains in even the most trivial diversions of life? Whatever our beliefs, we do not enjoy certitude, and the question keeps recurring in the most apparently insignificant choices.

Third, we wonder about being our true selves. We all have some idea of ourselves—how we look, what talents we have, how much energy we are willing to spend on various projects. But what we *think* we are and what we *really* are may be two different matters. This dichotomy is easy to see in people shopping in a department store as we watch them choose certain styles of clothes. In many cases we just shake our heads, knowing that they have an altogether unrealistic picture of themselves. Now and then, though, we face the dichotomy in ourselves when questions of our reputations are raised. It just may be true that I am spending my life thinking I am one thing when in fact I have always been quite another. But how can I tell? I do not know whom to believe, and I must spend my entire ambiguous life in this dilemma.

Fourth, we wonder about death and life. I am not speaking of our apprehensions about when or how we will die. I am speaking about this question of Euripides: "Who knows if to live is to be dead or to be dead is to live?" Socrates drank his hemlock with the conviction that it would be better to die with integrity than to live with compromise. St. Paul described himself as dead to the world and alive to God in Christ Jesus. Those men all recognized that life can be an illusion, that we can think we are alive while we are dead at the core, or that we can fear the death of something in us that in reality could never be life-giving. But what makes for life and death in this sense? We must each decide that for ourselves. A woman facing a hysterectomy must decide for herself, as must a student facing failure in school, or a playwright facing critical reviews.

These tensions underlie our ordinary moral choices. Existential tension is not the same thing as, say, the tension between solitude and involvement, between prayer and action, between deliberate malice and deliberate goodness, between the habits I have and a new kind of behavior. These are all recognizable options in acting. Choosing one eliminates the other. Let us call these passing tensions 'ethical' and call 'existential' the ongoing tensions between hope and fulfillment, between what is passing and what is permanent, between self-knowledge and self-reality, between death and life. Ethical tensions are resolved simply by choosing; the matter is resolved, for good or for ill. But existential tension is not resolved by choosing. It is heightened, because we cannot be sure whether good or ill shall come of our choices.

This heightened tension raises an even more fundamental question. Slowly it dawns on us that we have a basic choice to make. Will we accept a life of existential tension or will we reject it? Is a lifetime of moral uncertainty and continuous struggle with ethical questions itself worthwhile, or might it be better to keep the tension at bay, to surround oneself with the good behavior one is fairly sure of and forbid one's wonder from venturing into areas where ethical failures are almost certain? From this perspective, the authentic life appears to make us more prone to ethical mistakes than would a life of fidelity to the sound achievements of our tradition.

We cannot easily deal with this question from a purely intellectual framework. The vast majority of us deal with fundamental authenticity without ever using such technical terms as 'ethical', 'existential', or 'authenticity'. Instead, we use the softer mediations of symbols, those large images in the mind upon which we hang our hopes and fears. So let us look at how symbols work in moral consciousness. This will help us frame the question whether a life of existential tension is really life or not.

2.   Cosmos or Chaos

The most basic symbols in moral consciousness represent the pairs good and bad, right and wrong, better and worse, order and disorder. Let us refer to the positive sides of such pairs as Cosmos and to the negative sides as Chaos.[4] The capital letters are not meant to connote Manichaean demigods or Platonic ideas. Let them rather connote vivid pictures in the imagination. Cosmos is round, whole, orderly, bright, and alive. Chaos is fragmented, violent, dark, and decaying. We feel the fundamental questions of human existence more in our imagination than in our reflective consciousness. We approach every situation with the symbol-borne question, "Is this part of Cosmos or Chaos?" Cosmos stands for the universal order, whatever it may be, and Chaos stands for the breakdown of that order.

And so our questions about waiting, losing, self-reality, death, and so on, boil down to whether these unavoidable tensions of existence belong to Cosmos or Chaos. Remember that I am not speaking about the more patent question of how to act in situations; that is a matter of ethics and discernment. I am speaking about the underlying question whether a lifetime of struggling between two pulls is itself intrinsic to Cosmos. We do not have easy criteria for settling the matter. Think of mistakes of conscience, the suffering of the innocent (for that matter, the suffering of the guilty), blind alleys, mistaken judgments of fact, the slowness of development of individuals, inequality of opportunity over the face of the globe, and the maverick history of the human race. Is all of this Chaos, or might part or all of it belong to Cosmos? The wise see the difference, but even they do not easily live it out.

If we believe in the ultimate intelligibility of everything in the universe—a belief engendered more often by growing up in a home where trust and kindness abounded than by reflecting philosophically—then, in spite of the price we pay in suffering, we act on this principle: *Everything in the world is part of Cosmos, except the refusal to admit it.* In other words, we bear the frustrations involved in a universe of emergent probability whether or not fortune comes our way. We refuse to give up hope. But that is merely another way of saying that the only Chaos is to detest a life of moral uncertainty and to resent being subject to the merely happenstance. Emergent probability is the great equalizer of humankind. No one escapes its form of Cosmos. But it is also the judge of humankind because it condemns those who call it Chaos, making them loathe the order of their own souls.

The refusal to admit that everything belongs to Cosmos takes several basic forms. Let me mention four: Compartmentalism, Despair, Dogmatism, and Utopianism. There may be other forms, and these forms overlap somewhat. But these should convey the idea that all forms of deformation can be understood as a refusal to accept a world of emergent probability—or, in its symbolic terms, seeing all cases of happenstance and moral uncertainty as Chaos.

Compartmentalism is probably the most popular form of Chaos today. It is satisfied with islands of intelligibility in science, in scholarship, in art, in technology, in religion; but it makes no effort to import a question from one island to another. It seems to have imposed rigid restrictions on what certain courses in school may cover and what certain conversations at work may deal with. Economists are ignorant of ethics; ethicists are ignorant of economics. One team of medical doctors specializes in saving the fetus, another in destroying it. Dogmatic theologians tell us that Jesus instituted seven sacraments, while scripture scholars laugh at the idea. Why are we afraid to be corrected by other specialists? Because we think that ignorance is Chaos, that having to learn is a humiliation, that it is better to be certain about a few things than to suffer questions about everything.

Behind Compartmentalism looms Despair. I am not imagining the despair of being overwhelmed by emotional and social pressures, a despair that can lead to suicide. Rather I am thinking of the cynical judgment that nothing makes sense, or, if there is some sense to this world, God isn't telling. This kind of intellectual hopelessness follows Compartmentalism because, as one grows older, the island where things made sense appears to shrink as the tide of Chaos rises. In truth, of course, the rising tide is just as much Cosmos as the island, but Despair does not want to learn to swim. There is something in us that prefers the certainty of skepticism and the bittersweet pleasures of resentment to the darker agonies of waiting, of losing, of self-doubt, and of uncertainty about what is life and what is death.

The polar opposite of Despair is Dogmatism. Like Compartmentalism and Despair, it refuses to accept the struggle involved in Cosmos. But unlike them, it imagines Cosmos to be a universal and fixed set of truths. It correctly clings to the idea that if something is true, then it is impossible that it could also be untrue, in the same sense. So there is something firm to hold onto in a world of Chaos. What it cannot swallow is that all the truths we hold were reached by persons questioning their experience. If those questions lose their relevance in a later day, then so do the truths. Or, if the formulations of truths are cut off from their engendering experiences in history, then later generations will be handed judgments to believe without any guidance in understanding the experiences to which the judgments refer. Doctrines of Purgatory, of the Assumption of Mary, of the Resurrection of Christ, of the divine Trinity all originated in human experience. But who can easily name those experiences today? These and many other doctrines have been cut off from their 'existential' contexts because of a deep suspicion that human questions and struggles are part of Chaos. Dogmatists think that truth is a possession that eliminates the need for questions, as if questions were the enemy.

Utopianism, like the other forms of Chaos, rejects a life of mystery, struggle, and wisdom. But it stands head and shoulders above Dogmatism in its smug self-assurance. It loves the fantastic solution. It dreams of a realizable order in which basic questions and moral struggles are finally resolved. Eric Voegelin quotes Nietzsche: "The charm that works for us, the Venus eye that fascinates even our foes and blinds them is the magic of the extreme, the seductive force that radiates from all that is utmost."[5] It is serious about this dream, and has worked out practical steps for tricking the order of the soul once and for all, as if it could eliminate moral uncertainty and suppress all further questions forever. Marxists aim at changing the economics of production; Fascists elicit compliance by force; Positivists look for the right stimulus for the desired response. Even those who do nothing—because of some fear, or taboo, or just ineptitude—but who still entertain a dream of community without struggle and division, will sin against Cosmos, if only by yearning for an afterlife where there are finally no more questions.

The Cosmos, rejected by these and other forms of Chaos, does not stand fixed. It moves. We should not imagine the actual 'order' of the universe as a fixed recurring scheme, nor should we expect that the most ideal 'order' imaginable must be the attainment of a state of equilibrium. The order of the universe is a dynamic process with an increasingly systematic character, and yet its concrete destiny remains open. We, the family of human incarnate souls, represent its profoundest achievement because we are the only realities capable of understanding, judging, and evaluating. But the very spirit of inquiry that can bring us to accept the Cosmos and cooperate with it can also turn against itself, reject the movement of the soul, and thereby become the only thing in the universe capable of Chaos.

This is absurdly easy to talk about—Cosmos is everything; Chaos is the refusal to admit it. While this may answer the question of the intrinsic intelligibility of the universe, it can look vacuous if placed beside a question pressing on the fourth level of our consciousness. There the question is not about how the universe is structured but rather about how we ought to act. It is a question of whether we will honor and respect the limits imposed on us by the vagaries of coincidence and by our particular physical and emotional weaknesses. And we face the question every time we risk trying something new, or fall ill, or say farewell to a friend. Understanding the answer does not help much in loving the answer. And so we wonder, even after years of fidelity in the struggle, why the struggle does not abate. Is authenticity a war that cannot be won? Are there not people who have been toughened enough to deal with Chaos easily?

Certainly, fidelity to the transcendental precepts can become a habit. If I may adapt some wisdom from St. Ignatius Loyola,[6] those who are generally authentic find the movement within themselves towards Chaos to be like a drop of water spattering on a stone. It is violent and harsh. The movement towards Cosmos, even when it means pain, they find delicate and gentle, like water penetrating a wet sponge. For those who are generally unauthentic, the movements within feel exactly the opposite, so that authenticity feels harsh and unauthenticity a delight. Telling the difference between the two pulls can become a habit, and yet is it not always a struggle nonetheless?

The explanatory viewpoint reveals why. A universe of emergent probability brings forth new schemes, but with every new scheme the probabilities of emergence and survival of numerous other schemes change. We experience this change of probabilities in two ways. First, the concrete, familiar character of our vulnerabilities is constantly shifting. In some respects old difficulties can suddenly become easier to deal with, while in other respects, old strengths can suddenly falter and our weaknesses stand revealed.

The second way, however, presents the more basic and difficult tension. The experience of the spirit of inquiry within us is an experience of a movement towards an integration of otherwise scattered materials, ideas, and personal values. And when an integration with a high survival probability is reached, it tends to reduce the probability of emergence of some yet higher integration which might alter it in some fundamental way. No one likes to have his or her individual achievements absorbed into the schemes of others. And yet the dynamism of the spirit of inquiry, the very source of present achievements, can pronounce any present achievement outmoded.

To put it in a nutshell, we are tempted to remain faithful to transcendental achievements rather than to transcendental precepts. We prefer familiar data, hard-won concepts, truths received from tradition, and our cultures as we know them, rather than ongoing attentiveness, ongoing intelligence, ongoing reflection, and ongoing responsibility. The struggle is permanent because authenticity heads for relatively stable integrations, but relatively stable integrations can make continued authenticity difficult.

The existential problem is having to be dissatisfied with an imperfect world, and yet not hateful of dissatisfaction. To accept a universe of emergent probability means to let the spirit of inquiry roam across a battlefield, returning scarred and exhausted perhaps, but never mortally wounded by the combat. It means to let ourselves desire a human order which we do not clearly envisage, an 'order' which is not the enemy of inquiry but an ally, and yet an order that is within the reach of human achievement.

3. *Feelings*

Cosmos and Chaos are symbols, images representing the desirable and the undesirable. They reside primarily within consciousness and only derivatively in external artifacts, logos, mantras, mandalas, flags, and the phenomena of nature. Symbols function in everyone from childhood to old age, though hardly in the same way. As we grow up, what one person learns to love, another learns to hate, and even when two persons appreciate, say, the urbanity of a mounted police or a city park, one may respond with an active, serious respect while the other takes a more passive civic pride. The primitive images of Cosmos and Chaos, in other words, can each elicit hundreds of different possible affective responses from us: delight or dismay, joy or sorrow, exultation or wrath, sweetness or bitterness, patience or impatience, laughter or tears. All symbols, as long as they work, evoke feelings, and it is our feelings that first move us to like or dislike things in the world around us.

In the not-too-distant past, many of us emphasized reason so much that we thought feelings only blocked reason's clear vision of the worth of things. But is it not true that our emphasis on reason sprung originally from people feeling strongly about the matter? We can check the data of our own consciousness. Is there any person, any future project, any existing reality we appreciate which we did not first experience some feeling about? Feelings are not the final judge of value, certainly, but they surely are the initial movement within us towards that value judgment[7] and, once a judgment is made, it is our feelings again that consolidate our judgment and give focus to our attention, intelligence, reason, and responsibility.

It is our feelings, then, and not our thoughts, that give us our initial response to the worth of things. And it is our feelings, assisted by our thoughts, that elicit the cooperation of the whole of consciousness in concrete moral action.

It is very important, therefore, that we learn to recognize our feelings in everyday life. Here we can see how thought should serve feelings. Emotionally mature men and woman regularly think about how they feel. They realize that it takes time to name the feelings they experience. Growing up emotionally is a series of progressive differentiations in emotional response. Like a tree producing new branches every year, our emotional growth produces new feelings that regularly need to be recognized, named, and related to their older roots.

This is a task for thought. Feelings, after all, are just inner experience. Thought understands and verifies its understanding of this experience, transforming the merely felt into known feelings. However, thought can be mistaken. For a variety of reasons, we can misunderstand the affective data we experience and can pass judgments that may be too rash or too hesitant. The cavalier person will express more certainty than the data warrant, while the timid will express too little. So the task of knowing how we feel is ongoing and relatively difficult.

Still, we can take a few giant steps towards knowing how we feel if we employ a few important distinctions. Dr. Conrad Baars makes what I find to be a very useful distinction between *humane* emotions and *utilitarian* emotions.[8] (I am using 'emotions' and 'feelings' here as synonyms.) The humane emotions are direct responses to known objects perceived as satisfying or unsatisfying. He lists six basic types, coming in pairs. *Love* and *hate* (like and dislike, fondness and displeasure) are emotional states of pleasure or displeasure. They precede desire or aversion. *Desire* and *aversion* (wanting and revulsion, seeking and loathing) are emotional movements heading towards or away from objects. They follow love or hate but precede joy or sadness. *Joy* and *sadness* (happiness and unhappiness, delight and the blues) are emotional states that depend on whether or not we have attained the loved or hated, wanted or unwanted objects.

Utilitarian emotions, on the other hand, are not so direct. They are responses to known objects in view of any obstacles that stand in our way of attaining or avoiding them. Where we see pain and effort in attaining what we want, we feel either *hope* or *despair*, depending on how great the costs appear. Where we perceive some danger threatening our welfare, we feel either *courage* or *fear*, again depending on how great the harm appears. Finally, where we have already experienced, or are certain we will experience harm, we feel *anger*. (Each of these five utilitarian emotions, like each humane emotion, has a number of cognates or similar emotions.) The reason these emotions are called 'utilitarian' is that they are meant to serve the humane emotions. They do so with the assistance of insight and judgment taking the longer view and assessing the costs to be paid if the humane emotions are to work properly. They could be called the 'intellectual' emotions, and the humane could be called the 'instinctual' emotions.

Here are a few examples. If my favorite TV program has been preempted by a bowling tournament, my initial, humane emotion is disappointment (a form of sadness). Here the utilitarian emotion of hope or despair may intervene as I assess the prospects of finding my program on another channel. Or anger may serve to energize me to fire off a letter of complaint to the station as a way of trying to prevent disappointment in the future. Or, to take another example, suppose I experience a strong sexual attraction to someone. My initial, humane emotion is love and desire. But the utilitarian emotion of despair or even fear may intervene as I assess long-range possibilities.

Notice that these utilitarian emotions *may* intervene. There are many ways in which they can fail in their service of the humane emotions. In general, we can say that the utilitarian emotions fail us when they are not properly subject to insight. If I suppress my insight and thereby fail to take the longer view, then the humane emotions work without intelligence providing direction. Love and hate, desire and aversion, happiness and sadness are left up to mere chance and animal spontaneity. This happens regularly in people who were not taught as children to recognize their emotions and think things through. Their utilitarian emotions were never educated to provide the services needed by their humane emotions.

Furthermore, the utilitarian emotions themselves can become stunted in their growth because they contain too much instinctual element in them. For example, hope/despair become synonymous with love/hate when we fail to apply sufficient intelligence to sizing up obstacles. Likewise, courage/fear become synonymous with desire/aversion when we misgauge the amount of harm in a situation. Anger can degenerate into unthinking, raging aversion when it ceases to be a strategy of intelligence and becomes mere motor reaction.

One very common and specific way in which the failure of insight leads the utilitarian emotions to fail to serve the humane emotions properly can be seen when the utilitarian emotions are aimed directly upon the humane emotions, instead of upon the objects of those emotions. So, for example, a married woman may allow her fear of pursuing a career turn into a fear of the desire itself. She may effectively forbid the desire from entering awareness. Or a sick man may put so much hope in wanting to be healthy that he pins his hopes more on the power of his desire than on the advice of doctors. A teenager may "fall in love with love," that is, invest hope in the emotion of love rather than in the person loved. And surely we have all felt angry not merely at situations or other persons but at our own feelings of disappointment, of lust, of envy, and so on.

When crises arise and we need to sort out our emotions, it is very useful to admit all humane emotions into consciousness and allow ourselves to feel them—particularly such emotions as sexual desire, personal disappointment, instinctive aversion to certain persons, and lingering sadness.

Another way in which the failure of insight leads to a malfunctioning of utilitarian emotions can be seen in the phenomenon of "borrowing" emotions. This happens, for example, when we pick up the anger or the excitement of a friend about some object rather than being directly angry or excited about the object ourselves. No one wants to be a stick-in-the-mud, and so the temptation to borrow the emotional flow of the people one is with can be quite strong. And it can feel rather solitary to express feelings that no one else is feeling. But we each have a right and an obligation to attend to our actual feelings about things, admitting them at least to ourselves, if not also to others.

In a similar fashion we can even borrow feelings from *our own* habitual store of reactions to things. Our habitual feelings can often overshadow the actual transient feelings we experience towards specific objects at certain times. Insight is prevented from doing its job here because we are not paying attention to our actual feelings. The more we simply repeat old feelings in new situations, the more we become completely predictable and perfect stereotypes.

In all these cases, a vicious circle is set up. If we neglect a transient, humane emotion—let's say, aversion to old people—then insight has no data to play with. With no insight forthcoming, there is no chance for such utilitarian emotions as courage or fear to play an intelligible role in dealing with our aversion. So we may fake a great affection for the elderly or perhaps repeatedly find excuses for not spending time with them. The more we do this, the less we want to admit it, so even the faked feelings are not recognized as fake. We do not know what we feel and still less why we feel it. We effectively render the mind unable to determine exactly what we are feeling. So the mind becomes infected with a bias of which it is also unaware. In other words, when we fail to apply intelligence to our emotions, the emotions suffer first, but eventually the intellect does too. To know what we are feeling at any time may not always be a simple task. But it is quite a necessary one if we are to keep our minds and our emotions from turning to mush.

We have been talking about what psychologists call repression. In all repression, some emotion is neglected and we fail to advert to the neglect. But we should not get the idea that we neglect all desire or all sadness or all joy. Repression begins with a specific emotion about a specific object. So here we must acknowledge something very peculiar about our affectivity. Our emotions, both humane and utilitarian, can be detached from their initial objects and transferred to other objects. This transferability is what makes repression possible and gives us insight into how it works.

In repression, a desire or a repulsion has become detached from its initial object without our realizing it. The object of this original feeling—often parents, sex, or death—can be substituted by other objects more palatable to our affective sensibilities. But the desire for the substitute object lacks a certain proportion, so that we do not understand why we feel so strongly or so lackadaisical about various matters. We surprise both ourselves and others by our reactions. We may have suspected this uncoupling of feeling and objected for a moment but refused to look at it. Or we may have inherited a taboo from ancestors that forbade us even the thought that certain desires might be heading in a forbidden direction.

Let me give an example of how this works. It may help us understand ourselves and others by giving us key questions to ask.

Suppose, for reasons buried in childhood, you resent having to organize social gatherings. Whether you realize it or not, your subconscious has linked an affect with an image: resentment has become linked with organizing. Such a link between affect and image is precisely what constitutes a symbol. To recognize that affects and images can also be unlinked amounts to saying that symbols in the subconscious are divisible compounds.

74

Now suppose that you also love a good party. Love is the affect and the party is the image linked into a second symbol. As you can see, there will be times when these two symbols will clash, times when you are in the mood for a party but there is no one around willing to organize it.

Several possibilities follow from the clash. If you generally take on the task of organizing, you effectively unlink your image of organizing from the affect of resentment and attach it to the affect of love, forming a new symbol representing love for organizing parties. But that leaves a free-floating resentment meandering around the subconscious looking for an appropriate object—usually something more loosely connected with organizing. The less you acknowledge to yourself the existence of this resentment, the more likely you will earn a reputation for loving to organize parties and therefore you will heighten the tension of neurosis.

At the same time, the resentment is not asleep within; it takes a kind of revenge by refusing to organize even the smallest details in other parts of your ordinary life. Or, if even this kind of venting has been stopped, the resentment may build to the point of an uncontrollable explosion.

Of course this is not necessarily the only possible outcome of this repression. Instead you might generally refuse to organize parties. But then your free-floating love for fun erupts in surprising places and with surprising power.

Speaking more generally, a free-floating resentment, vindictiveness, or envy can lead to a genuine hatred of what we might otherwise deem a basic human value.[9] Reason may demand respect for soldiers, politicians, clergy, the aged, the good efforts of those who fail. But our guts, operating on the symbolic level and often ridden with repression, may detest such persons.

Likewise, free-floating fascination, lust, or desire can lead to an excessive love of merely penultimate values: money or sex or security. The point of recognizing the phenomenon of free-floating feelings is that it shows how important it is to understand first, and only then to evaluate. It is simplistic to condemn behavior we deem immoral. Much better, certainly, to grasp exactly what recombinant symbol is at work setting free the errant feelings and then devise a forum for responsible management of one's personal symbol system.

Psychoanalysis, surely, can help us understand our repressed affectivity. Analysts use techniques of free-association, hypnotism, and dream analysis to uncover the original objects of recalcitrant feelings. But we should not overlook the curative power of more ordinary and less expensive functions available to consciousness. The very process of dreaming lets affectivity relate to a wide range of objects without the prohibitions of a censor. Desires and fears appear in dreams in bald form, without the links of civility which, in waking consciousness, integrate them into a smoothly flowing dramatic pattern of experience. Likewise, our cronies—people with whom we complain about the state of things—allow us to let our affectivity loose and express itself far out of proportion without demanding too much hard realism. In similar fashions, the theater, fiction, art, and poetry give our affectivity free rein over matters of concern to all, and often bring us to the catharsis of hearty laughter or sorrowful tears.

Psychoanalysis may promise a clarity of understanding which dreaming, cronies, and the arts cannot promise, but it seldom has their sheer affective power. This is because these latter work directly within the symbol system, letting affects relate to their original objects in a lenient atmosphere that does not demand accounts and letting insight give direction to utilitarian emotions. However, where repression is long-standing and complex, these more ordinary and dramatic functions of consciousness do not have a great deal of analytic power for uncovering what those original objects of repressed affectivity were, and so some kind of psychoanalysis is needed.

To the degree that we do admit feelings into consciousness, we stop repressing them. But, as we saw already, our utilitarian feelings, prompted by the longer view of intelligence and reason, may still hold certain feelings in check. We call this kind of emotional governance suppression.

Suppression resembles repression, at least on the surface. In suppression, I *know* the initial objects of my feelings and, for cogent reasons, deem it inappropriate to go on feeling the same way about it. So I interrupt my emotional response to that object. I can transfer my affections to more appropriate objects.

Surely authenticity does not bind us to pursue every desire and obey every repulsion. So suppression will be as healthy or unhealthy as the measure in which the objects of my feelings merit the feelings. It will be healthy, for example, to suppress at least some natural revulsion to hard work. And it will be unhealthy to suppress the sting of conscience when driving a car too fast.

Notice, however, that while suppression appears akin to repression, they are only distant cousins. Where repression reveals a need for sheer analysis to determine the objects of my feelings, suppression raises moral questions of whether or not it is worthwhile to give in to certain affective pulls. Repression calls for intelligence while suppression calls for responsibility. Suppression, therefore, is the more crucial issue when talking about moral action.

Next we should investigate suppression more thoroughly and see how it functions to form or deform what everybody calls a 'conscience'.

4. Conscience

We spoke above about the need to name our feelings and to know their original objects because feelings are the initial impulses we experience towards recognizing and doing the good. But we also saw that some feelings move us towards the less worthy, and so we look to conscience to tell the difference. So, besides the difference between humane (instinctual) feelings and utilitarian (intellectual) feelings, we are recognizing a distinction between those feelings that respond to the truly valuable and those feelings that respond to the merely satisfying.[10] It is very important to notice, however, that we are not "making" the distinction. We are recognizing a distinction that everybody makes when they attend to their feelings. Let us look more closely at how this works.

We are all inclined to suppressing feelings that move us to actions which serve more the advantage of others than ourselves. We can habitually cooperate only with those feelings which lead to our own physical comfort, our own love of honor or security. Whether or not we admit it, we all work on a distinction between feelings that respond to the objectively good and feelings that respond to the narrow demands of our egos. No matter how morally refined we might become in our actions, we always face such questions as, "Should I get involved in this?" And we feel the tug between feelings that urge responsibility and feelings that urge mere self-satisfaction.

If we consistently try to discern the more responsible path, we consistently suppress feelings that respond to mere ego-centeredness. In so doing, we educate our feelings by empowering our intelligent, utilitarian emotions to direct our instinctive, humane emotions. However, those who are generally irresponsible are also educating their feelings, though teaching them the opposite lesson. They generally let the self-centered, instinctual feelings carry them away and suppress the more responsible, utilitarian feelings, which we know can be pitifully meagre at times. They learn, and eventually they believe with all their hearts, that "good" means nothing but "satisfying."

The point I am trying to make here is that both responsible people and irresponsible people attend to their feelings and suppress some in favor of others. So any person's conscience should not be thought of as some list of right things to do hidden in our moral psyches. Conscience is rather a system in which feelings, skills, knowledge, value judgments, and decisions are organized to work together. This organization is a developmental process and tends to head in either one of two possible directions, either towards the truly good or towards the merely satisfying.

This is why merely attending to feelings or a mere examination of conscience does not turn an egoist into an altruist overnight. This is why to move from hedonism or egoism to a life of responsibility and commitment requires a conversion, a *moral* conversion. And this is why it is so important to attend to moral education in our earliest years.

Responsible people gradually organize their feelings not only towards values as opposed to mere satisfactions, but towards some values as more important than others. They learn to rank their various affective reactions to the objective good.[11]

Generally speaking, that ranking becomes arranged like this. First there are the *vital* values of health, strength, and grace—preferred to avoiding the work involved in acquiring, maintaining, and restoring them.

Then there are the *social* values of cooperation and communication that help us maintain vital values by setting up economic, technological, and political institutions. So the vital values are preserved through commitment to social values.

Now responsible people are not content with just any social institution. They prefer institutions that give meaning and value to life, that direct our attention to beauty and give us the leisure to contemplate and appreciate the finer things. So they rely on *cultural* values to dignify human living. Cultural values, in other words, aim to insure the finest social and vital values.

But the recognition of cultural values only reveals more clearly the human person, how personal authenticity is the living source of all cultural values, and how love of neighbor is the chief fruit of a worthy culture. So *personal* values are more important than cultural values. Persons who are authentic are both the source and the object of cultural, social, and vital values.

Finally, there remains a higher value yet. We can call it *religious* value, but it means precisely the love of a divine object that simultaneously transcends all created objects of our love and drives us all towards the self-transcendence that is the source of personal values. We will deal with religious values more directly in the next chapter.

Remember that to each of these values there corresponds a distinct feeling. It is not an easy matter to recognize the different quality of these affective movements. Most of us tend to look for "that good ol' feeling" when we are about to leap. But the truly "good" feeling is often rather new. We need to get acquainted with it.

How do we learn to discern which feelings are headed which way? I would like to propose that a fully developed conscience dips back into past experience and remembers a few archetypical experiences of moral self-transcendence. In other words, besides storing up a memory of deeds which we consider good, we also learn to remember a specific combination of feelings and images which, although we seldom have accurate names for them, proved very real and immediate moral criteria by which we make decisions.

For example, we have all learned to associate certain feelings with certain deeds by watching someone else act morally and by feeling our hearts touched. Or perhaps, despite the personal odds facing us, we ourselves acted justly and earned a certain taste for justice and began from that day to depend on our new-found taste for it. In other words, the transcendental precept, Be responsible, is mediated to us to a large extent by the memory of a few key value judgments and their associated feelings, and these symbolic memories embody for us the actual ground of our own morality.

Since we lack ordinary names for these archetypical moral experiences that are specifically oriented towards the truly good and not the merely satisfying, let me propose four: *diké, eros, philia,* and *thanatos.*[12]

79

I am using Greek terms here to underscore the fact that they have their roots in Plato. But you will find that they stand for some very familiar experiences.

Diké means right order or justice. When we were adolescents, most of us learned the value of rules, both in games and in school. The good boy and girl would interiorize rules, thereby making themselves "good" persons. But the day eventually arrived when we realized that rules were made up by fallible people, our parents, teachers, and government officials. That is when we saw the bottom of things, that the rules of the game will be no better than the goodness of the persons who make them up. We experienced a new freedom to break rules, provided that we believed we were obeying an order within. We realized that real order in our homes and neighborhoods – indeed, even in our international relations – is not simply an orderly flow of particular goods and services. Real order also means acting from an ordered heart. And action from an ordered heart is the only foundation for a truly "right order."

Once we experience how external order results only from an ordered heart and that its purpose is to maintain ordered hearts, then we begin to bear within ourselves a new symbol for right order. This symbol stands not only for external rules and behavior but for internal order as well. It would resemble not so much ordered pigeon holes with everything in its proper place as an ordering process that moves the pigeon holes intelligently as each situation demands. Such a symbol serves for the rest of our moral lives to test our feelings as we encounter disorder. We possess a vivid memory, a feeling, an image, and a taste for this kind of self-transcendence that engenders true order.

Our second archetypical moral experience is *eros*. The experience of *eros*, in Plato's meaning of the word, is the experience of "It's not enough; there's more" within various experiences of human achievement. We may have achieved some penetrating insights; but we immediately pose further questions. We may have met the perfect friend; but we encourage such friends to become the better persons they want to be. In every sweet advance there lingers the bitter taste of limits. C.S. Lewis was fond of the German word *Sehnsucht* for describing this poignant longing that accompanies every touch of beauty.

The term *eros* may have become associated with sexual desire because sex provides such a good example of how our longing for more good leads us on to achieve that good. Sexual attraction between a woman and a man, for example, tends by its own dynamism to make them other-centered, through their children and through all the civic and cultural duties which eventually come with it. In scholastic terms, *bonum est diffusivum sui*: the good spreads itself around.

Surely the memory of this pull towards what is always greater can become a familiar experience as we successively try to meet our moral challenges in life. It can be so palpable at times that we dread its insistent demands.

Our third archetypical moral experience, *philia*, refers to a love different from *eros*. *Eros* aims always forward while *philia* is the lateral love we bear for the people with whom we seek to move forward. It is the experience of being part of a community of the maturing, the community of others who listen for truth in the soul and seek a good beyond their private spheres. It can be as few as two persons. *Philia* functions as a key moral criterion when, in the face of a decision (particularly a decision about what interior dispositions I will fight to maintain), I recall the face of someone with whom I have loved the good, the beautiful, the true; and I act in communion with him or her.

The mere memory of my companions in the struggle calls forth from me a courage and a self-sacrifice that not only helps me to grow morally but works to help the whole group grow. The moral fiber of a group is not merely the sum of the individual moral threads, as it were. The strength of each is enhanced by the memories of common commitment.

Finally, *thanatos* represents a certain class of experiences of self-transcendence connected with death. To acknowledge, often with a resigned nod, that what is good is more than just good for me, is to accept a servitude to an order that encompasses me and my life, an order for whose sake I spend my energies, and an order to which I am obedient even unto death. It is the order of true values. It will go on without me. There is no need to affirm an afterlife to justify the expense of doing good in this life. The good—what is truly good—is justification enough, even under the present conditions whereby the truly good is so often missed and the merely apparent good so often chosen.

We often experience this commitment to the truly good when someone we love dies. At the center of our sorrow stands a consolation, a pride in the fact that during their time on earth they lived not merely for themselves but left their mark in the goodness of their lives. And we know very well that many of these good acts involved winning interior battles, not for the sake of publicity or success, but for goodness' sake alone. Such is the experience of *thanatos*.

If, as I am suggesting here, our conscience is formed or deformed by key experiences such as these, then calling these experiences to mind and telling them to others help us locate what truly moral feelings can feel like. After all, our love for sheer fun and enjoyment, for recognition and applause, while they may be truly good at one time, may not be so good at another. And such love by itself cannot tell the difference. We have been blessed with another love, the desire for the truly good, and we must train ourselves and our children to tell the difference.

We have been regarding conscience as a system that refines its own capabilities as it successfully meets existential challenges. But it would be a mistake to think that conscience grows only in response to challenges. The precept, Be responsible, is meant to urge us not only to respond to ethical dilemmas but to invent, create, and play as well.

In a well-developed conscience, after all, the power behind the creative impulse is love of neighbor. When we care for another person, we search out ways to act on his or her behalf. We prefer to share what we have with our friend rather than keep it to ourselves. We like to be inventive in finding ways to please our beloved. We are creatures made to love and care for persons. Being moral is doing that. Being moral is fundamentally being in action for another. Anyone who is not doing that is immoral, even though he or she gets in nobody's way.

For example, in international relations we speak of the "immoral" acts of aggression and building of nuclear stockpiles. And they are immoral. But not just because it narrows the elbow room of other countries or even threatens the livability of the earth as a whole. Nearly all thinkers on nuclear morality think this. They imagine human freedom means being 90% free of any control and 10% restricted for the sake of everyone else's 90%. This outrageous picture imagines that humans are animals who like to do all sorts of crazy things, and that this is all right, provided only that your craziness does not get in the way of mine. But these belligerent acts are immoral first of all because they are a failure to act in love and care for others. So it is ridiculous to talk about whether nuclear deterrence might possibly be moral. It is not. It is a last awakening of a conscience, long comatose, that failed to enhance the lives of others on an international scale.

The internal system we call a conscience exists only by a continual expansion from a love-needing, super-ego dominated consciousness of the child to the love-giving, conscience-dominated consciousness of the adult.[13] Once a conscience settles into merely applying the principles it has already learned, it begins to atrophy. A vigorous conscience continually directs its intelligence to discover how to share, how to welcome, how to enhance the lives of others. This is why truly good people are outraged at the sort of moral reasoning that claims to find certain circumstances in which a lie, a murder, or a war could ever be called "moral." These are nothing but the terrible price we pay for a long season of the immorality of lovelessness.

Before going much further, we should mention at least something about the love of God here. The connection between morality and religion may not be a very clear one, particularly if we look at the history of religions. But we can look into consciousness and discover a surprisingly clear connection between conscience and loving the transcendent.

The very fact that our conscience is expansive by nature tells us that we long for a good beyond criticism. This is a powerful piece of evidence that we are already in love with something that transcends ourselves and transcends every human achievement. We spoke of this above as *eros*: the feeling that "It's not enough; there's more." This *eros* is not a passive hope; it is an active force that catapults us out of our narrow perspectives and pitches us into the realm of the finest.

Now when we discover this *eros* for ourselves and let it do its work on us, we want this for others too. So we do what we can to help our neighbors discover and embrace this movement towards the finest in themselves. In this way we discover a paradox: the more I love my friend, the more I experience my own solitude. For what is absolutely the finest thing in the world is not absolute cooperation and agreement between us. It is rather that each of us, as far as possible, obeys the *eros* in his or her spirit.

In the next chapter we will examine how the love of God integrates the movement of conscience into a higher movement yet. For now we ought to summarize what we have covered so far.

In this discussion of conscience, we spoke of moral conversion and feelings, of moral development, of the affective criteria in decision-making, and finally of the expanding and loving nature of conscience. Some readers may be uneasy over the fact that moral criteria are precariously perched on affective development and on the chancy business of conversion. They may want to see something more secure—if not a set of do's and don't's, then at least a few inviolable principles. But let me say at once that the only inviolable principle is the transcendental precept, Be responsible, and that we put this principle into practice not through a logical deduction in one case after another, but through the attentive, intelligent, reasonable, and responsible actions of a large number of men and women over a long period of time. That is the nature of the beast we call 'conscience'.

In our study of authenticity, feelings, and conscience, we have concentrated on the subjective side of doing good. Now we can look at its objective side and see how it relates to the subjective. What is the human "good" towards which conscience looks?

5. The Human Good: A Process View

By calling our topic "the human good," we run two fundamental risks. First, we are apt to think of nothing but good objects: a good car, a good vacation, a good spouse. We are letting our imaginations restrict our intelligences here. The "good" is not always visible, nor is it simply "out there," an object without somebody wanting it. Every 'object' considered good is *considered* good by a subject, a person. This is very plain to see when we watch, for example, two car buffs argue the "objective" merits of a Mercedes-Benz over a Rolls-Royce. We simply cannot talk about objective worth of things without also talking about human persons, their value judgments, and the kinds of moral bias that may be distorting those judgments.

The second risk we run is the Platonic expectation that we are going to study something abstract, something all "good" things must possess. Goodness here is conceived as something reality may or may not possess, a kind of metaphysical stuff that good things have and bad things do not. This makes goodness something somehow above real things, something reality participates in to the degree that real things are truly 'good'. But *goodness*, like *whiteness* or *happiness* does not exist. There are only good movies, white blouses, happy children.

So we have to think of the utterly concrete when we discuss the good.

We can avoid these materialist and idealist mistakes by thinking of the good in terms of process.[14] And the process we have in mind is, quite simply, the process of choosing good things as it really occurs among us. We want to understand the ordinary structures of the entire process—taking in the subjective aspects as well as the objective, the social aspects as well as the individual, and the question of moral rightness vs. moral bias. For the most part we will leave out of our discussion such natural 'goods' as earth, sunshine, and all the subhuman processes that human process relies on. Our interest is in the good things humans choose or reject. Then, once we have understood *what* goes on when we choose things, we can cooperate more intelligently and realistically with the process of doing good in our world.

We begin by noticing that every concrete instance of something we consider a human good is an event-conditioned thing. Our intellectual conversion ought to expect this. Imagine a few examples: a pizza, a car, a lovely vase of flowers, a refreshing swim. We would not have these things to enjoy were it not for certain events going on. Someone had to make the pizza. Someone had to decide on what make and model of car. Flowers need planting and picking. And there had to be the proper pipes and valves to deliver water to the pool.

Among this vast array of conditions that makes every particular good thing possible, we can see two major kinds of conditions.

First there has to be some setup, some routine, some institution, some scheme of recurrence that brings forth a certain kind of particular good *regularly*. So, for example, a pizzeria, an auto industry, a skilled eye that arranges the flowers in an enhancing vase, and a city water department all have as their purpose the continuous production of particular good things. The same is true for every language, every set of customs, every cultural or religious ritual, and every educational system, whether the size of a Michigan State University or a mother teaching her child the ABC's. These are institutions aimed at the *ongoing* production of goods.

Lonergan calls this setup the 'good of order'. It is not the particular good things themselves. It is rather the set of events that keeps the particular goods flowing regularly. The good of order is absolutely invisible. But if you need convincing that it really exists, compare a country with an expanding economy to a country with a faltering economy. Compare a society with laws to a country without laws. Compare an industry at work to an industry on strike. The good of order exists when a large set of activities is ordered; and it does not exist where activities are not ordered.

What are the events that keep particular goods flowing regularly? Principally, human insights. Imagine a young boy who spots a silver dollar under a sidewalk grating. By an initial insight he fixes a wad of gum on the end of a long, narrow stick in order to lift the coin out. If he is successful, a second insight hits him: keep the stick; there may be more lost coins waiting to be rescued beneath other gratings! This second-level insight sets up a coin-rescuing institution to keep the coins coming in. It also educates such utilitarian emotions as hope, expectation, and perseverance to overcome any difficulties that may appear. We enjoy such secondary insights every time we arrange our rooms or buy the tools of our trade. We aim at facilitating more regular enjoyment of good things.

The same insight required to set up an institution is also required to participate in it. If you own a garlic press or a home computer but do not understand how to use them, you will not be able to enjoy the efficiency they can provide. But to the degree that you do gain these insights and take advantage of them, you become a changed person. You learn new skills. You learn new habits. Your instinctual, humane emotions about particular good things become educated, utilitarian emotions about the institutions that keep them going. Among the people who know you, you might gain some reputation for being a gourmet cook or a systems analyst.

So the first major condition in which we find particular goods is that they normally are connected to an institution, usually to a complex of many institutions. And by 'institution' we do not mean some building with a company name on it. We mean a set of insights, skills, habits, and feelings oriented to the continuous flow of particular things that people want. The second-level insights produce and maintain the institution, but the institution incorporates all its participants into a recognizable, cooperating social body.

The second major condition in which we find particular goods is that they are desired by persons who may or may not be morally converted.

A friend of mine once remarked, "My needs never cause me a problem; it's my desires that get me into trouble!" The implication, of course, is that we ought to discern what we really need and not merely drift with the winds of desire. Moral conversion aims to accomplish this. A commitment to true needs—which often includes the need to put the good of others before our own—is a commitment to getting an upper hand on mere desire. This is what being responsible means.

A particular good thing, however, can be desired both by responsible and irresponsible people. The philanthropist and the miser both want money, but for vastly different purposes. We all know that when people say a movie was "good" or a party was "terrific," they reveal as much about their own moral makeup as about the movie or party.

If particular goods are always found in personal moral horizons, then so will the institutions that keep the particular goods flowing. We approve or disapprove not only of particular things but also of habits, of customs, and of organizations depending on what "valuable" means to us. If it means the maximization of personal pleasure, we will approve of hedonistic institutions. If it means the maximization of the truly worthwhile, we will disapprove of hedonistic institutions. By the same token we will approve or disapprove of our utilitarian emotions, the emotions shaped by intelligence. If our hope/despair, courage/fear, or anger are educated to serve mere self-centered desire, we may or may not find that acceptable, depending on whether or not we are morally converted to the truly valuable.

So, besides a social order based on insight, we also have a cultural order based on value judgments. The social order is built on the insights, the insights into how to cooperate to keep the particular goods flowing, while the cultural order is built on the value judgments that weigh the worth both of the particular goods and of the institutions that produce them. These two orders are not distinct communities of people. Rather, they are distinguishable orders within any community. Of the two, the cultural order plays the major role in making a community human. For a community based merely on shared skills and insights is like a gear with well-fitting cogs: no cog complains that the gear may be turning for the wrong purposes. A fully human community shares a sense of common purpose. The members agree on the worthiness of its common goals and usually have a say in determining what those goals ought to be and how well they are being pursued.

In most of the cases we have experienced, we find an annoying tension between the social order and the cultural order in a community. The social order specializes in planning, organizing, exploring the possible, and trimming away the fat of inefficiency. But it is interested only in the means to produce things people want, not in the objective worth of those particular goods. The cultural order, in contrast, is interested in the ends. It specializes in evaluating, in criticizing, in enhancing whatever is worthy, and in excising whatever is worthless. The tension between the social and cultural orders is relatively permanent because insights and value judgments both occur in the same person, and every person experiences both an impulse to insight and an impulse to value judgments. Insights open up possibilities that value judgments cannot dream of, while value judgments give purpose to insight and render us more than mere machines. Only a regular obedience to the transcendental precepts by each member of a community can successfully direct brilliant insights towards worthwhile ends.

We have seen how the particular goods we desire belong to three invisible but very real sets of processes, or schemes of recurrence. On the immediate level, good things are simply the objects of people's desires. But there is also the institution that produces the particular good to be considered, along with the education of feelings and the socialization it effects. And there is the cultural order that passes judgment on the worth of the things desired and of the institutions, habits, skills, and emotions that produce them.

By way of a review, you may find it helpful to study the chart:

Three meanings of "good"	Three corresponding operations in the person	Three dimensions of affectivity	Three dimensions of community
1. Particular good things	Experienced desires, needs	Humane, instinctual emotions	Collective desires, needs
2. Good of order	Insight, skills, habits	Utilitarian, intellectual emotions	Social order, institution, the setup
3. True value	Value judgments, commitments	Moral conversion	Cultural order, personal relations

What is important to realize is that every particular good thing in the world is like this—whether a pizza, a car, a vase of flowers, or a swim. Every social institution in the world is like this—whether a language, a law, an agreement, a habitual feeling, or a social symbol. And every cultural force in the world is like this—whether a sonata, an editorial, a prophetic outcry, or love of neighbor.

Once we see that every particular good is linked into a social order and a cultural order, and that the desires, insights, feelings, and value judgments on which they rely are processes within persons, then we will be better able to understand our world and to guide its development. Let me suggest five canons that ought to guide any reflection on concrete situations.

First, the business of doing good in the world is a moderately, but not impossibly, complex process that is simultaneously individual and social, subject to bias and yet naturally expansive to overcome not only the erring that is so human but the malice that is so human as well. If we overlook any of these elements when we read our newspapers or history books, or when we make plans for the future, we are bound to overlook something good.

Second, the starting point of any investigation ought to be the particular goods. A community does not set up its values first, a functional organization second, and then start to crank out the goods. Rather, a community wants some particular goods or services regularly, and as it organizes to achieve this goal, it also evaluates and, if necessary, adjusts the goal. This is the nature of all community, whether it be a couple in love, a family, a religious order, a city, an athletic club, or what have you. When we want to understand such a community, we begin with the particular goods, grasp the guiding insights that keep them flowing, and then name the underlying values that seem to be at work.

Third, just as it requires insight to *create* an institution, so it takes insight to *understand* that institution. (And remember, by 'institution' we mean any and all kinds of agreements aimed at getting good things regularly; it does not have to be public or legally recognizable.) One does not understand a setup by reading propaganda or studying written laws or contracts or constitutions. One understands it by grasping why particular goods and services flow the way they do. The reality of capitalism or communism, of Democrats or Republicans, of Catholics or Protestants, of patriarchy or feminism, of my family or yours, is revealed only when we understand the concrete, functioning insights that make them cohesive bodies meeting desires for particular goods.

Fourth, the good of order is stable by nature. It resists changes in procedures because these render certain skills obsolete. Changes in the setup shake up an entire social order because they upset utilitarian feelings of attachment and loyalty, they alter the pecking order in the community, and they put strains on interpersonal relations. Even more stubbornly does the good of order, the institution, resist changes in long-range goals. This is because institutions specialize in insights, not in value judgments. They thrive on efficiency and quantities, not value or quality. Therefore, anyone contemplating a change in how things are going to work ought to give serious thought to the adaptations required in people's skills, feelings, friendships, and—most importantly—insight into the new order. Unless all the members grasp the overall picture, they will be unable to provide the many supplementary insights that concrete situations demand.

Fifth, just as it takes moral conversion to *create* a culture committed to true value, so it takes moral conversion to recognize a converted community. Again, one does not recognize conversion by just reading texts or watching behavior. One evaluates the particular goods, the setups that produce them, and even other evaluators. Imagine, for example, that a small-town library plans to sell all the books which were not borrowed for, say, ten years. We could tell more about that town's moral commitments by surveying the titles read and the titles unread than by reading its newspaper editorials or pamphlets from its Chamber of Commerce. And yet, while one person may conclude that the town is rather morally upright, another may conclude that it is rather decadent. This leads us to the dialectical situation in which evaluators are evaluating each other's moral sensibilities. In our final chapter we will say more about how to deal with such a dialectic. For now it is enough to recognize that no one of us can really stand outside a situation and pass moral judgment on it without becoming part of the evaluation situation.

The foregoing process account of the structure of the human good, brief as it is, is meant to account for the origin of all the goods humans produce. You will likely find this analysis cogent enough, but you may have difficulty passing judgment on how correct it is. It is very important for your spiritual integration, however, if you at least let this view challenge some of the more materialist and idealist views that you may have absorbed along the way.

The materialist imagines that goodness is a visible or palpable force pulsating within good things and evoking our appreciation or desire. "You can just *feel* it!" The materialist has little notion of how buying a sewing machine imposes an order on one's affectivity and involves one in a specific social class. Nor do we find in the materialist any great concern to distinguish true need from mere desire. "If I want a sewing machine, and I can afford one, why in the world shouldn't I get one?" Nor is there much concern to distinguish personal commitment from mere cooperation. "Sure, I work for a nuclear weapons plant, but that has nothing to do with what I think about nuclear war!" In many cases such as these, the materialist thinks the good is just "already out there" and that is all there is to it.

The idealist is more astute. He or she is convinced of the difference between good and bad but deep down believes that there is an ideal way for all people to get along together. In light of the overall ideal, we can deduce what the ideal behavior is in this or that situation. "If people would only realize that true community is based on *trust*, then. . . ." The fundamental problem about being moral becomes a matter of determining what the ideal really is and to be intelligent enough to see how we ought to proceed towards it. Thus Marx envisioned a world built on communism, and Comte envisioned a world built on scientific progress. To the idealist, the good is some abstract possibility that we try to discover, and once we discover it, then we *deduce* what social institutions ought to be set up to pursue it.

In contrast to materialism and idealism, we are saying that goodness does not lurk in objects nor in an ideal possibility. The human good is an ongoing process by which desires are organized by insight and both are given direction by moral conversion. It is a process notoriously vulnerable to both error and malice. And yet it is also malleable under the force of the transcendental precepts, Be attentive, Be intelligent, Be reasonable, Be responsible. When these are obeyed, error and malice are gradually overcome and the truly good gradually emerges.

The ultimate court of appeal, therefore, is neither how desirable a thing looks nor how rational a possibility seems to be. To deal with disagreements on the worth of particular goods and of our institutions, we evaluate the persons on either side. Morally converted persons readily recognize and respect one another. They may disagree on procedures, but they quickly move to the level of shared purposes, where they expect to find agreement. From there they hope to collaborate in creating procedures amenable to the common good.

Those whose moral conversion has been retarded feel at least a respect for and usually an attraction to the worldview of those more developed. They are learners and have developed at least the humility to acknowledge it.

The greatest difficulty is with those whose moral conversion has hardly begun, who barely know the existence of a converted horizon. The greater they are in numbers, the more likely they will win the day. They cannot be argued out of their faith in mere desire because they do not put faith in argument; their faith is in mere desire. Nor are they easily attracted out of it by the example of good persons. Even if they desired to be such admirable persons, they feel no desire to walk the path that truly admirable men and women have always walked, a path that often detours around mere desire.

Our discussion has brought us to a point that everyone recognizes very well: A good situation tends to get better while a bad situation tends to get worse. But it has also laid bare the nature of the problem of how to consistently bring the good about. Once a family or a nation grows to the point of self-centeredness, how can it be turned around? To what can we appeal?

There is more to this difficulty than meets the eye. The unconverted come in several different forms, and so there will be different strategies to deal with each. But in order to deal with this properly, we ought to look more closely at how in general a community or a situation improves and how it breaks down. In other words, we ought to look more closely at the nature of historical progress and decline.

6. Historical Progress and Decline

An improving situation in human society is a spiral of events.[15] The operators that keep the spiral turning and rising are the transcendental precepts, Be attentive, Be intelligent, Be reasonable, Be responsible. As long as they are working in the people involved, a situation tends to get better.

For example, if we consider any concrete social situation that is generally improving, we will still find within it a set of problems. But the improvement going on has a specific character. Attention has uncovered one of the problems. Intelligence has produced explanations of the nature of the problem and has suggested solutions. Reason has tested the explanations and the suggestions to make sure they are realistic. Responsibility has evaluated the costs and benefits to all concerned and has applied the best available solution. This is how the situation became improved. The improved situation, of course, has its own problems, but they are fewer in number. And the fewer the problems, the higher the odds become on the next turn of the spiral that further application of the transcendental precepts will spot anomalies and apply apt solutions. So, where we find authentic men and women in a good situation, we find that their situation tends to get better and that they tend to respond to difficulties more quickly.

A worsening situation is also a spiral of events, but the spiral turns backwards and downwards. The reason is that at least some of the transcendental precepts are being ignored.

Thus, given a concrete situation with its normal set of problems, no one may want to attend to certain parts of the problem, so these parts of the problem continue. Or the people involved may be aware of the problem but understand it merely in mythical or shortsighted terms, and again the problem continues but is now compounded by misunderstanding. Or they may look at a number of explanations and proposals but be completely unrealistic about picking the one that meets all the relevant data, which only makes them further out of touch with what is going on around them. So the problem is further compounded by illusion and the unrealistic remedies it endorses. Or they may see exactly what the problem is and what ought to be done about it but either fail to act or apply some irresponsible remedy, and then they have the further problem on their hands of a failure in moral nerve and a remedy that makes no sense. At the next turn of the spiral, the odds become worse that the transcendental precepts can be effectively applied to the worse situation. So a bad situation tends to get worse and the responses to difficulties occur more slowly.

We have been considering an improving situation and a worsening situation. But this is a somewhat abstract way of looking at it. Concretely, our human situations are mixtures of upward spirals and downward spirals. The same particular goods, as we saw, can be pursued by the converted and the unconverted alike. An institution that provides funds for the needy also provides funds for the greedy. It remains true that progress will result only from obedience within and that decline will result only from disobedience within, but it is very difficult to discern one from the other in actual cases, let alone in one's own soul.

Lonergan has analyzed situations in which elements for progress have blended with elements for decline and has found four types of bias to which we are always prone: neurosis, individual egoism, group egoism, and intellectual shortsightedness.[16] We should look at each of these. They represent permanent tensions in the consciousness of all people, good or bad. And because these biases are our own permanent possibilities for ruining good situations, they represent the same sort of evil which Scripture and tradition have called Original Sin. This analysis, however, does not ask how we got this way, as the story in Genesis does. It only attempts to understand how situations in fact get worse. What follows, then, is an explanation of four ways in which we normally suppress the work of the transcendental precepts in us.

1. Neurosis

The chief mechanism in a neurosis is repression. As we saw above, an affect can be unlinked from its original image and linked to an alternate image. This can occur without our knowledge. Popular wisdom has proclaimed that we are afraid of certain feelings. But this is not quite accurate. The feelings emerge eventually, even though attached to some alternate image. We see anger, lust, grief, sorrow, and the like expressed all the time in today's culture, running at a pitch far out of proportion to their objects.

A more cogent case can be made for saying that what we are afraid of is the original image. And the reason we fear certain images is that they will bring an unwanted insight into ourselves. The reason we do not want certain insights into ourselves is that understanding will demand a change in the routines that provided us some elementary security. This is a case of an integrator system challenging an operator system.

Repression does not prevent us from looking at such images altogether. In fact, a really efficient repression allows us to look at them directly and to deal with them smoothly. The chief work of repression is simply to prevent us from letting an image appear in its original affective setting. That is why the techniques of free association, psychodrama, and conversations with these image-figures often have surprising power. They allow the original image to appear in its original dramatic setting and thereby stimulate in us questions about it.

The kinds of images we are talking about, we must not forget, are not some abstract, gothic images of coffins or sexual organs, but the concrete childhood memories of watching someone in the family die or hearing stern warnings from some repressive teacher not to touch "down there."

A repressive mechanism develops compulsive routines, stylized or ritualized circuits around a feared dramatic image. It does this to compensate for the more demanding adaptations which intelligence would suggest. In vital areas neurotics do not understand themselves and are misunderstood by others, because of these hardened routines. So they choreograph a secondary set of stylized or ritualized dances, equally unintelligible to others and intelligible to themselves only as canny ways to appear in public without being taken for a fool. In this way they develop a protective system. In specific areas they appear rigid, compulsive, repetitious, almost religiously obedient to some inner law. Their employers, friends, and relatives feel obliged to create routines of their own to respect that inner law because they care for the neurotic and want to get along without incident. Everybody is convinced that these adaptations are necessary, but nobody understands why. And every scheme which is aimed merely at breaking down the protective routines without pinpointing the unwanted dramatic image only makes the situation worse.

2. Egoism

The egoist resembles the neurotic inasmuch as everyone feels constrained to make adjustments in order to keep the peace. But the egoist is up to some self-centered scheme knowingly, and so what is needed is not insight but moral conversion. And since moral conversion is no automatic process, the forbearance and the adjustments of others continue, but with the added exasperation over the fact that everyone knows very well what is going on.

Until the egoist decides to change, acquaintances try various tactics, ranging from stinging the conscience to the application of tender loving care. While the squeaky wheel gets the grease, their own valuable intellectual energies are being drawn away from larger concerns.

The conversion of the egoist in their midst can become a habit, even a pride. A family can spend all its moral capital on reforming one person and so justify their neglect of concern for their neighbors and for world affairs. They feel conscientious, but their narrow moral horizon restricts their intellectual inquiry. They read little, vote without intelligence, and swallow clever propaganda whole hog.

So the individual egoist is a dried-up well when the community needs insight into the common good. But the very efforts of the community to reform its resident egoist also render it that much less likely to get the insights it needs to meet political, economic, and social crises beyond its doors.

3. Group egoism

Group egoism, like individual egoism, works by regularly suppressing insights into the good of outsiders. And like the individual neurotic, a self-centered group creates a style and a set of rituals meant to dignify this refusal to consider the needs of other groups.

But when we look at the broad scale of history, and at the worst miseries that civilizations have inflicted on one another, the role of neurosis and individual egoism in destroying a community pale in comparison to the bias of one community against the welfare of another. Even a Hitler, who was both a neurotic and an egoist, needed German nationalism and Aryan pride on which to build his Reich. Many neurotics and egoists can be healed in a relatively short period. At worst, their malady does not last longer than their personal lifetimes. But the bias of a group does not depend on how long its individual members live. In nearly every historical case we can think of, the bias of a group lasts the lifetime of the group. And the lifetime of the group is usually ended only by the vengeance or greed of some other more powerful group, which will have its own brand of self-centered bias. Truly moral communities hardly ever result from the reformation of a previously selfish community. They nearly always spring from prophetic leaders who gather members from among the disenfranchised in other communities. Or else, like Israel, they undergo a reform with only a small remnant of the original community and do so at the terrible cost of breaking family and economic ties.

The reason that group bias is so impervious to healing is that there is a tension between intersubjective feeling and practical intelligence.

Intersubjectivity is conservative and stabilizing by nature. It revels in consistent behavior, codes of etiquette, nostalgia, long-term commitments, the steady development of loyalty, and the ready means for knowing who belongs and who does not. Practical intelligence pulls in another direction. It is progressive and destabilizing by nature. The more intelligence is given free rein over practical matters, the more it sees room for improvements, suggests alterations in the institutions that provide particular goods, streamlines some procedures and cancels others—all of which tends to change familiar ways of doing things.

This tension between intersubjective feeling and practical intelligence normally should be resolved by the mediation of objective value judgments provided by a rich culture. But as often as not the wisest voices in a culture prefer those changes that provide the most good for the most people, not just for their own people. On the surface that can look like disloyalty to the community and is often made out to be such. So the easier path is simply to entertain those practical insights which do not put any strains on group feeling but instead provide more group cohesion.

So a given group may be quite creative and visionary on its own behalf but overlook insights into the good of other groups and even regard other groups as nothing but means to its own end. As long as the group remains in power, its insights are the operative ones, while the insights of the oppressed groups, intelligent in themselves, are blocked from implementation. The dominant group recognizes that only by power can it maintain its own hegemony on putting ideas into practice, and so it bends its intelligence also towards manipulating the economy, organizing its military forces, and refining the technology by which the oppressed groups can be efficiently rubbed out the minute there is trouble. That diverts just that much intelligence away from attending to the dominant group's internal problems, and, barring a violent revolution, the external oppressed group has only to wait while these internal problems bring the dominant group to its knees.

4. Commonsense shortsightedness

A fourth bias or distortion of intelligence to which we are all prone is a bias against taking the long-range view. "Good common sense" specializes in practical-mindedness, adaptability, and quick results. But common sense does not specialize in history or philosophy or literary criticism or theology. It prefers to raid these territories every once in a while and rustle a few insights to meet concrete situations. It distorts these insights without realizing it because it tears them away from a fabric of related insights and tries to patch them onto a quilt without design. It thinks that its greatest wisdom can be condensed into mottoes and displayed on posters.

So common sense suffers two permanent limitations. First, it regularly fails to think in terms of history—to learn lessons from the past, and to look further than tomorrow when planning for the future. We see evidence of this in the nuclear power industry's persistent failure to deal with problems of safety and disposal of toxic wastes. We see it in the failure of automobile companies to produce efficient automobiles. We see it in the refusal of industrial cities to diversify their works and so avoid the usual fate of a one-industry town.

Behind this first limitation of common sense lies the second. Common sense does not have the sense to recognize this first limitation. In other words, by not recognizing its own problems, it thinks itself omnicompetent. Only when people also possess the uncommon sense that is willing to take the longer view do they willingly subordinate their common sense to an in-depth study of the human species.

Why is common sense so limited and blind to its limits? Again, because of the tension between intersubjective feelings and practical intelligence. Intelligence by itself has the drive and the norms for understanding profoundly complex problems. But as each of us grew up, we specialized not in the intellectual pattern of experience but in the dramatic. Our minds were oriented to meet the immediate intersubjective demands of hearth and kin. So our intelligences stay myopic. We readily deal with the immediate, and we suspect that anyone who withdraws into reading history or discussing philosophy is evading issues.

Obviously we are making a case here for the hard work involved in dealing with theoretical and scholarly issues. So far we have simply made the raw assertion that common sense fails to take the long-range view, and anyone can deduce that this probably results in short-sighted solutions. The case can be made much more forcefully if we look at how the persistent dependence on common sense creates progressively absurd situations. Let me present a domestic example.

Imagine a husband and wife with two children. And suppose the husband drinks heavily—a two-martini lunch with a few more before dinner and a nightcap before bed. As we can expect, he will not have his wits about him when he eats with his family. At first his wife and children will avoid issues that might enrage him. Then the children will arrive late for dinner and leave early, staying out later to avoid contact. He becomes concerned and angry towards them, and he tries all kinds of inducements to win back their respect, ranging from strict discipline to expensive gifts. His wife sees the problem and nags him for drinking. As it often happens in such cases, the children resent their mother for the grief she seems to cause their father.

Notice the insights at work. The children are shrewd enough to avoid certain issues, and they intelligently spot the negative effect which their mother's nagging has. The mother understands that drinking is the problem. And the father himself is quite practical-minded in his efforts at mollifying the children. But these insights all head in different directions. They do not form a coherent whole. The reason, of course, is that the husband will not acknowledge the root of the problem, and no one understands what remedies have proved effective for others. An organization like Alanon makes it its business to teach the long-range view to families. Their aim is to help a family build insight upon insight into a coherent whole. The fundamental insights come from research, and the implemental insights come from the particular family involved.

So, because of one fundamental oversight there arise many practical solutions which are incompatible with one another. The father lays down rules requiring the children to stay home, while the children create excuses to escape. The mother harangues the father because the family is breaking up, while the children see the family breaking up because the mother harangues the father. Further adjustments are applied to these adjustments, and in the end either the family breaks up altogether or it is held together by sheer tyranny.

What we see in this family is also true of corporations, nations, and entire civilizations. Insight has the capacity to discover the roots of problems and to learn from human mistakes. It functions by complementing fundamental insights with further insights into present situations. This takes time and hard work, but this is how a culture becomes wise. When there is a neglect of long-range vision and fundamental insights, then practical insights merely meet those aspects of fundamental problems that apply to one's immediate situation.

In the middle of this series of unrelated adaptations, common sense is looking desperately for a guiding principle that will hold everything together. It is already apprehensive that down the line there lurks either a complete collapse or a brutal dictatorship. And common sense nearly always clings to the principle that "We must face facts!" The facts, after all, are the real problem, and what is needed seems to be the courage to look the problem directly in the eye.

Recall, however, what we said earlier about a fact. A fact, if it is of any significance, is a human understanding of human events. So in reality, when we think of ourselves as facing facts, we are really just attending to human interpretations of human activities. In both the activities and in the interpretations there likely occur the biases of neurosis, egoism, group bias, and commonsense myopia. Common sense fails to see this, fails to see a need to discern the intelligible from the absurd in human situations and so will naively crank out insights that leave the absurdities untouched and thereby add even more absurdity to an already deteriorating situation.[17] In short, common sense is not enough sense.

So we ought to approach all human situations with a critical eye and resist the commonsense impulse to accept the givens of a situation as uniformly coherent. Even psychologists and sociologists tend to act as though all human problems are intelligible. They are not. They do contain an intelligible portion which analysis can illuminate, but they also contain an unintelligible suppression of attention, intelligence, reason, or responsibility; and that requires therapies of mercy and forgiveness. Jacobo Timmerman, a Jewish critic of Israeli policies, was told to face the facts, to "Take it or leave it." His reply was perfect: "I will not take it, and I will not leave it."

There is more to be said about the combined spirals of progress and decline. Our analysis so far has revealed how important it is for all people of common sense to subject their common sense to the lessons of history and philosophy, and to resist the resigned attitude that is willing to accept things as they stand. But our analysis has also shown that things as they stand contain a permanent set of biases that will forever drag against the upward dynamics of human attention, intelligence, reason, and responsibility. But this is by no means the end of the story. Fortunately there is yet another factor to which all good men and women turn. We need to talk about love.

Discussion Questions: CHAPTER THREE

These questions are designed to test how well you realize the ramifications of the material in this chapter. Their answers will rely also on materials from chapter 2. Again, although my own replies (which are by no means definitive) can be found in the appendix, please attempt to write out and/or discuss your own replies without relying on mine.

Question 1

Karl Marx has provided a method of critiquing ideologies that even some Christian theologians find useful. In brief, one of the major insights of Marx is this: the particular goods that men and women desire and the skills they learn are not generated from within their own psyches. They are conditioned by the economic order, the arrangements of the forces of production. In Marx's view, the capitalist system shapes the psyches of individuals without their realizing it. It alienates workers from their own selves by imposing desires and skills which make life comfortable for the wealthy stockholders and which prevent the cultivation of desires and skills that might dignify the lives of workers.

This is a very useful critique, not only of capitalism, but paradoxically of the present forms of communism as well. However, there still remains a danger in it. Compare Marx's conception of the human good to Lonergan's.

Question 2

Suppose a teacher friend of yours writes you a letter about her situation at school:

> Our principal is a real power politician, and people really don't like it at all. He makes all the decisions himself and gives only the appearance of consulting the rest of us. Last month he pretended to ask our advice about the need for a new music teacher, while in fact he had already signd a contract with a friend of his without telling anybody. Unless we can get him out of here, the faculty will be in revolt. Teachers will quit. Or at least they will drag their feet on every issue. The whole institution will break down. Any advice you have will be greatly appreciated!

What advice would you give her? Can you back up your advice with any of the theoretical materials we have presented? In what sense is her view "factual"? Is the principal really the "problem"?

Question 3

Suppose now that your teacher friend sends you the following letter a few weeks later:

> Thank you so much for your letter. Your explanation of how our principal/faculty problem is a *system* has been very helpful. I took the risk of showing it to the principal and he was surprisingly open to looking at the problem with us. The trouble is, we don't know where to begin. So I'm asking you for further advice. Do we just spend a weekend sharing our hopes and fears? I'm afraid that even if we do that we still won't be able to put our finger on the problem. I wait with bated breath for further wisdom!

What advice would you give now? Can you give reasons for that advice drawn from our study of the structure of the human good?

Question 4

The distinctions between instinctual and intellectual emotions, as well as between repression and suppression may be helpful for an individual's emotional health. But what has it got to do with the 'spiritual integration' of a community? Surely this ideal involves more than just emotional health for individuals. What is it about the ministry that makes it so important for a minister to understand his or her own feelings?

Question 5

In Lonergan's structure of the human good, there is a dimension of community called 'personal relations' or the 'cultural order'. It appears to be the communal aspect of a person's moral conversion. These relations correspond to a person's value judgments and commitments in the same way that the social order relates to a person's insights, skills, and habits. What does that mean, concretely?

Also, the term 'personal relations' has many commonsense connotations that perhaps do not apply here. Can you spell out what the technical term means? Can you give examples of how these relations among people are the substance of what is finest in a culture?

Notes to Chapter Three

1. Lonergan's summary treatment of much of these same issues can be found in *Method in Theology*, Chapter Two, and "The Human Good" and "The Subject" in W.F.J. Ryan and B.J. Tyrrell, eds., *Second Collection* (London: Darton, Longman & Todd, 1974), pp. 69-86, esp. 79-86.

2. See "The Response of the Jesuit as Priest and Apostle in the Modern World," *Second Collection*, pp. 165-187, esp. 165-170.

3. Here I am expanding on Erich Voegelin's notion of 'metaxy'. See his "Gospel and Culture" in D.G. Miller and D.Y. Hadidian, eds., *Jesus and Man's Hope* (Pittsburgh: Pittsburgh Theological Seminary, 1971), vol. II, pp. 59-101.

4. This distinction between Cosmos and Chaos relies initially on Eric Voegelin. I have transposed it somewhat by regarding them strictly as symbols in order to locate them within Lonergan's generalized empirical method. While 'cosmos' appears in most of Voegelin's writings, the contrast with 'chaos' seems to be only in an unpublished work, "Wisdom and the Magic of the Extreme: A Meditation" © Eranos Yearbook, c.1976.

5. Ibid., p. 7. I am also indebted to Voegelin for his critique of Dogmatism and Utopianism in this same work.

6. See *Spiritual Exercises of St. Ignatius*, trans. Louis J. Puhl (Chicago: Loyola University Press, 1959), para. 335, p. 149.

7. I depend here on Lonergan's *Method in Theology*, pp. 30-34, who in turn acknowledges his dept to Dietrich von Hildebrand and Max Scheler.

8. Conrad W. Baars, *Feeling and Healing Your Emotions* (Plainfield, N.J.: Logos International, 1979), pp. 14-26. See also John Macmurray's excellent little work, *Freedom in the Modern World* (London: Faber and Faber, 1932), esp. pp. 145-154.

9. For reflections on the phenomena of free-floating feelings, see Max Scheler, *Ressentiment*, trans. W. Holdheim (New York: The Free Press of Glencoe, 1961) chap. I, pp. 43-78.

10. See *Method in Theology*, p. 240.

11. Ibid., pp. 31-32.

12. Here I depend originally on a few hints given by Eric Voegelin, *New Science of Politics* (Chicago: University of Chicago Press, 1952), pp. 64-66.

13. See John W. Glaser, "Conscience and Superego: A Key Distinction," *Theological Studies* 32/1 (March 1971), 30-47. Reprinted in John J. Heaney, ed., *Psyche and Spirit* (New York: Paulist, 1973), pp. 33-55.

14. In this section I am trying to give a fuller account of what Lonergan treats under "The Structure of the Human Good" (Section Six, Chapter Two), in *Method in Theology*, pp. 47-52.

15. Here I fill out Lonergan's "Progress and Decline" (Section Seven, Chapter Two) of *Method in Theology*, pp. 52-55.

16. See *Insight*, pp. 218-242.

17. Ibid., pp. 229-232, 630. See also John Dunne, *"Realpolitik in the Decline of the West," Review of Politics*, 1959, 131-150, for an excellent historical account of how "facing the facts" has destroyed much of Western culture.

CHAPTER FOUR

Loving

We now turn our attention to love because something in us is convinced that in the human drama, love plays the leading role. In fact, any discussion that leaves love out of the picture would be grossly unrealistic and, by default, might even idealize a rational life with no heart.

Over the centuries a lot of ink has flowed out on the subject of love. But even the best of works often leaves us with more awe than understanding. So we should be very clear at the outset what our aims are. Our aim is understanding. We want to grasp which of the many movements in our consciousness is love, and we want to understand how that love functions. No doubt, we will not understand everything about love, but at least we can understand where understanding leaves off, and at that point we can gaze in reverence at the mystery. Mystery there is, but there is no sense in calling 'mystery' those elements that understanding can grasp.

In our chapter on Knowing, we saw that to understand anything, we need to understand the processes that condition its existence. That is, we gain insight into things not by an imaginative reconstruction, nor by the ability to draw a diagram, nor by personal skills in the use of the things in question, but by a grasp of the recurring processes that keep the 'thing' functioning as it does.

This focus on process is absolutely fundamental. It may not provide an immediate guide to how we ought to love in concrete situations, but it will provide the kind of long-range view which, as we have just seen, common sense usually fails to take. At least the long-range view will help prevent us from making a lot of mistakes. At best it will give us solid ground on which to build the social and economic structures which are needed to support love.

Now that we have reached the topic of love, we have reached the absolute core of all human knowing and acting. Just as all our knowing takes place only in moral contexts, so all our moral decisions take place only in this larger context of love. The work we did in chapter 2 concerning how we know was only a first approximation to the reality of human knowing. It was enough to clarify how we should proceed, but it hardly exhausted the topic of knowing. Likewise, the work we did in chapter 3 concerning how we feel, decide, and act, also enlarged upon how we know, particularly about how we know *values*; but it too was just a further approximation to the full reality of human knowing and acting. As we shall see, all our knowing is primarily a form of religious love and, at the same time, a form of love for one another.

Please do not expect that we will exhaust the topics of knowing, acting and loving. The best we can do is determine what the main features of human self-transcendence might be. As I say, our aim is understanding. That understanding will be largely structural in nature and relatively incomplete. But it will also be relatively stable inasmuch as you will be led to locate and distinguish within yourself the fundamental movements of love from which spring faith, charity, and hope. These, in turn, will be shown to be the concrete setting for all our moral commitments and intellectual achievements.

So let us begin to look at *love*. The word, we must not forget, is a human invention fashioned to circumscribe a definite set of human experiences. But to which set of experiences, of all the experiences of consciousness, does the word aptly refer? How can we avoid introducing a romantic, Platonic, Victorian, or individualistic understanding of love which we may already carry within us? Certainly we are aware that many people call "love" what we would call "selfishness" or "mere need." But how can we isolate the unrevisable core meaning which we believe exists? This is our task: to locate a certain set of experiences and to understand them as contained within all experiences called "love."

We will try to locate the core experiences of love first by recognizing that being in love constitutes a fifth level of consciousness. We will see that just as the moral level of consciousness envelops the three cognitive levels, so being in love envelops the moral and cognitive levels together. Following Lonergan's definition, we will treat religious conversion as a "falling in love with God."[1] Then we will assign some key technical terms to the basic elements in love; namely, mystery, faith, charity, and hope. Finally, having created such a model of love's elements, we will examine the process by which love both integrates the spirituality of an individual and redeems the situations of social decline in history.

1. Loving

What do we do when we love? Two features appear immediately.[2] For one, we feel benevolent. That is, we feel ready to give to someone else, or we really desire someone else's welfare. This benevolence lies behind concrete acts of caring, and any act that might appear to be "caring" would not be love unless it sprang from interior benevolence.

The second feature is appreciation. It differs from benevolence insofar as it does not focus on what good can be done, but rather on the good that the person actually is. Appreciation is welcoming; it is happy with; it is content.

Notice that benevolence and appreciation alternate. We provide care for someone until we are content with how things stand for the person. But while we may rest in appreciating how things stand, we never rest for long. Benevolence desires to have even more to appreciate, and it takes the steps to bring it about. So benevolence and appreciation are the right and left footsteps on a journey. These two forms of love continually replace one another as love seeks to have ever more value to appreciate.

This dynamic, alternating process of love comes from a third kind of love that forms the backbone of appreciation and benevolence. Let us call it 'transcendent love'.[3] It is a force and a process which, although it may center on this or that person, still is on the lookout for more goodness, more beauty, other persons, fuller community. Without this dynamism, all the appreciation and benevolence we could muster towards this person or that group would be limited; and because it is limited, it would be unable to promote further goodness. Appreciation for what is would dominate the benevolence that hopes for what more might be. In other words, the love of friendship or fellowship seems to be the product of a more transcendent love for order, for beauty, for reality, and for goodness. These are abstract terms, I realize. But they do not stand for mere concepts which we love. They stand for concrete possibilities which we desire for those we love. After all, is it not true that at the far end of every thought, every question, every decision, every human project there always stands a person or a community for whose sake we are attentive, intelligent, reasonable, and responsible—even if it be our very selves? And yet this love of specific human persons is only a moment, a phase, a plateau, of this larger process of transcendent love.

Transcendent love, therefore, is not separate from the love of human beings. Nor is it love for abstractions. It has concrete reality as its object. Transcendent love is not merely an emotion either, although it can express itself through emotions. It is the movement we experience within us that seeks the absolutely highest value possible for real men and women. It is the dynamism, the motor that moves us to wake up and be attentive, to wonder and be intelligent, to reflect and be realistic, to deliberate and be responsible.

While we have tried to stress that transcendent love has concrete reality as its object, we must add an important observation. Those objects remain partly obscure to benevolence and appreciation. The goods we want for our friends do not exist until we bring them about. And when our friends enjoy the desired goods, our appreciation is always under the cloud of moral uncertainty; we can never be sure we have appreciated the truly valuable.

If the concrete objects of benevolence and appreciation are partly obscure, then all the more so is the 'object' of transcendent love itself. We refer to the obscure yet very concrete object of transcendent love as 'God'. By this word we mean one whose value and goodness are absolutely beyond criticism. Since 'personhood' is the highest value we know, we think of God as a person. But God is not a 'person' in the exact sense that you and I are. As the ultimate object of transcendent love, God is not the object of our benevolence, as persons are. (How can we wish goodness for one who has all goodness?) Our total response is appreciation, an appreciation that is absolutely without criticism and yet an appreciation for one who is yet obscure.

Notice that while we are all accustomed to our own *images* of 'God', here we are trying to understand the process of our souls from which comes all the concrete meaning of that word. All the meaning of divinity is derived from our experience of transcendent love.

Finally, we must recognize that this pull of transcendent love tugs against a counterpull. The very meaning of self-transcendence is that we commit ourselves to becoming different selves than we are. So the existential tension, which we saw in our last chapter, between a relative fidelity to transcendental achievements and an absolute fidelity to transcendental precepts is also, and fundamentally, a tension between humanity and divinity. The restlessness of our souls is a divine restlessness.

Our commitment to self-transcendence can take the form of a moral conversion in which we dedicate ourselves to a life committed to true values rather than mere satisfactions. It can deepen through an intellectual conversion—either explicit or implicit—which clarifies the difference between a major authenticity that relies on the transcendental precepts and a minor authenticity that relies on transcendental achievements.[4] It can deepen further through a religious conversion that recognizes divine movements in the soul that heal (from love downwards) what the soul's creative movements (from experience upwards) cannot successfully create.[5]

Such a multi-leveled tension between present contentment and future hope can generate the biases of neurosis, egoism, group selfishness, and short-sightedness. But the tension is also and primarily the concrete possibility and power behind every transcendental achievement.

Let us pause here and summarize what we have covered so far. We have tried to establish that 'loving' refers to the experiences we call benevolence and appreciation, and more basically to the experience of a dynamism that transcends each of the particular objects of our attention, intelligence, reason, responsibility, and love. We think of this transcendent object as a 'person' and we call this one 'God'. Now we must look at *being loved*.

2. Being Loved

How do we know whether or not someone loves us? It is not merely a matter of whether or not others tell us that they love us—they may either be lying or they may be mistaken about what love really is. We still have to make our own judgment about the truth of the matter.

What criteria do we use when we make such a judgment? On the evidence of their kindness, partly, but acts of external caring do not necessarily spring from internal benevolence. We depend partly on our own feelings, but our desire to be loved all too easily sees love where there is none.

There is one great clue about how we determine whether we are loved. It is found in our doubt that we are loved truly. Recall what happens when we doubt another's love. We hear words of love, but we tell ourselves that the other person does not know the "real" us. We think that if he or she knew us as we really are, we probably could not be truly loved.

The enormous mistake here is the presumption that we know ourselves better than anyone else. Or, to put it more precisely, we think that we know what is truly valuable in ourselves better than anyone else ever could. Obviously we do know more facts about ourselves than others do. But it is not the *number* of facts we know about ourselves that makes us doubt another's love. We doubt another's love because we think they do not know the *significance* and *worth* of those facts as well as we do. But there is a great deal of evidence from people in love that the opposite is the real truth—that someone who loves us has a better, a more accurate judgment of value in our regard than we ourselves do.

The upshot of this is that when we come to know that we are loved, we do not go exclusively on the basis of evidence—the evidence of kind deeds and loving words. Somewhere in the process we have to make a decision. The decision is about whether or not to believe the person. It is a risk. We may decide to believe that he or she truly loves us and later discover that this was a mistake. And yet this is no warrant for not believing anybody. There is no knowing whether or not we are loved that can avoid the act of deciding to believe, in spite of the risk. We cannot prove it to ourselves. We can only commit ourselves to believing it.

So the act of decision is an integral part of letting oneself be loved. Without it, another person's love for us remains unrequited.

This is fairly clear in the acts of love we have called appreciation and benevolence. We make a *decision* to trust the other person's words and acts of love. But what about transcendent love? What about this dynamism of pull against counterpull that we constantly suffer? Once we realize that this force is a basic instance of loving, we are naturally drawn to the question of whether that which we love loves us in return. Love always seeks to know the beloved in an intimate way. So the question naturally arises, "Does what I love, when I love anything, love me?"

We can expect that in pursuing this question philosophically we will find some evidence to support the judgment that we are loved, but we can also expect that we must come to the juncture of decision — that we will have to decide to believe that we are loved or not.

What evidence, then, do we have that the transcendental object of all our human intending (all our wonder, questioning, appreciating, and so on) is also in love with us? There is the evidence of the universe, of course, the order and beauty of creation. But, like the classic "arguments" of Aquinas, the evidence and the explanation do not form compelling proofs. We could go on and look at the many incidents in our lives that have been evidence for us that we are loved by a transcendent Thou. Each would have his or her own story. But besides these stories, we share a common gift that is incredibly powerful in helping us see that we are loved. The gift is simply the fact *that we love*.[6] That is, this transcendent dynamism which underlies all our appreciation and benevolence is itself a gift. It is not something we created. It was there before we knew it. It is the source of the questions whose answers brought us to knowing it. And it seems also to be an integral part of the cosmic process of a burgeoning universe of giant galaxies and fields of wildflowers.

So here we find ourselves, stricken with the relentless tension of a transcendent love. It came as a gift and as a challenge. It is a principle of our lives. We did not create it nor did we choose it. We cannot even successfully reject it. Our loving itself may be the gift of a lover.

3. Being in Love with God

Will we believe it? The answer to the question whether or not we are loved by the object of our transcendent love does not require our decision in order to be real; we may be loved and deny it. But it does require our decision if we are to *know* we are loved.

If we decide to believe, then we can see that our lover is unlike any earthly lover. I might love you with all my heart, but you did not give me my love. This lover comes to us by giving us our power to love, and nobody on earth ever did that. With transcendent love, we can imagine ourselves caught in a great circle of love, beginning from the One who loves us, pouring this thirst and desire into our souls, and pouring from our souls towards absolutely all goodness, truth, beauty, and order — which is what this One is. Our love is Alpha and Omega, both the source and the object of our loving.

For this reason, we cannot find an apt comparison to express the love we are caught up in. It is not a 'friendship'. It is not a king-servant relationship. Nor is it well represented by metaphors of thunder or whisper. Scripture uses these and many other comparisons because it is searching and not finding. The sheer plurality of metaphors for the dealings between Divinity and Flesh should convince us that they are incomprehensible. Better than metaphors are stories, accounts of divine action in human history. These do not explain much in a theoretical mode, but they do bear the elements of transcendent love in a compact, symbolic, and forceful manner.

Unfortunately, while stories and myths have the power to maintain our hope within a godless world, they do not function critically to help us sort out what is actually going on when we love in this way. They may help our conviction, but they do not directly help our understanding.

That is why we would like to suggest that the expression *love of God* refers exactly to the pull of transcendent love and to nothing else. That is, our love for God includes our experience of raising questions, of wondering, of appreciating, and preeminently of our longing; and at the same time it is also God's loving gift to us. It is God's way of giving the divine self to us. The very word *God* cannot have any meaning to us outside of our experience of this transcendent tug. All our data on the one we call "God" lies in this ever-widening yet increasingly urgent search.[7]

Now, not everyone recognizes that their own longing is a transcendent love. There are the self-styled secularists who take their stand on honesty or realism or responsibility. But what a pity that so many secularists avoid anything smacking of religion for no other reason than their own fidelity to this inner drive towards honesty, realism, and responsibility. Whose fault, pray tell, is that? Conversely, many self-styled religionists, who profess a love for "God," somehow manage to suppress their wonder, curiosity, and natural awe, replacing them with narrow opinions, dogmatic pronouncements, and high-minded moralizing. Can this be love for God? In reality, we believe, it is the humble who shall see God, the meek who shall inherit the Kingdom. In other words, it is those who trust that their inner makeup is tailor-made for God who find God.

To be religiously converted is to give oneself up to this love and subordinate everything to it. Right here, however, we ought to clarify the status of "religious conversion" in our intellectually converted approach to spirituality. By religious conversion we do not mean an event pinned down to a certain point in time, like Paul being knocked down on the road to Damascus. That meaning is more appropriate to the storyteller's questions about when and where something happened. Nor are we after a description of conversion that will enable us to recognize it in others. That would be helpful for a spiritual director, but not for us, at least not directly. We are primarily seeking an explanation of how conversion works in consciousness. An explanatory grasp of conversion, we believe, will give us something that storytellers and spiritual directors usually lack, namely, an understanding of *how* the love of God works to redeem the human race.

Also, if religious conversion means the subordination of all conscious activity to transcendent love, then we should make a distinction between an implicit and an explicit conversion. In an implicitly converted horizon, a person does indeed subordinate everything to a love which is transcendent, but he or she has not asked the question of where this love comes from and to whom it is directed. Such a person is in love with God and does not know it. In an explicitly converted horizon, the person has objectified the term of his or her experienced orientation, usually thinking of it as a Thou, and usually convinced that this Thou is responsible for planting the seed of love in the first place.

As we hope to show, both the implicitly and the explicitly converted horizons make authenticity more possible and more likely. (Indeed, have we not often noticed that the authenticity of some "non-believers" puts many a "believer" to shame?) What the explicitly converted horizon gives, then, is not a corner on the authenticity market. It simply gives a Thou, a Someone, a named and loved term of an orientation. And for those knowingly in love, it makes an enormous difference in how they ponder life's mysteries; it gives them a Thou to talk with. And yet we must admit that it does not make the struggle for authenticity a great deal easier.

Once we recognize that at the core of our love for God lies this surprisingly familiar habit of wonder and longing, we find a kinship with those strange men and women we call the mystics. They turn out to be not as strange as people think. At times, sometimes while we are praying, but sometimes when we least expect, our own attention wanders from the concrete objects that surround us and attends to something vague and beyond. Our preoccupation with the concepts and symbols that carry a world to us recedes into the background of our consciousness. At these times we experience a movement that heads beyond all the things and the persons we love. It is the simple experience of the dynamism without attending to the everyday objects to which that dynamism ordinarily attends. It is an experience that is far more common than most people believe.

This experience of movement without any known object can be a sweet and delightful blossoming. Usually it is a rather sober and quiet opening of the soul. Often enough it verges on the painful. It simply hurts to be in want and to long for we know not what. It ought to hurt. We share in God's love for a business unfinished. We yearn for the tying up of all loose threads, and this yearning is God's work in us.

Do the so-called mystics experience something different than this? A good question. We would have to ask the mystics. If they did not experience at least this, we would have good reason to call them frauds. Their supposedly mystical experiences would not connect with the rest of their lives, and the God they claim to have met would remain no part of anyone else's experience. But when we do put the question to the mystics, we should be careful. Your average mystic has not bothered much with cognitional theory, so he or she may talk as though the experience was like "seeing" God; although such giants as Teresa of Avila and Ignatius of Loyola seem careful to deny that it was like seeing.

This very common mistake, thinking that a mystical experience has to be like looking at something, leads students of mysticism and religious experience to ask whether mystics in all cultures "experience" the same divine object. But experience only gives data, and in mystical experience all the data is data from inner movements, not from outer presentations, not even from remembered or imagined images of outer presentations. When the mystics claim to know something in mystical experience, their understanding and judgment have intervened to name what happened, whether they realize it or not. The names they settle on will nearly always be drawn from their prior religious tradition. A Moslem does not see the Blessed Virgin Mary in a vision. And

114

yet, when the mystics have sufficient greatness of soul, their understanding transforms the traditional meanings and reveals a new profundity to human dealings with the divine. John the Evangelist transformed the meaning of *life*. Paul transformed the meaning of *church*. Augustine transformed the meaning of *memory*. And Jesus, of course, gave an awesome and yet very concrete meaning to the word *love*.

So the primary transcultural question is not whether all mystics saw or heard the same thing. It is whether they all experience the same inner movement from attention to intelligence to reason to responsibility and to a transcendental love whose brilliance at times can obscure everything else. And it is relatively easy to see that the answer here is yes. If this is true, then when we study mystics, we must shift our attention from their inner *experience* to their culturally conditioned *understanding* of that experience. There we need to make a hermeneutical analysis of their understanding of what happened, particularly how their often metaphorical language relates to the categories that can be grounded through the analysis of interiority that we have been doing. And at that point the existential question often emerges for ourselves, namely, whether their understanding of the movement between humanity and divinity so far surpasses our own that we are drawn to undergo a metanoia ourselves.

Many problems of unbelief among basically good people occur because they expect their experience of God to be "more" than this, or other than this, something so significantly beyond human existential tension that existential tension would vanish. A thorough moral conversion would help here. That is, the more ready we are to entertain the belief that what is truly valuable may not be free from hurt, then the more likely will we recognize God's gift of the divine self in our very darkness and longing.

We can now specify the fifth and final 'transcendental precept'. Beyond the precepts, Be attentive, Be intelligent, Be reasonable, and Be responsible, we also experience *Be in love*. We should take care, however, to understand this love precisely as the transcendent love we have been talking about here, and not merely the more familiar love we feel for one another, a love which transcendent love always includes, but always transcends as well. As we will see, it is this fifth precept, Be in love, that gives us the power to obey the other four.

Taken together, all five constitute the source of full human authenticity. All other laws, precepts, wisdom, insights, and heroic deeds originate with these five "Be-attitudes."

4. Mystery

Let us refer to the end-point of our transcendent love as 'Mystery'. We also call that end-point 'God', and think of 'God' as a person, but we have already seen how the term of our transcendent love is quite unlike human persons because it is also the source of our loving. And besides, in our Christian tradition we have learned to speak of God as being not one person but in fact three, though *person* here is clearly an analogy. Even to call God an 'object' of transcendent love would mistakenly suggest that we already know the One towards whom our love heads. But our transcendent love does not *result* from knowing the divine pole; on the contrary, everything we know about that divine pole is the result of that transcendent love at work in us.

So, although the word *God* must remain in our worship and in our everyday language, we will use the word *Mystery* in our analysis of how religious love functions. It puts the focus on the divine precisely on how we experience it. For we want our intellectually converted talk about the divine to be talk about human experience too, particuarly about our experiences of being pulled where we would not go and being awestruck at this faithful obedience as we see it in others. We do not want to imagine ourselves as so chummy with the divine that we forget that One's eternal incomprehensibility and our utter impotence to do anything by ourselves.

Let us turn this Mystery around in the light as we might turn a jewel. If we examine this jewel through a functional analysis of our inner processes, we see different facets for each different level of consciousness.

On the level of attention, we experience ourselves as open to any possibilities whatsoever. On the level of intelligence we keep asking questions that explain how or why, firmly expecting all things to be intelligible. On the level of judgment, we bow to the stubborn independence of reality; reality *is what it is* regardless of what we think. On the level of decision, we strive for a good beyond criticism.

Our wonder works on the presupposition that there is really a difference between ideas that make sense and ideas that do not, between truth and falsehood, between better and worse. Furthermore, these transcendentals quite possibly may converge into one single transcendental. We certainly act as though each of the things we put our minds to ought to be simultaneously intelligible, real, and good. By *Mystery* we mean precisely that transcendental which lies behind and within all reality—something whose intelligibility, existence, and goodness is not an instance of or a manifestation of these transcendentals but is identical with them.

This 'Mystery' must also be the *source* of all intelligibility, existence, and goodness, since it is the source of our search. In other words, the Mystery must be completely intelligent, must be the fundamental condition on which all other existing things depend without having any external conditions on which it depends, and must be a willing, benevolent, and appreciative source of goodness.

As we turn this jewel, we realize that all these facets are facets of transcendent love. Transcendent love is the light refracted into human goodness, realism, intelligence, and attention.

How shall we look at the light itself? If you will allow me to stretch the metaphor a little further, that light comes in three primary colors. We are all very familiar with these "colors," but, because they easily blend with one another and refract at every level of consciousness, we do not always catch their raw brilliance. I am talking about those three virtues which tradition has recognized as having the divine One as their source, the virtues we call theological. I am talking about faith, charity, and hope.

No doubt you recognize faith, charity, and hope as Paul's list of divine gifts. It does not occur as a triad in any other Biblical work.[8] But there is evidence that Heraclitus seems to have recognized these three approaches to the Divine as "other than" the rational approach.[9] Can we presume that they may be part of human capacity and still insist that they are gratuitous gifts from the Divine? I see no reason why not, especially once we recognize that all humans are "pulled" by transcendent love. And, if we define them clearly, there is ample evidence that faith, charity, and hope abound in this world. Indeed, we will see that these were the missing elements in our analysis of human social decline and so will form the structural basis for understanding how redemption works.[10]

Let me briefly describe these three, just to help us locate the kind of 'knowledge' we possess that does not emerge from the upward deployment of attention, intelligence, reason, and responsibility—which we usually refer to as "rational"—but which emerge downward from transcendent love directly.

Faith is knowing where real good lies. It recognizes a value in creation, in other persons, and in God, even though it cannot explain how. When we look for guidance in pursuing the transcendent Mystery behind all event-conditioned things, faith is that intuition which knows which people are worth listening to, which authors are worth reading, which movies are worth seeing.

Charity is loving other persons. At least as Paul uses the term in his triad, charity is *not* the direct transcendent love for the Divine; it is interpersonal love of neighbor. But when we fall in love, we sense a value in other persons that we can never explain rationally. And as we grow in love, we learn, like Flannery O'Connor, to be touched by even the most grotesque human beings and to let ourselves be enveloped by Mystery there.

Hope looks to the future, to the unknown, and remains steadfast in confident expectation even though by any rational analysis the odds may seem insuperable. We cannot explain why we hope, but we do, without even insisting that the good for which we long arrives before we die.

So the transcendent love we bear for Mystery is a fruitful love. We touch this Mystery consciously when we find ourselves with more faith, charity, and hope than we thought were in us. As I say, they blend, particularly when we fall in love or are confronted with human tragedy and find that we trust reality, we count on one another, and we hope in historical process far beyond what common sense warrants. So the precise meanings of these virtues seem to overlap. But there are differences between them, and if we can spell them out we will be able to understand how divine love penetrates human consciousness and redeems human wreckage.

5. Faith

Lonergan defines faith as a judgment of value born of religious love, and he describes it as the "eye of love."[12] According to his definition, the old Catholic emphasis on the statements of what we believe would not properly be called faith. Lonergan's definition is closer to the old Protestant emphasis on trust in God. Faith is the prior act of appreciation or evaluation that discerns and welcomes God as the transcendent Thou in both nature and history. It can gaze on the stars with gratitude. It can welcome the stories of what God has done for humanity. It can discern concrete proposals (such as turning the other cheek and walking the second mile) as worth committing oneself to. It discerns what to believe in a religious tradition. It has the power to discern the relative importance of, say, Jesus' Resurrection and the miracles he performed, or the relative importance of various ecclesiastical pronouncements. Faith discerns the transcendent value of everyday activities. Far from excluding good works, faith does not live except by discerning which works are good. All these concrete objects of faith are seen in the light of a single question: Of what transcendent value are they?

Of course, as we grow in our religious lives, we accumulate a vast knowledge about the transcendent worth of things. Insofar as this knowledge is habitual and operative, we say we have a living faith. Nowadays, it is extremely important to pay attention to and name this element of our religious living. We can forget that we have faith, and, having forgotten, forget to nourish it. Faith can be regarded as something abstract, or as merely a set of statements we are supposed to subscribe to. Faith can be replaced by a blind trust in a heavenly God that fails to sort out the difference between earthly good and evil. To name faith as the eye of religious love is to understand that our love for God has a new eye for value; Paul calls it "the eyes of the heart" (Eph 1:18). To nourish faith is to get into the habit of weighing the value of everything against our felt love for God.

According to this view, our faith is no different in structure from the way our human loving guides our commitments. Falling in love gives a new appreciation of the value of other persons, not for what they can do or for how attractive they look, but for the simple value of their persons. It is in the light of their value as persons that we are concerned about them and care for them. In both human friendship and divine love, love as welcome and appreciation naturally overflows into love as care and concern. It is in this same light that we see the value of believing in the love others profess for us.

And yet, religious faith goes beyond friendship and family love. Religious faith originates in an orientation which we experience *before* we know God, while the eye of friendly love originates in the love that follows *after* we know a friend. Faith regards even human love from the vantage point of transcendent love; for example, when we desire a good beyond criticism for our friend, or when we revere in our friend that same orientation to absolute Mystery.

Faith is not the same thing as good will. I can want to do the right thing and to recognize truly good actions in others. I can even be quite willing to sacrifice my own well-being for the sake of some worthwhile cause. But without the eye of the heart in love with God, there is no ultimate "for whom" that I look to and no one but myself willing the good I will. Certainly we all experience the tugs of conscience. But unless we acknowledge that tug as a love which divine Mystery has planted in our hearts, unless we yield to that love's universal scope and uncriticizable values, then our good will maintains a rather provincial and short-term outlook. Without faith, good will is terribly prone to contraction. By itself, conscience need not desire the universal good willed by a personal God; it would be enough to desire the good of one's own family and friends. So the good will of one family would counter the good will of another, and history would teach again the harsh lessons about the larger common good. And even should the greatest possible number of people will the most common good, there would be no guarantee that anyone wills the good for the sake of a divine Thou.

Faith works not only in the realm of common sense, giving us the practical discernments of value and truth we need every day. It also works in the realm of theory, revealing values and truths that are fundamental enough to be the ground on which a psychology, a sociology, an economics, or a political theory can stand.

Take economics for example. Marxist economics is built on the judgment that human consciousness is shaped *primarily* by how we gear our economy and our personal lives to produce material goods. Western liberal economics is built on the judgment that all human wants are legitimate; only those need to be held in check which interfere unfairly with the wants of others. Religious faith denies the validity of both these judgments. It sees human consciousness as shaped primarily by self-transcending love, not economic forces, and it holds a critical, not a liberal, attitude towards human wants and desires.

Similar examples could be given for the other human sciences, but our point is that faith not only can but actually does work on the theoretical level. It gives believers the convictions about human nature which not only run counter to the fundamental convictions in other theories but can serve as foundations for workable theories themselves.

6.   Charity

By 'charity' we mean our experience of love for a known person or community. We do *not* mean the transcendent love in its primary sense; that love seeks long before it finds its beloved. Charity, along with faith and hope, is an overflow of transcendent love and then, by return route, a direct link to divine Mystery.

We sense that Mystery in passing flashes of love for people around us. We also sense it when we reflect on the dedication made by parents for their children—how children rarely learn the half of the sacrifices their parents have made for them, how no child could ever "return the favor" of being brought to birth, reared, and then let go, and how parents are eager to spend their sustenance and livelihood for these children's sake anyway. We sense the Mystery in a citizen's love of country, a soldier's willingness to die for the freedoms of others, and in the quiet dedication of those people in schools, hospitals, and the like who clean the offices, type the letters, mind the boilers—the people who give an institution its "soul."

However, for the greater part of our lives we forget what a miracle a person or a community of persons really is. Familiarity may not always breed contempt, but it does breed a spiritual drowsiness. We grow accustomed to the wonders of human intelligence, realism, and commitment; or perhaps we are just disappointed that they fail to reach the profundities they seem destined for. And the drowsier we grow, the less astonishment we inspire in others, so that a family, a staff, a city, an entire culture can find its wonder smothered by routinized relationships, by the drudgery of hard work, and by thought-stifling propaganda and advertising. But then along comes an Anne Frank, who gazes at a small square of blue sky from her sequestered window and learns again that people are miracles. Charity keeps breaking through, like the little wildflowers, through the cracks in our cemented pathways.

We have all known what it is to love others, and surely we remember not only the moments when that love shimmered in the presence of Mystery, but also the long dreary periods when we worked out that love in practice. In other words, sometimes the sense of Mystery is keen, but ordinarily it is dull. What makes the difference between the keen and the dull? If charity is so intimately related to divine Mystery, then why should it get so dreary and mundane? Should we allow it to?

Earlier we considered the difference between appreciation and benevolence. That distinction can help us here. When we appreciate some person or community, we value what they are, whereas in benevolence we value what they might become. Appreciation is love as welcome; benevolence is love as care. Appreciation rests with what is; benevolence moves towards what ought to be. We saw how appreciation and benevolence alternate as people in love knit a life together. Benevolence, however, is instrumental. It values good food, gracious atmosphere, and even certain persons not for their own sake but for how they might enhance those other persons we appreciate. Appreciation is the end; benevolence is the means.

More often than not, benevolence suffers the dreary part of love — as we tediously build the conditions that will dignify the living of those we appreciate. Benevolence draws on attention, intelligence, reason, and responsibility — on human savvy, in others words — to move further towards a love at rest with the beloved. Appreciation, on the other hand, is the mysterious part of love. It draws not on human savvy but on transcendent Mystery to see a divine beauty where the world sees only human ugliness.

Appreciative love gives benevolent love a transcendent purpose. That purpose can give the dreary part of love a divine meaning. So a genuine charity should always have two characteristics. One, it ought to revel in naked appreciation for other persons from time to time. Without that, our benevolence becomes a treadmill of pointless obligations. Two, our charity ought to experience the treadmill anyway, the tedium of keeping our promises and meeting our obligations when the glow of appreciative love has dimmed. Unless our appreciative love of neighbor activates our responsibility, our reason, our intelligence, and our attention, we could hardly claim to love with our whole heart and soul.

To continue to care for others when our appreciation grows dim, we fall back to faith, the eyes of the heart, which insists on seeing transcendent value even in the dark. Without faith, charity towards the neighbor washes away on the first rainy day. With faith, charity keeps surprising itself on how much self-sacrifice it is willing to endure and towards how many different people it is willing to pour out active, caring love.

7. Hope

Lastly, there is hope. We are drawn towards divine Mystery by the transcendent love that is in us. By our faith, we discover where that Mystery has penetrated the human sphere. By our charity we love and care for that Mystery as it is embodied uniquely in individual persons and specific communities. Yet the story goes on; the end is not yet in sight. And so we hope.

But what is hope? Can we understand it in terms of operations of the subject? Following the pattern of Lonergan's definition of faith, I propose the following definition: Hope is a confident desire born of religious love.

As desire, hope longs for the fullest good and the unadulterated truth. It pines for a glorious outcome to human history. It yearns to see the face of the Mystery that incessantly draws it. Hope thereby complements natural desire—the pure desire to know and the pure desire for good that belong to our natural capacities—by unabashedly hoping for what is absolutely best.

Earlier we named hope as one of the utilitarian (intelligent and reasonable) emotions that gives direction to the humane (experienced, instinctual) emotion of raw desire. But, considered as a movement springing from faith and charity, hope has a further and a higher meaning. It is a virtue, not just an emotion, which flows from the responsible and loving levels of our consciousness to resolve the ambiguities of biased experience, understanding, and judgment. It accomplishes this through moral and religious conversion. It is through these conversions that the virtue of hope gives direction to the utilitarian emotion of hope (as well as to despair, to courage and fear, and to anger), which in turn transform natural desire (as well as aversion, like and dislike, happiness and sadness).

Hope's desire is confident because of faith. Faith gives the judgment of fact that there is a way out of our difficulties, and so hesitant desire is rendered confident even though outcomes remain obscure.

The carriers of hope are not the carriers of faith. Faith—value judgments born of religious love—is fundamentally constituted by cool judgment and is expressed in firm canons. So we support faith by meditating on the objective values of the Beatitudes and on the objective truths of our creeds. In difficult times we fall back on our store of personal wisdom and fundamental beliefs concerning what life is all about. Hope, in contrast, is carried by imagination and affectivity. We support hope by affective contemplation on the Coming of the Kingdom, by liturgical rite, song, incense, art, and architecture. Hope dips into the world of symbols (particularly into dreams, the cosmos, and the culture) to produce the anagogic symbols that alone can represent the mysterious work of our mysterious God. It is through anagogic symbols that hope also resists the vast pressures of social decay and the gnostic, absolutizing instinct of humanity in all ages.

Now some people might wince at the suggestion that we should identify faith with cool judgment and hope with warm feelings. But there is a very good reason for making the distinction. Have we not found that common sense is very much inclined to use feelings as the litmus paper for faith? And is it not correct that when a person is battered by the storms of many feelings, the best spiritual directors emphasize the raw truth, the plain facts, the hard reality of God's love? No doubt, faith is supported by feelings, but we must not think that faith is primarily feelings. Faith is judgment. It is by judgment that we reach the real world. Hope supports faith by giving the initial affective movements towards value judgments, and it consolidates faith by the felt expectations of a confident desire embodied in anagogic symbols. In brief, then, the necessity for distinguishing and relating faith and hope is nothing more than the necessity for distinguishing and relating judgments and feelings.

So hope is about felt expectations. Hope has as its object not the positive realities that faith and charity reach but rather the negative aspects of what is yet to be reached. Now our religious lives are negative experiences in two basic respects. There is the negative reality of Mystery, the Cloud of Unknowing, the apophatic way of prayer, the hiddenness of God. And then there is the negative reality of sin, the absurdity of suppressing the transcendental precepts and the unintelligible situations that result. We fail to comprehend Mystery

124

because it has a surfeit of intelligibility to be grasped; and we fail to comprehend sin because it has no intelligibility to be grasped.

But in the concrete, God actually lets us get away with murder. We are allowed to inflict such atrocities on ourselves that sin begins to look like a part of Mystery, a positive power with a trans-historical will of its own which no human being could ever fathom. Likewise, the Mystery we call 'God' can begin to look like sin during those dark hours when we share in Christ's Gethsemane of being abandoned by God. At any given moment, we cannot be certain whether our terror is an ordered response of a creature to its creator or a disordered response of our biases and illusions. Hope enables us to carry on without certitude about the present. It gives rather an assurance about the future for those who hope. Hope does not eliminate fear, but it does help us differentiate our fears by distinguishing the fearful darkness of sin and the fearful darkness of divine Mystery. Hope enables us to expect an eschatological day when we will see God face to face, and when the darkness of sin is entirely banished.

Sin does have immense force in the world. It can take on a powerful cultural sway when a civilization is in decline. So, to keep our hopes up, we tell one another the stories of God's work in our lives. We enhance our worship with songs, art, incense, drama, procession, and ceremony. The liturgies that really work are always those whose tone or feeling bring hope—not, as many liturgy planners seem to think, those whose theme or thoughts are most clearly articulated. The themes and thoughts may give liturgy a direction, and, God knows, we need direction. But it is tone and feeling that give the affective power we need to live in a culture laced with secularism.

Hope counters sin not only at the level of our culture but within the most recondite of individual temptations as well. After all, when we suffer temptation, we do *suffer*. We endure, at least for a while, the counter-pull towards what we know is wrong. Then like a second surge of doom, we begin to wonder how long we can endure. Little by little we suspect that we are going to give in anyway. At this point temptation has firmly lodged itself as a felt expectation. We expect to give in, and, often enough, we do. But hope is a felt expectation too, in the direction opposite to sin. Hope resists the expectation that we will give in to temptation by envisioning the victory of Mystery over sin. And the richer the eschatological symbols we have available in our tradition, the more we will be able to desire with confidence that the Kingdom will come, the Heavenly Banquet will begin, Jesus will come again upon the clouds to judge the living and the dead, and so on.

8. Religion

In the midst of many a discussion on how effective religions may be in the world today, an old insight keeps reappearing. One realizes that we should conceive of religion not in terms of the behavior we call religious, nor in terms of how people use language. Religious behavior and religious language often just paper over gaping holes in spiritual substance. And it is the substance that counts. This insight peters out right here because the substance of religion has been the subject of considerable debate among psychologists, sociologists, anthropologists, and theologians. But, following Lonergan's leads, we have been trying to work out a model of subjectivity that is relatively verifiable and broad enough to serve all these disciplines. So, now that we have defined faith, charity, and hope as the first fruits of transcendent love, it seems appropriate to attempt a process analysis of what goes on in people we call "religious."

Faith, charity, and hope originate on the fifth, the topmost level of consciousness. Their most obvious appearance, however, occurs on the fourth level, the level where we weigh alternatives and commit ourselves to responsible courses of action. Our faith reveals what those valuable courses of actions are and which persons will be good guides and good company. Charity moves us to appreciation and benevolence towards others. Hope inspires reliance on specific people and institutions to bring about what the heart longs for. In other words, faith, charity, and hope have concrete, known objects on the fourth level.

But they also have a very concrete object on the fifth level too, though it is not "known" except as the obscure term of transcendent love. What makes the fifth level distinguishable from the fourth is that the term of our longing remains obscure yet attractive. At this level we can discern the more hidden but more fundamental workings of faith, charity, and hope. Faith is valuing the term of the orientation. Charity is actively moving towards this term in praise and thanksgiving and wonder. Hope is depending on the term to be also the source of everything good we can long for.

Since 'God' is obscure, we represent divine Mystery by symbols, and so we talk to God and worship God as if divine Mystery were somehow an appropriate object of human attention, intelligence, reason, and responsibility. The truth, of course, is that our talk and worship originate not in human knowing but in a divine impulse, and they look to One whom human savvy will never comprehend fully. Even in what we call the Beatific Vision, as St. Thomas pointed out, a creature cannot fully grasp the absolutely unconditioned source of everything created.[13]

This movement towards divine Mystery produces a new existential tension. Recall the four existential tensions we spoke of above — having to wait, to lose, to be onself, and to die. Besides these, being in love means that we simultaneously experience the divine Mystery as close and far, intimate and remote, immanent in consciousness and yet transcending all known objects. Religious consciousness sustains this tension with great difficulty. Recall, for example, the Corinthians' monument "to the Unknown God" and their scorn at Paul's preaching that we now know this God. They comfortably fell on the side of God's transcendence. In contrast, the Pharisees emphasized a divine righteousness based on the Law so much that they could hardly hear of a divine reality unpredictably at work in Jesus. They comfortably fell on the side of God's immanence. We can see a similar one-sidedness in Arianism. Apparently Arius and his followers felt forced to call Christ a creature, made by God, because of their keen awareness of God's transcendence. And, falling on the other side, we see gnostic groups all over the Near East clinging to a secret knowledge bringing God within the firm grasp of human minds. So while religious conversion does bind us to God in a more profound way, it also reveals to us more clearly what a profound difference remains between God and ourselves. Unless both this closeness and this distance are present in the religious sensibilities of believers, we can suspect that their religion has found the illusory peace that will not admit a divine tension in consciousness.

We have been speaking thus far of the structure of religious consciousness. But while we have argued that this structure belongs to all human consciousness, we must also acknowledge that not everyone realizes it. In other words, among people who are fundamentally authentic, there is a difference between religious persons and non-religious persons. Non-religious persons may well experience faith, charity, and hope on the fourth level and many will cooperate with these virtues more or less during their lives, but they do not also let them find a transcendent Thou on the fifth level. Still, for the non-religious, the movement of faith, charity, and hope at least moves towards the quiet discovery of a transcendent, loving, mysterious Thou, and they can become religious. For the religious, the same movement normally returns them to the known world as the field upon which they must surrender to transcendent, loving Mystery, because they learn that the Divine Thou wills the good of the world and wills their cooperation and participation in that work, that labor of Divine love.

Still, whether or not persons happen to become explicitly religious, their faith, charity, and hope will move them to "lose themselves" in that paradoxical process by which they also "find themselves." There is no question that all major religions and philosophies have recognized the value of a self-loss, but neither is there any question that self-loss has always been easily identified with self-hatred, self-punishment, and other perverted degradations of the human person. So we should scrutinize this notion of self-loss to see if we can discover its intrinsic intelligibility. If we can, we will possess a personal, grounded, and intelligent standpoint on such dominant religious notions as "dying to self," "poverty," "mortification," "self-denial," "the negative way," and so on.

What exactly do we lose when we "lose ourselves" in a religiously authentic way? We have already seen that religious authenticity means obeying one's experience of transcendent love, particularly as it overflows into faith, charity, and hope, regarding both the created world and the divine Thou who is the source of that love. But to obey a Thou who is not ourselves means to lose ourselves as "private."

For example, spouses in a good marriage will respect one another's privacy, autonomy, and growth. Even as their love matures over the years, their individual solitudes will grow more poignant than ever. God, however, does not respect privacy. Yet God does not "listen in" like a spy. God is the source and principle of our yearnings, the spring to which we retreat when we say we want to be "alone." This is true whether or not we realize it. And this realization is easy to suppress, particularly when we feel guilty and imagine ourselves as cut off from God and utterly on our own.

It is this imagined "private" or autonomous self—which faith reveals as an illusion—that we lose when we surrender to the divine Thou. Self-loss is the loss of the truncated self that does not yet realize that it is never alone. It feels like a genuine loss because the gains in self-image were honestly made, or at least were necessary for psychological survival. And yet it is not actually a loss; it is a further gain which demands a thorough shake-up and total re-deployment of the forces of consciousness.

The illusory, autonomous self is a very concrete self, constructed through attention, intelligence, reason, and responsibility—though not yet known by the knowledge that comes from religious love. It is a self with a story, a history, a self as jealous or as eaten up by the desires of the flesh or as beaten down and depressed by aimlessness, a self that seems irreversibly linked to one particular, familiar set of human burdens. It can even be an apparently humble self or an apparently arrogant self. The point is that we can build up a knowledge of ourselves *by* ourselves. That is, we can be relatively authentic in coming to self-understanding, but fail to go all the way to religious authenticity and let faith, charity, and hope see what attention, intelligence, reason, and responsibility do not see.

This is not to say that having a self-image is unimportant or wrong. We would not be psychologically healthy if we did not build up a relatively stable and acceptable self-image. But there comes a point in our adult religious lives when we feel drawn to surrender that self-image to divine Mystery. This means two things. It means letting Mystery guide us to become a new self, a self we may not have envisioned or even wanted to become. And it also means realizing that the self-image we have already built up is probably way off the mark. It means letting go of our certitudes about what our best and our worst deeds have been. It means waiting upon divinely inspired faith in us to notice those graced moments where Mystery has moved in our lives.

So religious self-loss is not just the loss of something we love or possess. It is the loss of the very mechanism by which we decide what is worth loving and possessing. We trust divine Mystery with the movements of the soul—faith, charity, and hope—which have the power to detach us from absolutely anything in this world and to attach us to anything else. We begin to attend to these movements and grow sensitive to them. In decision-making, we count more on these movements of attraction or repulsion than on analysis of cost-effectiveness. Even when we witness the examples of holy men and women or when we read classics in religious literature, we depend on these inner movements to discern where true divine values and meanings lie.

What then is the place for mortification in a religious life? The reason for self-denial, for fasting, for a life of evangelical poverty or of commitment to a celibate community is by no means a matter of punishing ourselves. On the contrary, their sole justification is *to refine our sensibilities to resonate with divine movements in the soul.* Even when the saints took on strict corporal penances for their sins, they did so because they wanted to become attuned to God, and they knew what a constant struggle self-surrender really is.

9. Christianity

There are many religions and Christianity is one of them. We do not want to argue whether Christianity is a better or a worse way to God, but we should understand what it is about Christianity which makes it one of a kind. I say we should understand, and by that I mean a grasp of the intrinsic intelligibility, the inner sense, of historical Christianity. That is, we are not passing judgment on how well it works nor looking for ways to improve it. We are simply asking the question, What is Christianity?

We can deal with this question quite expeditiously, now that we have located and named some of the key elements in religious consciousness. What makes Christianity unique is that Christians have exercised *absolute faith, charity, and hope towards Jesus of Nazareth.*

By faith, they recognize a value in Jesus which cannot be surpassed, not even by the divine Thou, because Jesus is divinely worthy. By charity they will love the neighbor after the pattern of Jesus' own self-sacrificing love, a love that is not afraid to lay down one's life even for one's enemies. But what is more, they love the person of Jesus not merely with the appreciation and benevolence one gives to a neighbor but with the same charity one owes to the transcendent Thou. By hope they put their stock in the community begun by Jesus and confidently desire an eschatological day when Jesus will "come again" to subject all history and nature to himself and submit them to the divine Thou.

Eventually the councils of Nicea and Chalcedon established that whatever is true of the 'Father' is true also of the 'Son' (except 'Fatherhood').[14] This affirmation has become solidified—we might even say rigidified—into the affirmation that Jesus is not only human but also divine. Yet what is this affirmation but a third-level judgment of fact proceeding from fourth- and fifth-level involvement with divine Mystery in the person of Jesus of Nazareth? It is the spelling out in cognitive terms of the experience of absolute faith in this Jew, absolute love for this man, absolute hope in the future of this crucified preacher.

The proposition that the human Jesus is also divine is a true proposition. But we do not grasp the meaning of this truth unless we repeat the inner experiences of those who first formulated it. As most commentators point out, this orthodox dogma was the inevitable implication of two movements in the souls of the faithful.[15] Christians were giving Jesus the same glory and worship which they knew belonged to the all-transcendent God (*lex orandi, lex credendi*). And they also turned to Jesus as the only person in whom 'salvation' from the power of sin could be found—again, a salvation they believed came from God alone (the 'Principle of Salvation'). To express the same movements in terms of the structure of consciousness, we can say that Christians turned to Jesus with the same faith, charity, and hope that belong to God alone. This is what Jesus' 'divinity' actually means with regard to believers. What 'divinity' means in itself, of course, is as opaque to human insight as the utter transcendence of God itself.

Christians therefore know themselves as moved by God, through the gifts of faith, charity, and hope, to recognize Jesus and to see the world anew. So they know God to be not only (1) the transcendent term of an orientation but also (2) a known person in history, and (3) as the inner love that stalks divine Mystery. Mystery remains shrouded in a cloud, but that same Mystery gives itself to human history in the mysterious person of Christ Jesus, just as it gives itself to human consciousness in the mysterious gift of transcendent love which overflows in faith, charity, and hope. Christians, therefore, know God as giving the divine self in two manners.

This has an immediate relevance to the Christian doctrine of the Trinity. The Christian finds 'God' (1) in the person Christ Jesus, (2) in the inner impulses of transcendent love (called by expectant Jews the "Holy Spirit"), and (3) in the term towards which that love seems to head (called by Jesus "Father"). The Christian does not think that Christ Jesus is identical to the Holy Spirit or to the Father. Jesus worshiped the Father, and, like us, was moved by the Holy Spirit to do so. Therefore, without necessarily giving it much thought, Christians have always known God as doubly self-giving. They have counted on the person of Christ Jesus and on the inner movements of the Holy Spirit to bring them into union with the God they love. In brief, the Christian religious experience is the experience of the theological virtues springing from the inner transcendent love of God and directed outward towards Jesus of Nazareth. It is this experience of a double self-gift that eventually led dogmatic theologians to speak of God as "three." But as we can plainly see, simply calling God "three" easily trivializes the experience. Perhaps something like "doubly self-giving" or "doubly assuring" would keep the Christian religious experience at the heart of trinitarian doctrine—where it belongs.[16]

Other religions manifest the same structure as Christianity, even though they obviously do not preach the same content. We can see that they depend on inner spiritual process to lead them to recognize which paths to walk, which spiritual leaders or guides to follow, which written works convey divine Mystery. In other words, they too depend on a divining spirit within the soul to discern divine realities in history.

I have been fortunate to discover an independent verification of this doubly assuring structure of religious consciousness in the work of Claudio Naranjo.[17] He has studied the basic forms of prayer evident in world religions and finds that they fall into three classes. These classes, as you will see, are not merely descriptive. They emerge from a process analysis of the data of consciousness, which, of course, is "right up our alley."

First, there is the Way of Surrender (or Self-Expression). One meditates on the spontaneous contents of the mind and heart. It is receptive, orgiastic, surrendering, inner-directed. It centers on the individual and remains in the present. It emphasizes freedom, transparency. This method usually pictures the self as a *channel* for God rather than, say, the self as *united* to God. It revels in archetypal experiences: the journey into the underworld, the ascent to heaven, dying and rising. When it comes to expressing the experience, we find visions, revelations, prophecy, sensations, glossalalia, automatic writing, spirit possession, and clairvoyance. The technique is to overcome the difficulty of attending to one's consciousness without controlling

132

or creating it. Breathing exercises and experiments in artistic expression are used. Evil spirits within have to be faced, since often they prove to be friendly in the long run. The novice has to redirect evil desires by giving them expression, converting enemies into helpers, devils into guardian angels.

Second, there is the Way of Forms. Here one meditates on some externally given symbolic object: a mandala, a mantra, a monstrance. It is "medi-tation" of something between God and us—for example, the polarity of yin-yang or the contradiction of the cross. One assumes the attitude of order, of regularity, of lawfulness, conforming oneself to God's will or surrendering to Tao (Way) or Dharma (Law of the Universe). Its asceticism involves ego-dissolution, nirvana, sacrifice, detachment from desires as well as from things and actions. The supreme action is non-action. It is typically pious, conservative, and traditional: "Here is the truth; assimilate it and make it yours." It seeks absolutes, principles, laws, theocracy. And it is past-oriented. The problem, of course, is that the symbol for God can become just the veil that hides divine mystery from us.

Third, we have the Negative Way. One meditates by denying the ultimate validity of the other two ways. It is a higher integration of the other two and is usually found to some degree in both. Total detachment is required, letting go of everything, external symbols as well as inner movements. Its negativity is complete: nonviolence, nonlying, nonmisappropriation, noncraving, nonpossessiveness, and so on. Zen is the typical example. Just sit, with no idea of self and no urges to work on anything, even including the prayer. One accepts oneself as Buddha without knowing it.

Notice that the Way of Self-Expression emphasizes what we have called transcendent love, the inner movements that occur in the world of immediacy. The Way of Forms emphasizes the perceivable objects of faith, charity, and hope—the outer realities mediated to us by our acts of meaning. Both are recognized as partial inasmuch as they each head towards the Negative Way that denies them exclusive ultimate validity. Another way of reading the same data is to see that both the Way of Self-Expression and the Way of Forms do have an ultimate validity when taken together and regarded as making real contact with the incomprehensible One of the Negative Way.

We can draw at least two conclusions of great ecumenical importance from this analysis. First, although not all religions have made this double movement the substance of their doctrines, it is nonetheless easy to discern them at work in their practices of prayer. Christianity, therefore, shares the identical inner spiritual processes with all religions. It differs from other religions in recognizing Jesus of Nazareth as the person in whom the entirety of one's experienced faith, charity, and hope can be directed.

Second, the old division of prayer forms into apophatic and kataphatic should be expanded. They do not articulate well enough their structural correlatives in consciousness. What has been called the apophatic form of prayer does correspond to the Negative Way of Naranjo's study, the prayer that relinquishes any claim to univocal understanding. But the kataphatic form has two distinct forms within it—the Way of Self-Expression and the Way of Forms, corresponding respectively to the world of immediacy and the world mediated by meaning. With this threefold distinction in mind we can much more easily talk with non-Christians and find, if not an acknowledgement of Jesus as Lord, at least an acknowledgement of a doubly assuring God.

10. Evil and Redemption

We have been moving upwards through the levels of consciousness. In our chapter on knowing we looked at experience, understanding, and judgment and saw how they combine to enable us to reach knowledge of reality. Then, in the chapter on acting, we looked at decision, the fourth level of consciousness, and analyzed how feelings, images, memories, value judgments, repression and suppression worked. We saw how incapable individuals and communities are of bringing about sustained moral progress as long as they depend only on the resources of the first four levels of consciousness. So in this chapter we moved to the fifth level, and we examined how transcendent love is the backbone of all levels of consciousness and how it produces faith, charity, and hope.

We are now in a position to see how these theological virtues actually redeem human evil. But before doing that, let us review what we have already learned about what exactly this evil consists in.

Recall how, in our account of Lonergan's analysis of historical progress and decline, good situations tend to get better and bad situations tend to get worse. The reason, we saw, is that disobedience to the transcendental precepts not only makes each particular situation slightly worse but also decreases the odds that our obedience to the transcendental precepts will be effective in the deteriorated situation. And, finally, recall the four general forms of disobedience within: neurosis, individual egoism, group egoism, and anti-intellectual short-sightedness.

We do not spontaneously think of evil this way, but if we are to resist evil intelligently, it is very important that we keep this vision clearly in mind. Evil is not the world order that allows for blind alleys, slow development, mistaken judgments, and so on. As we have insisted, that world order is intelligible and good, albeit painful and demanding. Everything is Cosmos, we said, except the refusal to admit it.

Nor should we let ourselves slip into the naive illusion that evil is nothing but the awful things we humans do to one another—the lies we tell, the wars we wage, the hurts we inflict. As any high-school sophomore will point out, there are always circumstances in which such normally prohibited behavior is allowable and sometimes even necessary. We should be outraged at evil behavior, of course, but unless we see exactly what makes the behavior evil, we will rage against the wrong enemy and apply all the wrong remedies.

Fundamentally, human evil is disobedience of the transcendental precepts, just as *the* fundamental moral action is to obey them. Redemption, therefore, will not be a *release* from a world in which we must learn through our mistakes and suffer pulls and counterpulls in consciousness. Nor will redemption be primarily an end to *behavior* we deem immoral. Primarily, redemption will be a liberation within consciousness which, far from taking its stand on prohibitions, will take its stand on continual creativity. It will be eager to attend to what is going on, to ask why and how, to test ideas and proposals against reality, to invent ways to enlarge the common good, and to love and worship divine Mystery.

Once we let divine Mystery into the picture we see that disobedience within is the same thing as hatred for God. There is no getting around it. If God comes to us through the gift of transcendent love, and if that love operates through the transcendental precepts, then to suppress them is to reject God's gift of the divine self. It is a double rejection, as we might expect, since to reject the movements of the soul within us will mean that we will also fail to realize the potentialities, intelligibilities, realities, and values available from without. Fenced around as we are by divine love, we realize that the smallest inner disobedience is also an interpersonal rejection of God—something all the great mystics have come to know.

Is it outrageous to suggest that when we resist the movements of self-transcendence in the soul we thereby hate God? If God were nothing but some almighty and invisible friend in the sky, yes, it would be outrageous. God's reaction to our inner disobedience could be at most some kind of pity as that divine onlooker watched us destroy ourselves. But God is the love that moves every man, woman, and child within consciousness. So it is not outrageous to call inner disobedience hatred of God. It is a rejection of the divine One for whom everything in us longs.

Fundamentally, therefore, the essence of human evil is simultaneously the disobedience of the transcendental precepts and a rejection of the divine Mystery being offered as an interpersonal gift. We have hinted that redemption of this evil will consist in obedience to the transcendental precept, Be in love, and an acceptance of the redeeming movements of faith, charity, and hope which follow. Let us now look at what redemptive effects these theological virtues have over all the levels of consciousness.[18] By doing so, we will be sketching out, in a formal but absolutely fundamental manner, what our 'spiritual integration' really is.

We will be fairly compendious here. There is far too much to say about how being in love integrates the rest of human spiritual process. Keep in mind that many of the integrating functions we will describe here also work in people who have not yet acknowledged the loving source of their love. That is, we are looking at the intrinsic intelligibility of redemption in people whether or not they think of themselves as in love with God. Finally, since we are moving "downwards" from the fifth level of consciousness, it may be of help if we number these levels from five down to one.

5. Being in love, of itself, is a process, a dynamism, a first principle from which flow a great many interior operations—wonder, awe, puzzlement, questions, appreciation, deliberation.

It is given, already going on, but not because we have perceived its object. Indeed, we do not perceive any objects whatsoever except inasmuch as this process prompts us to attention, intelligence, reasonableness, and responsibility. And when that is done, we are still left longing for Mystery.

The best objects it can find are human persons and human communities. Yet these are not enough. They are not loved simply in themselves, but only insofar as they bear, in partial ways, the infinite intelligibility, truth, and goodness we long for. Yet, friends are not lost because we go beyond them; friendship is integrated from above into divine love.

4. The immediate effects of being in love are felt on the fourth level of consciousness. There, being in love gives faith, the eyes of the heart, which perceives values that surpass explanation. It is faith that discerns the reliable guides in life. It is faith that recognizes the news in the Gospels as "good" and the community of believers as guided by the "Holy Spirit of God." It is faith that gives the fundamental convictions about human nature (and its drive towards the transcendent) which run counter to the theories and ideologies by which nearly all our reigning institutions rationalize their raping of the human person. In other words, faith is redemptive of theory as well as of common-sense practicality.

Through faith, a person "in" love discovers the profound mystery of other persons and makes loving commitments that last a lifetime — indeed, that cost a lifetime. That is, faith produces charity.

Being "good," after all, is really not enough for us. Not because we have not been good enough but because we need someone to be good *for*. Once we let transcendent love find human persons to love, we see a purpose in life beyond being practical and efficient, or being a contributor to a process of communication of information and goods. That larger purpose is simply to love. Our principle of selection changes — selection of what to say in a group, of how to spend a Friday evening, and so on. It is now a method controlled by love and purpose, where intelligence is instrumental. We let go of the habit of selecting according to mere intelligence — what will work most efficiently — without posing the further question of purpose and value. We no longer oscillate between meeting a chain of responsibilities, necessities, and obligations and, on the other hand, loafing, relaxing, storing up for the new round of duties.

Charity towards one another takes priority over the self-indictments that come from our consciences. John the Evangelist makes this poignantly clear. "Only by this (loving one another in deeds, not just in words) can we be certain that we are Children of Truth and be able to quieten our conscience (hearts) in His presence, *whatever accusations it may raise against us*; because God is greater than our conscience, and He knows everything. My dear people, if we cannot be condemned by our own conscience, we need not be afraid in God's presence" (1 Jn 3:19-20). In other words, our love for God and for neighbor gives our moral lives an inner guide and a concrete outer term that, in effect, forbid us passing judgment on ourselves by our own initiative.

Faith and charity together enable us to withstand the dark forces both of God's transcendence and of human malice. Faith assures us that sin has no ultimate power, and charity points to the next steps to take in this Valley of Darkness. In other words, faith and charity produce hope.

Hope backs up decision-making with a courage to take risks and a stamina to withstand setbacks. Hope moves towards a future that we do not clearly see, but it assures us that we can trust transcendent love within us and those guides in our world which faith discerns are reliable. So we could say that even though we *do not* know where we are going, we *do* know how to get there.

3. Being in love leads to being reasonable; it makes us more realistic human beings. This third-level liberation of reason may not be as evident as the liberation of morality on the fourth level. Still, its effects are profound and absolutely necessary for our full liberation as otherwise biased human beings.

Just as on the fourth level, being in love leads to such concrete judgments of *value* as "It is better to suffer evil than to do evil," so here on the third level it leads to such judgments of *fact* as "God's Spirit is at work in every person" and "The world is indeed a gift from the living God." Such judgments of fact are part and parcel of our faith, giving us an antidote against the biased intelligence that moves merely from experience upward.

Being truly realistic does not mean hard-headed practicality; nor does it mean the smug conviction that the real is quite obvious. Quite the contrary. Being in love naturally leads to the radical realization that what appears to the eyes is not the real world. We experience a readiness to entertain invisible possibilities. Herbert Butterfield, the historian of science, has noted that scientists who happen to be Christian, or at least religious, are more ready to entertain questions about the non-obvious, the unexpected, the outrageously implausible.[19]

Usually this conversion to intellectual realism begins when we fall in love with another person and experience the sudden evaporation of a lot of comfortable and secure views about reality. The conversion deepens when we have to accept ourselves as we really are, with all our concrete limitations. We are forced to face this reality because we know that our beloved knows, and sees, and accepts. That self-acceptance can then lead to a readiness to look upon the world with an open mind. Then we discover ourselves as searchers in a very real world, and that this universe is a friendly place. We also discover that many of the assurances given by politicians and corporations are complete lies.

2. Being in love leads to a more effective intelligence. Because we are knowingly in love, and more responsible and more reasonable, we become more able to ask why and how. Not that our IQs are raised; IQ is a measure of intellectual potential only. But we are enabled to realize more effectively the intellectual potential we have. This is because we feel less threatened to admit that we do *not* understand. We become like little children asking the how and why questions that most adults are ashamed to ask.

Hope, in particular, enables us to endure the unanswered question. It counsels us not to jump to facile explanations that at best only suppress the question and at worst compound the problems.

For persons engaged in scientific or scholarly fields, there is a readiness and a desire to understand the real order of all things. One knows that God has ordered the universe, but this order is still rather elusive. A lifetime spent uncovering this order is recognized as a worthwhile expression of divine faith, charity, and hope. In other words, religious fundamentalism, which belittles understanding and cherishes the simple view, is really a failure in religious love.

1. Finally, being in love leads to a transformed attentiveness. The very experience of how religious conversion cracks open the horizons of our responsibility, our reason, and our intelligence, giving them an orientation to uncriticizable goodness, the absolutely real, and the completely intelligible makes us aware that all data is data on God. Every-

thing speaks. "The world is charged with the glory of God." And we are rendered attentive in a wondering, loving, respectful, and awe-struck way.

There is even a paradoxical readiness to be inattentive, a readiness to fall asleep in the assurance given by faith, charity, and hope that divine Mystery will keep watch. "In vain you get up earlier and put off going to bed, sweating to make a living, since God provides for the beloved as they sleep" (Ps 127).

11. Pull and Counterpull

Finally we ought to say a few words about spiritual consolation and spiritual desolation. Even though transcendent love has the power to integrate the levels of consciousness from above, we do not experience this power all the time. Sometimes we suffer a counterpull that resists the workings of transcendent love. Those who know the pull cannot deny that there is the counterpull as well, even though they may not use these terms. People familiar with spiritual literature usually speak in terms of consolation and desolation, terms used by St. Ignatius of Loyola in his *Spiritual Exercises*.[20] But the reality appears to be the same. We experience two primary and contrary movements in the soul, one experienced as an increase of faith, charity, and hope, and the other experienced as their decrease. So, to round off our discussion of how being in love with transcendent Mystery actually works in human consciousness, let us situate 'consolation and desolation' within the framework we have been constructing.

Consolation, like desolation, is an experience of a rather total movement of consciousness. In both, feelings play a key role, either making virtue easy or making it difficult. If we are not experiencing strong currents of affectivity either way, then we do not think of ourselves as in consolation or in desolation. We are in a time of tranquility. Feelings are not pulling strongly in one direction or another. And yet we have to be careful not to think of these movements as nothing but our own feelings. Spiritual classics treat them as movements "from without." There is wisdom in this. If we were to think of consolation as our own feelings, we would count as our own what is really a divine gift. And if we were to think of desolation as "from within" ourselves, we would too easily count ourselves as essentially a source of evil rather than as persons subject to temptation "from without." (The notion of good angels and bad angels has served us very well here.)

So let me suggest that consolation is *the experience of faith bringing forth the fruits of charity and hope.* Hope is necessary in this definition because consolation is carried by feelings and yet is not identical to feelings. The feelings serve to confirm our expectations that all will be well and to give momentum and direction to our attention, intelligence, reason, and responsibility. Charity is a necessary element because in consolation we experience a power to love God and neighbor which we did not generate by ourselves. That power makes us ready and willing to give ourselves to others in sincere love and genuine care. Faith, as we saw above, is the "eyes of the heart" that sees divine values in human affairs and is the source of both charity and hope. It is faith that gives us the glimpse of divine Mystery in persons and communities, thereby making charity possible. And it is faith that grounds expectant feelings in the firm judgment of fact that sin has no ultimate power and will not prevail: and this is our hope.

On the opposite end, let us consider spiritual desolation as *the absence of movements of faith and its normal fruits of charity and hope.* With hope diminished, our feelings for God, neighbor, and virtue no longer carry us along. With charity diminished, we experience little power to act for the sake of others. With both hope and charity diminished, our faith stands still and naked, making the discernment of divine Mystery in others difficult and rendering our confidence in the future rather shaky. We are left with nothing but the judgments of value and the judgments of fact which we have appropriated from our religious heritage and from our own past struggles. In other words, we are left with the content of faith but without any experience of its movement in the concrete present.

Obviously, a time of desolation is not a good time to have to make a decision. But it does offer us an opportunity for some precious spiritual booty anyway. For one thing, desolation is a humbling experience because it reminds us that charity and hope, as well as our faith itself, are gifts beyond our control. (Who can ever become humble without being humbled like this from time to time?) Also, desolation can serve to strengthen our faith. When we are forced to rely on the values and truths embedded in our tradition, they very often take on a newer and a more solid meaning. That too is no small thing.

Besides times of consolation and times of desolation, there are also times of relative tranquility. What is going on here is that faith is indeed alive and moving, but it is not making itself felt directly in movements of charity and hope. That is, we do experience keen perception for discerning divine values—usually with the help of our traditions and commitments—but we simply do not experience an unusually strong power to act on behalf of others nor an unusually strong feeling of confidence about ultimate outcomes. In their absence we simply have to rely on the judgments of value and of fact which faith brings forth. Normally we need to test these judgments against reason and against the wisdom of our community, just to make sure we are not subverting the self-transcending nature of consciousness and becoming spiritual screwballs. And, if the judgments are sound, there usually occurs a subsequent 'confirmation' by way of consolation in the future.

Need I remind anyone that consolation is not always pleasant? And that desolation is not always unpleasant? We may be moved to leave our familiar surroundings and our friends and to dedicate ourselves to caring for some outlandish folks on the fringes of society—a rather unpleasant movement of faith, charity, and hope. Or we may feel tremendous grief over our own sinfulness. These are full-blown consolations. On the side of desolation, we may feel giddy with excitement at a party or blissfully content after a few Manhattans. If these tend to diminish faith, charity, and hope, then they are pure and simple desolations. I have little doubt that most good people know how to deal with these movements, but not everyone understands them in terms of consolation and desolation. I simply wanted to bring it in here lest our highly analytical treatment makes us forget what our moral conversion has taught, namely, that the truly good is not always merely satisfying.

What we have treated so far may serve well enough for us to locate what Ignatius calls consolation and desolation within our model of the self-transcending subject. Our next task is to analyse how consolation and desolation work in the different levels of our consciousness.

If the divine pull works on us through all five levels of consciousness, then there must be five discernable manifestations of consolation. The first four have perceived objects. So, for example, on the level of attention we can feel drawn to notice certain promising-looking data; we can gaze expectantly at ordinary data waiting for it to reveal its extraordinary secrets. On the level of intelligence we can enjoy the lightsome pleasures of insight; we can experience the sage's understanding of the meaning of life. On the level of reason, we can bow to the limits of reality; we can welcome the truth in spite of its costs.

On the level of responsibility, we can embrace worthwhile proposals and rejoice over good deeds and good people. Of course, these four tend to combine by nature so that we tend to experience all four levels cooperating in a harmonious expansion.

The fifth level of consciousness, as we have said, has no 'object' in the sense that we must recognize it before we are drawn towards it. So there is a kind of consolation that feels like sheer autonomous movement beyond the objects we know. It is often accompanied by strong pleasurable feelings of happiness, but not always. Sometimes the movement seems almost devoid of ordinary feelings. In their place we find the experience of an awe, even a kind of dread, and yet an irresistible attraction. But we trust the movement because, as we learn by experience, the more we manage to attend to it in prayer, the more easily we can liberate the other levels of consciousness to work unhindered by inner limits of fear and insecurity.

Ignatius of Loyola points out that in this latter consolation, which goes beyond the objects we know, it is not even possible to doubt its source and direction.[21] And even the mere memory of it can help us weigh alternatives at later times. The other kind of consolation—the kind that responds to known objects—may be a relatively dependable guide for perceiving divine values, but not absolutely so. He cautions us to scrutinize the entire course of that kind of consolation because, in the case of people who are going from good to better, the movement can actually diminish faith, charity, and hope in the long run, turning consolation into desolation. How this spiritual bathos works is anybody's guess. My own guess is that in the misleading consolations we are responding not to the real objects at hand but to our memory of similar objects in the past, objects which may in their time have brought a dependable consolation. It is a case of borrowing feelings from ourselves, but feelings which are not really appropriate responses to realities at hand.

If consolation, or the divine pull, is somewhat discernable over five levels of consciousness, then so too for desolation. On the level of experience, the counterpull can render us stubbornly oblivious of important data. On the level of intelligence, it can smother our intellectual curiosity. On the level of reason it can harden us in narrowmindedness, prejudice, and rigid fantasy about what is real and what is not. And on the level of decision, it can constrict the normally wide range of our benevolence and appreciation.

Is there a fifth level darkness? If there is, it ought to manifest itself in disgust with anything connected with striving, hoping, longing, growing. It would be a despair so complete that even anger or fear would not seem worth the effort. It would be a total entropy of the soul. But is there such a darkness? In my own limited experience and reading, I believe there is, but it lasts for only very brief periods. Before long, we get frustrated, angry, anxious, or afraid. And even though these feelings are far from satisfying, they are a sign of hope that the transcendental precepts have gotten under way and transcendental love is on the move again.

What should a person do while in desolation? Ignatius suggests several things. We should remember that desolation can serve to make us humble and to strengthen our faith. We should avoid quick decisions. We should remember that desolation does not last; consolation "will soon return" in those who work against its downward drift.[22] (This is surprisingly difficult to believe when one is actually in desolation.) We work against that downward drift, he says, by some careful self-analysis to see if we might have brought it about by slacking in the struggle; we should also intensify our prayer and mortifications.

I would like to add my own bit of advice here, which can be expressed in terms of the transcendental precepts. Just as in consolation, we let the precept 'Be in love' take the lead, so in desolation we should try mightily to Be attentive. Desolation is a trial of waiting and endurance. To be attentive during this time means watching for where divine Mystery might break through our dulled perceptions. We should watch attentively not only for the movements within our private consciousnesses but also, and often more importantly, for the breaks in the routines of our lives. I'm thinking of slowing down and being attentive to the flowers, the quiet slant of light through trees, the rough beauty of a carpenter's hands. And I am thinking of those requests that people put to us during desolation in which we are asked to do something quite out of character for us. Being attentive to these "breaks" in the obviousness of reality very often cracks open divine Mystery before our eyes, and once again our life stirs to see its Beloved again.

During the last twenty years or so there has appeared a greatly increased interest in how the practice of discerning spirits can help a person or a community make concrete choices according to "the will of God." For the most part the work done has been theologically sound and quite practical. But very few theologians have examined how the practice of discerning spirits can also enable us to choose between two interpretations of the same event. For it often happens that prior to making decisions we settle on one particular understanding of a situation without much inquiry as to whether our biases might be blinding us to the full reality.

Let me give an example. A few years ago I spent some time teaching at a university far away from my home. By the end of the term, as often happens, I was aware of the many shortcomings of the institution and of some of the people I had worked with. I felt frustration and was anxious to get out of there. At the same time, I had met some wonderful people with whom I had tasted some of life's poignant mysteries. It is no oversimplification to say that I had two contrary feelings about the time I spent there. Resentment pulled in one direction and gratitude in another. And I had two stories to choose from—either "The semester was a drag" or "The semester was a grace." The truth of that semester, like the truth of any human situation, was not some fixed set of outer data that just waits for somebody's correct perception. The truth was a struggle of movements within me between two interpretations of the same data.

Notice how this choice of one story over another can turn not only one decision but often years of decisions in a biased direction. The stories we believe about ourselves carry plots with them that predetermine thousands of choices without our realizing it. If I were to think of myself as constantly frustrated I would become resentful and my interests would turn less to trust and more to control. On the other hand, to regard myself as constantly graced would move me towards letting go of control and walking with more trust in other people and in the providence of God.

So while recent studies on discernment of spirits have examined how one person or a community of persons make one sound decision—strategic though that decision be—we also ought to examine how one person or a community of persons chooses its stories, because the stories we choose to tell about ourselves can shape a lifetime of decisions.

Discussion Questions: CHAPTER FOUR

Again, here are five questions to test your knowledge of the material from this chapter. Please refer to the chapter for your answer before looking at my response in the appendix.

Question 1

George is married to Dianne. He accompanies her to church often, but not because he believes in God. He believes that it is good to support his wife in her beliefs and that religion does do some good in the world. On one particular Sunday, he hears the text about Jesus driving the money-changers out of the temple. He hears the lines, "Zeal for thy house has eaten me up" and "Destroy this temple and I will raise it up in three days." What do you imagine George thinks "zeal" is? How do you think he interprets Jesus' reference to his resurrection? What sense will he likely make of this text? Discuss how an exegete's religious conversion or its absence enters into how he or she interprets scriptural texts.

Question 2

In all of the Old Testament, there are only two or three references to an afterlife spent in bliss, and these occur only in the books written a few hundred years before Christ. So it appears that the Israelites believed in God, loved God, counted on God, and lived moral lives without any hope of a personal reward in the next life. Indeed, they expected that after they died, they would be consigned to a Sheol where no one praises God. For example:

> For in death there is no remembrance of thee; in Sheol who can give thee praise? (Ps 6:5)
>
> What profit is there in my death, if I go down to the Pit? Will the dust praise thee? (Ps 30:9)
>
> Dost thou work wonders for the dead? Do the shades rise up to praise thee? (Ps 88:10)
>
> For Sheol cannot thank thee, death cannot praise thee; those who go down to the Pit cannot hope for thy faithfulness. The living, the living thank thee, as I do today. (Is 38:18)

How can this be squared with their profound love of God? Try to answer the question in terms of transcendent love and its fruits.

146

Question 3

Theologians ever since Luther have speculated on what happened to God when Jesus died on the cross. Did God suffer? Certainly the Old Testament shows God at least changing moods quite often. And any theology that has impact for our world today ought to conceive God as changing in some respect. But, on the other hand, Thomistic/Aristotelian metaphysics insists that God not only does not change but cannot change. How can we reconcile these two views of God?

Question 4

When Jesus was asked which was the greatest commandment, he answered "To love the Lord your God with your whole heart, your whole mind, your whole soul, and all your strength. And the second is like it: to love your neighbor as yourself."

Christian tradition has always linked the love of God with the love of one's neighbor. Even such mystics as Teresa of Avila and Ignatius of Loyola were never so drawn to God that they did not grow more and more practical in their love of neighbor. How are we to understand these two objects of our love? In terms of the structure of consciousness, how are they a unity? Why is it that deeper mystical union with God seems to produce deeper commitment to one's brothers and sisters?

Why, in other words, does faith always demand justice?

Question 5

Tim visits his spiritual director and describes an experience he has had of tremendous unity with nature and, for all he knows, with God. Eventually he asks the director, "Is this truly a spiritual experience or just a psychological experience?"

If you were the director, how would you answer Tim's question? Would you lean towards calling it spiritual? Only psychological? Spiritual *and* psychological? Would you have to wait until you see what fruits it produces?

Discuss this in terms of the different levels of consciousness.

Notes to Chapter Four

1. *Method in Theology*, pp. 105–107

2. I am following the Thomistic distinction as articulated by F.E. Crowe. See his "Complacency and Concern in the Thought of St. Thomas," *Theological Studies* 20 (59), 1–39, 198–230, 343–395.

3. I call it 'transcendent love' to distinguish it from love that already knows its beloved. Transcendent love moves in us before we reach any knowledge of God. See *Method in Theology*, p. 106.

4. *Method in Theology*, pp. 79–80

5. See Lonergan's "Healing and Creating in History," in Eric O'Connor, ed., *Bernard Lonergan: 3 Lectures* (Montreal: Thomas More Institute, 1975), pp. 55–68. This splendid article is the very first one I recommend to students interested in spirituality and Lonergan.

6. Here I am following the provocative lead given by Lonergan in *Method in Theology*, p. 109.

7. Again I am following a lead given by Lonergan. "Now an orientation to transcendent mystery is basic to systematic theology. It provides the primary and fundamental meaning of the name, God." *Method in Theology*, p. 341.

8. See Tibor Horvath, "A Structural Understanding of the Magisterium of the Church," *Science et Esprit* 29/3 (1977), 286.

9. See Eugene Webb, *Eric Voegelin: Philosopher of History* (Seattle: University of Washington Press, 1981), p. 115.

10. On how faith, charity, and hope function in redemption, see *Insight*, pp. 696–703, 718–729 and *Method in Theology*, p. 117.

11. The category of 'Mystery' I am using here is in large part due to Flannery O'Connor's reflections on method in fiction. See her *Mystery and Manners*, ed. Sally and Robert Fitzgerald (New York: Farrar, Straus & Giroux, 1957), *passim*, but esp. 87–118.

12. *Method in Theology*, pp. 115–118.

13. See Karl Rahner, "Thomas Aquinas on the Incomprehensibility of God," in David Tracy, ed., *Celebrating the Medieval Heritage: A Colloquy on the Thought of Aquinas and Bonaventure; Journal of Religion* 28 (1978) Supplement, S107–S131.

14. See Lonergan's "Origins of Christian Realism," in W.F.J. Ryan and B.J. Tyrrell, eds., *Second Collection* (London: Darton, Longman & Todd, 1974), p. 251.

15. See, for example, Maurice Wiles, *The Making of Christian Doctrine* (Cambridge: Cambridge University Press, 1967), pp. 62–113.

16. This is the gist of my short book on prayer from a Lonerganian perspective. See *We Cannot Find Words: The Foundations of Prayer* (New Jersey: Dimension Books, 1981).

17. "Meditation: Its Spirit and Techniques," Part I of *On the Psychology of Meditation*, by Claudio Naranjo and Robert Ornstein (Part II), (New York: Viking, 1971), pp. 3–132.

18. I am expanding on the leads given by Lonergan in "Healing and Creating in History," pp. 55–68, esp. 63–66.

19. "The believer in Providence can be prepared for any surprises. The Christian need put no limits to the Creator's versatility." See Herbert Butterfield, *History and Human Relations* (London: Collins Clear-Type Press, 1951) p. 141.

20. *The Spiritual Exercises of St. Ignatius*, trans. Louis J. Puhl (Chicago: Loyola University Press, 1959), para. 316, 317 (p. 142).

21. "When consolation is without previous cause ["without any preceding preception or knowledge of any subject by which a soul might be led to such a consolation through its own acts of intellect or will"] there can be no deception in it." (*Spiritual Exercises*, para. 330, 335). Also: "It often happens that our Lord moves and impels our soul to one particular course or another by laying it open—that is, speaking within it without the sound of any voice, raising it all to his divine love, without our being able to resist what he suggests, even if we wanted to do so." See Hugo Rahner, ed., *Saint Ignatius Loyola: Letters to Women* (New York: Herder and Herder, 1960), p. 334.

22. "When one is in desolation . . . consider that consolation will soon return," *Spiritual Exercises*, para. 321, (p. 143).

CHAPTER FIVE

Storytelling

They say that extroverts talk in order to think, and introverts think in order to talk. But everyone talks. We talk to one another about our children, our jobs, our friends, our hobbies. We brag; we lament; we entertain; we joke; we inform. We discuss the problems of our country, of other families, of the local school, of our city. We talk about ourselves, testing to see if our perceptions make sense to someone else. In part, this is an effort to learn the truth about ourselves. But we also talk simply to communicate, to keep in contact, to maintain the interpersonal links that bind us one to another. Even when we are by ourselves, we hold imaginary dialogues in which we manifest the truth of things to a person who will listen, even if that person be only our selves.

By far, most of our talk comes from an urge to tell a story. We use our minds more for telling stories than for all other purposes combined. Experts in the most theoretical fields may work in the intellectual pattern of experience for long periods, but their imaginations and hopes long for the scene in which they can shout their "Eureka!" and join their colleagues in an interpersonal celebration. Mystics return from their cloud of unknowing and talk, perhaps in halting terms, perhaps with prophetic force, but always in narrative style.

Besides the fact that everybody tells stories, there is a further reason why we should examine storytelling here. So far we have seen that religious self-transcendence is the fundamental power in the soul. Whether explicit or not, it blossoms in moral self-transcendence, and that in turn fructifies in intellectual self-transcendence. But none of these occur in the unconnected individual. They occur while we tell our stories, and our stories help them occur. In other words, by talk-

151

ing about storytelling, we do not arrive at some additional reality that only a few people reach; we arrive at the fullest reality of our lives, the living context of every human struggle.

Without stories, we would have no way to symbolize, let alone to understand, what happens to us. Stories bear both the known and the unknown, both the cogent and the ambiguous, both sin and grace. They allow us to deal with truth even when we cannot understand it. And they bind us together in a common desire to hear the truth spoken in love.

There is mystery here. We Christians have come to know God as self-uttering and self-hearing. The obscure yet ever-close object of our love is one who speaks and one who listens. So the true meaning of love, found as it is only in God, contains an essential element of storytelling. This means that by the transcendent love we feel surging in our own hearts we each share directly in divinity when we open our mouths to talk. To speak is, in a mysterious way, to do what God does of necessity.

In what follows we will attempt the chancy business every theologian faces: how to talk about divine Mystery in intelligible terms. On the one hand, we must be careful not to think we can explain Mystery. On the other, we must be equally careful not to call Mystery those things which Mystery impels us to understand. But at least we now possess a model of subjectivity that accounts for the *human experience* of transcendence, even though it cannot account for the transcendent itself.

Were we literary critics, we might speak of characters and plots, comedies and tragedies, suspense and surprise. These form some of the structural elements of stories. But we are not literary critics. Generalized empirical method directs us to understand what the *experience* of hearing a good story is like, and then to relate those experiences to one another in an intelligible manner. After all, it is the fascinating elements in the narrated experience, not in the structural elements, that shape the characters and create the plot. Good storytellers usually have in mind some rather elusive or subtle turn of events they want to portray. The events are not always obvious. In fact, the stories that bear retelling usually point to the events *within* the souls of people that shape the more visible events that take place *between* them. So we will begin by defining the inner events that make great stories great.

1. *Mystery and Mysteries*

In our preceding chapter, we defined the word 'Mystery' as the transcendent term of the movement of our souls—preferring it, for the time being, to the word 'God'. But because concrete events can do more than anything else to stir those transcendent movements in our souls, let us call the more crucial events 'mysteries'. I am not thinking here of detective mysteries; these are puzzles that admit clear answers. I am thinking rather of the impenetrable events portrayed in the "mysteries" of the Rosary, or the "mystery" plays of medieval times.

So a mystery in this sense is an event in which a human is touched by the divine, regardless of whether or not its story talks about "God." The stories that speak of mysteries in this sense symbolize for us, in palpable, concrete terms, our contact with the singular Mystery we are made to love. We find examples of this everywhere in our tradition. Israel praises God by telling stories of what God has done. Each Evangelist has his own narrative about the mysteries of the life of Christ. The Church tells of the lives of the saints. Each one of us tells of a personal call to holiness, of when and where it happened. Even within a more secular narrative, we are touched by the story of an anti-nuclear demonstrator speaking so gently to belligerent police officers you would think they were "family." Or we find some poignant piece of fiction, and we read the story to a friend in the hospital, knowing very well that it says something absolutely true about real life in a way that factual reporting never could. Like the one Mystery, each of our mysteries holds ever more meaning and can be told and retold without exhausting it. Mysteries, in this sense, are always about what Scripture calls salvation or redemption because they save us from meaninglessness and redeem us from despair.

The know-it-alls among us are impatient with good stories because they prefer certitudes to mysteries. They hope to slice some moral from the heart of a story or enshrine some pithy line on a poster. But such categorial reductions of good stories can never exhaust their meaning. Flannery O'Connor has made this point well: "When you can state the theme of a story, when you can separate it from the story itself, then you can be sure the story is not a very good one."[2] And yet on the other hand, no single event or set of events, nor any of their stories can ever exhaust the total potentiality of complete intelligibility, existence, or goodness. So 'events' that we find important enough to tell a story about stand halfway between what Scholastic philosophers call the categorials and the transcendentals. In other words, good stories are more than we can handle, and yet they fail to slake our thirst for Mystery. Good stories, like good liturgies, span the chasm between divine Mystery and human reckoning.

Not all human events are expressed in stories. And yet this does not necessarily mean that only certain events are mysteries and that the rest of life is just ordinary or obvious. But we often act as though this were the case. We think of certain "religious" events as so extraordinary that we think the normal laws of physics and history had been abrogated for a brief, astonishing moment. We then tend to call such events "divine interventions," as though we had been, up to that point, surrounded by the obvious and not really living in a universal darkness packed with divinity but masked by ambiguous color, sound, movement, and smell.

So we must seriously consider the possibility that all events are mysteries. They bring reality upon the mind, but the reality passes on, leaving the mind with more questions than answers. For the religious lover, all events are the words of a lover. They possess no intelligibility except that which comes from a loving intelligence. These events which are real depend completely on an existence that cannot have been called into existence but lovingly calls all things into existence. They do not possess any worth except what is positively intended and appreciated, desired and welcomed by a lover who cannot will anything but the good. And these events, these "words of a lover," are salvific words because they reveal life as a tightrope and yet beckon us to walk forward anyway.

It is no easy matter to sense the mysterious in every ordinary event. Among Christians it has been customary to refer to doctrines and miracles as "mysteries." For example, the divinity of Christ is a mystery; the raising of Lazarus is a mystery. But we should be careful not to associate mystery with mere perplexity in our minds. In their origins, mysteries are historical events that waken our wonder. And the historical event itself is a saving encounter in a specific time and place with the one transcendent Mystery. When it comes to teaching doctrines about God and establishing certain doctrines as authoritative, we always come back to the stories of the events. Likewise, miracles and visions, however impressive, are neither the exclusive nor the normal way in which we encounter divine Mystery. They may seem "mysterious," but they are not necessarily "mysteries" in our sense, because they often lack the transcendent punch of even an ordinary "I'm sorry; will you forgive me?"

Also, I do not think it is helpful to speak of the Church as *a* mystery, or of a person as a "something" which is among the mysteries. Not that they are not involved in mystery; quite the opposite. But in order to understand the Church and a person as related to divine Mystery, we really do not get very far with a mere philosophical analysis of static relationships.

You will recall from our chapter on knowing that we grasp the intrinsic intelligibility of "things" by understanding the events that condition their existence. In a similar fashion we reach the divine Mystery in ordinary 'things' by seeing the unique *historical* events that condition their existence. This explains why we are more effectively impressed by a story than we are by a formal analysis. It is the narrated event that brings the Mystery of God home. In other words, the "mystery" of the Church or of any human person has to be understood within the framework of something historical—that is, "storied." It is difficult to believe that Christianity could survive in a culture that emphasized its doctrines and codes of behavior but never told any stories. Indeed, maybe that is why Christianity is not surviving in some cultures.

If by 'mysteries' we mean practically any events in which humans encounter the divine, then we can expect to find faith, charity, and hope at their core. These, after all, are exactly the movements of the soul which respond to divine Mystery and which we cannot rationally produce or explain. It is because of the faith, charity, and hope in us that the story of the event amazes us. For example, a story of someone seeing value where another misses it (faith), of commitment and fidelity beyond what can reasonably be expected (charity), or of long-suffering without a great deal of assurance that everything will turn out for the best (hope). It is not that all amazing stories have to be success stories. The story of Judas can shake us just as thoroughly as the story of Peter. Both are about salvation. But just as long as we can sense that these movements of the soul are at stake in a story, we are on tiptoe to see its outcome.

Part of the universal power of mysteries lies in the fact that hearing the story of the event can become another mystery. That is, the event of *hearing* about an encounter with God can itself become an encounter with God. For example, as Israel recited past deeds of the Lord or as Paul preached the past events of Christ's Paschal mystery, hearers encountered the living God in their present and were converted. Or to take a more extended example, many early Christians, having heard the Good News, became chaste. Augustine, having heard the Good News and of their chastity, became chaste. Millions of Christians since then, having heard the Good News and of early Christian chastity, and of Augustine's chastity, became chaste. It is in this fashion that mysteries reproduce themselves, as the 'event' of the original encounter expands into an ever-broadening and all-encompassing story of God encountering souls in flesh and blood. The mysteries of our faith, then, are not finished events. They are open events. The self-sacrifice of Jesus truly lives, not merely as a model for us to imitate—it is that—but as a growing organism continuing to live in history, making not many mysteries but ultimately one mystery.

Now besides looking at the future of mysteries as they are retold, we should also look at how they began. I have been speaking as though the original historical event, the 'mystery', occurred before any story of the event emerged. But let us look more closely at the beginnings of the story. Is there really any event we can properly call historical in which the people involved did not already have some understanding, in dramatic terms, of what was going on? Perhaps Moses on Sinai or Jesus in the desert encountered God before they told anyone else the story. But unless they themselves understood the 'event' as a story, their experience would have remained just experience. The story, then, is already present in any historical event. An event literally would not mean anything to the people involved if this were not the case. This story-making activity is present in all significant historical events, not merely religious ones. But what this says about religious mysteries in particular is this: In claiming that God has encountered us in this time and place, we must recognize that the original story-making activity is intrinsic to the encounter. God cannot begin to mean anything to us except as protagonist or antagonist in a story. Any properly human effect God can impress on flesh depends very strictly on storytelling.

Right from the beginning, then, religious experience is always a matter of insight into the meaning of the experience. That insight, in

156

turn, is made possible only by faith, the "eyes of the heart." And that faith is made possible by the love we bear for transcendent Mystery. So the stories in our religious tradition are made possible by both an outer occurrence and an inner love. Indeed, it is this inner love that wants to bring the mystery of an historical occurrence to the open expression of story. And as one generation succeeds another, the storytelling itself becomes the outer historical occurrence of kerygma addressing the inner love and faith of an historically continuous community.

2. *Fiction, Emblem, History*

Now there are many different kinds of stories, ranging from pure fiction on one end of the scale to critical historiography on the other. And yet, despite the surface differences between fiction and fact, we usually find a common spirit, a common goal in both the spinners of yarns and in the scholarly historians. The common goal is not to make up stories, certainly, but to get in touch with that part of human life that is mysteriously unrepeatable.

For historians, the unrepeatable is what defines their field of investigation, distinguishing them from the sociologists, the anthropologists, or the psychologists. These latter specialize in finding patterns or laws at work over a number of different events. Historians do offer some explanations of a general nature, and the best historians will discover and identify developments that were unnoticed even by the participants in a certain sequence of events. But even these developments possess a unique character, so that both the quirks in an individual's behavior and the strange turnings of a community's development just stare us in the face, repudiating anyone who might say "I told you so."

We humans are, all of us, idiosyncratic. We are odd, even to ourselves. No one of us understands much of what he or she has done, still less what he or she will do when we encounter life's next surprise. Moreover, when our private purposes get thrown together with the purposes of others, the outcomes seem to go beyond the purposes of any one of us. Hegel marvelled how this conglomeration of human intentions produces results that nobody intended. But he flinched in the face of this mystery; he felt that we should imagine a "Cunning of Reason" working some transtemporal process of historical advance.

A more realistic approach to history ought rather to end up amazed, dumbfounded, revolted, or awestruck over what goes on in the human soul. The more realistic the historian, the more respect will be paid to the uncategorizable, the grotesque, the queer, the fascinating. We readers of history should be profoundly moved at the potentialities that lie within the reach of our own kind, and I am thinking not only of the horrors of genocide but also of the wonderful strangeness of those people who never seem to fit. Individuals are far more diverse in their values than advertising and statistic-gathering companies would have us believe. These are the people who actually live the lives of a culture, making the culture a profound yet always elusive object of inquiry.

In the manuals that explain how historians do their work, we usually find a distinction between the written 'history' that appears in book form and the actual 'history' that the book is about. Historians investigate actual history and produce written 'histories'. Now there is more to this distinction than meets the eye. Most world leaders, and other people for whom self-importance is very important, can be found everywhere in written histories. After all, they aspire to go down in history, meaning in the books and in the memories of ordinary men and women. But the actual history that goes on under the eye of the historian moves much more along the lines of those people whose self-image is *not* important. The "Will of the People" is surely a larger factor in the unfolding of a culture's history than are the individuals intent on following or shaping that will. It requires a conversion of sorts to see this and to accept it, particularly if one is enamored of one's own self-image. True, people for whom self-image is important are usually influential. They do make an impact. They do make written history. But historians have to be ready to see the difference between progress and decline. They need to see that progress results not from narcissists but from authentic persons and that decline results from inauthenticity, whether in the famous egoists or in the secret ones. This is what actual history is all about. It is a drama in which four billion people play a part and everyone is trying to write the script as the scenes unfold.

Writers of fiction also concentrate on the unrepeatable, but they do so in a way that complements the work of historians. The fidelity of historians to making sense of evidence sets a limit as to how far they can probe the inner intentions, fears, and hopes of individuals. The evidence of human interiority, after all, is notoriously ambiguous. Often enough we feel constrained to render our interior thoughts and feelings ambiguous on purpose. The fiction writer sails right over that limit and freely constructs inner worlds that give some sense to outer behavior. The story ought to be plausible, and so the writer's own inner experience is the major resource for making that sense. But it need not be predictable. On the contrary, the best writers know very well how surprising the human spirit can be, whether with malice or with grace.

So it can be said that there is truth in fiction. But by "truth" we do not mean an accurate reporting of evidence, nor even a plausible explanation of the events that really happened in a specific time and place. Truth in fiction is about the actual *possibilities* of the human soul. Truth in profound fiction is particularly about the soul's *mysterious* possibilities, which is the same as saying that fiction rings "true" when it deals with the soul's stretching towards self-transcendence and with how people negotiate their faith, charity, and hope. Fiction seldom talks in these terms. Even our own definitions of these terms had to be drawn from fictional accounts of how we experience these movements of the soul that surprise us. But is it not the case that fiction fundamentally makes palpable the human struggle to discern value amid chaos (faith), to honor the mysterious in another person (charity), and to endure life's troubles (hope)? Whether or not the characters in the story succeed does not matter. The good story is concerned with seeing, not with teaching lessons. So the truth of fiction can be tragic as well as comic, ironic as well as romantic.

Lying halfway between historical accounts and fictional accounts, there is yet a third major kind of story that bears elements of both fact and fiction. I am thinking of what cultural anthropologists call the "myth." But since this term often connotes pure fiction, perhaps it would be better to speak in terms of 'emblem' and give it a definition of our own.

An emblem is an event understood as an instance of an archetypical event. For example: Russia "Declares War." His parents were "Lost at Sea." She was "Born Again." This is the "Paschal Mystery." Couple finds "Buried Treasure." Lincoln "Freed the Slaves." He was "Possessed by the Devil." Like fiction and history, emblems too can touch mystery. To understand this it will be helpful to compare emblems with histories.

A history is an event understood as something new and fresh. It does not admit of headlines and capital letters. It is full of context, names and places, the flow of time, interruptions, dead ends, and ambiguity. In contrast, an emblem is a portrayal of an event as though its archetype occurred before. It will contain familiar patterns and clear lessons.

Here are some common examples. A Christmas dinner, as it is actually being eaten, is a history. But it quickly passes into an emblem, joining all the Christmas dinners gone before and those yet to come. The day Mother and Dad met was likewise briefly a history but soon became an emblem. Liturgy is meant to be an emblem. It should take history and lift it up to purified form, inserting the everyday into the eternal. Newspaper headlines are usually emblems, and in the for-profit-only newpapers, the stories beneath them are too. Headlines in the more serious papers are less often emblematic, and their stories try to fill in all the relevant context.

Emblems leave us in quite a different frame of mind than histories. Emblems tend to eliminate questions about what the people involved thought about the matter as it was unfolding. Histories rather tend to lay out data that may or may not prove relevant. Emblems reinforce old lessons. Histories do not so much teach a lesson as temper enthusiasm, qualify judgments, delay reactions, wait upon wisdom to respect the impenetrable. Still, the study of history always runs the danger of slipping into emblems. We often read such headlines as "El Salvador Is Becoming Another Viet Nam" or "The P.L.O. Want Another Holocaust." The truth, of course, is that there was only one "Viet Nam" and only one "Holocaust." But their tragic nature urges survivors to learn a lesson for the future, lest "it happen again."

Both emblems and histories honor the mysterious, though in different ways. Emblems are not fussy about details. Any clue that even suggests an emblem is enough impetus to canonize the story in archetypical form and leave behind any evidence that fails to fit. So emblems honor the mysterious by oversimplifying, which carries with it the hope that beneath life's complexities reality actually *is* simple. History, in contrast, tries to respect all the data, without any rigid canon of selection. So there is a surfeit of palpable detail; the air is redolent with a smell we cannot name; we are left wondering about what everything means. Histories are pieces of eternity with strange-shaped edges. So histories honor the mysterious by pointing to a thousand unexplainable pieces, while emblems carry all eternity in themselves. History, in that sense, is an ongoing inquiry, while emblems are finished answers. Histories are conjectures. Emblems are successfully told stories, final and certain.

Still, neither emblem nor history can exhaust the meaning of an event. Each halts before the mysterious in human affairs in its own way. The emblem oversimplifies the story. It places the story in a myth of eternal recurrence, but the myth does not explain anything; it serves as a mere heuristic for the realities that lie hidden beneath what appears on the surface. History does attempt to explain things, but it unabashedly leaves all sorts of loose ends; it regards all of history as a single whole, though what the connections may be is anybody's guess.

Among the Gospels, Mark's leans towards the historical while John's is more emblematic. In Mark we find details that are never followed up: Jesus' mother and relatives try to reach him; Jesus commands a cured blind man not to enter his village; a young man is stripped of his linen cloth and runs naked out of the story. All of this heightens the effect Mark wants to impress on us: "Who is this, that the wind and sea obey him?" In John, on the other hand, the man born blind reappears, as do Mary, Lazarus, and Mary Magdalene. Each of the five miracles in John comes to a nice finish. We are not left wondering "What happened *after* that?" But the miracle-stories are signs of something mysterious *above* that, something that recurs in the lives of all who seek God. And yet, in spite of these differences, each kind of story packs its own kind of dynamite. The historical accounts of salvation leave us with an overwhelming sense that something profound really happened, and that our normal expectations can be blown apart at any minute. Emblematic accounts give us an assurance that what happened is of enduring significance, that the ordinary contains the extraordinary. In most Christian stories, histories make us feel less secure while emblems make us feel more secure.

All three forms of stories—fiction, emblem, history—usually talk about misfortune and sin. And insofar as they do, they also raise hopes for redemption from these evils. The better historians, the ones who avoid projecting emblematic myths onto concrete events, very gingerly suggest why things happened and hardly ever predict what will happen. They are more interested in human character or the lack of it, in the intricacies of a particular sequence of events. And yet, they cannot delve very deeply into the mysteries of human persons without running the danger of speculative psychologizing. So they tend to treat both evil and redemption as emerging from an inner depth of specific people which is left as inaccessible.

As we saw above, these inner depths are the province of fiction. Fiction writers do not speculate on what people silently think and feel; they just tell us. They easily portray some people as mean or malicious and others as weak and afraid – a distinction beyond easy reach of the historian.

Emblems, too, can be very bold. They can represent outer calamity (Napoleon's Waterloo) or inner struggle (Benedict Arnold, Traitor). In any case, they offer simple pictures of both sin and grace. Since we have dealt with sin and grace ontologically, perhaps we should also look at how well or poorly our emblems for them represent what is really going on.

3. Emblems of Evil and Redemption

From Old Testament times up to our recent past, spiritual writers relied heavily on emblematic stories for talking about evil. The source of evil was a powerful and cunning person called the Devil, who assails all people, from Judas to Jesus, with temptations. The final end of evil was considered to be an Apocalypse. For some that meant an actual day of the week in which the world as we know it would collapse and some completely new evil-free existence would begin. Today, we have some reflective distance on such emblems. Both believers and non-believers recognize that the stories belong to myth, not history, though believers also recognize the value of such myth for talking about the mysterious character of redemption within history.

But emblems of the Devil and Apocalypse have recently given way, again in the minds of both believers and non-believers, to another pair of emblems, Neurosis and Economic Forces. The guilt of the individual over wrongdoing has been forgiven by Freud; it is Neurosis that deserves the blame. Likewise the social guilt over social evil has been forgiven by Marx; Economic Forces deserve the blame. The Day of Reckoning for human living has become the Psychological Depression or the Economic Depression. Even though neurosis and the economy surely deserve the best analysis we can bring to bear, they have become overwhelming personal and social emblems that fix our attention on a clearly defined enemy, a conspiracy, an It that is guilty, not us. We are still trying to say "The Devil made me do it."

Redemption in these latter-day emblems is proclaimed to be a matter of psychoanalysis or sociological research, in which the root of evil presumably will be uncovered, followed by an intelligent therapy or social reform. But both this analysis and this redemption, like some extreme forms of belief in Satan and the Apocalypse, give evil a reality it would not otherwise possess.

In chapter 4 we pointed out that basic human evil is the disobedience of the transcendental precepts Be attentive, Be intelligent, Be reasonable, Be responsible, Be in love. Fundamentally, therefore, evil is not the positive existence of some power or force, even though when we are in the dramatic pattern of experience it may feel like it. Basic evil is the absence of events in our consciousness which ought to be occurring. So any emblems of evil that suggest a concrete existing origin—whether as the person of the Devil or as a psychological or social mechanism—always run the Manichaean danger of dividing the universe into the two equally real and opposing forces of good and of evil.

Having reified evil, these emblems then suggest that evil must be understandable (on the correct inference that if something exists, there are reasons or causes for it). So psychologists and economists analyze. They expect that all problems have explanations and that once they hit upon a correct explanation, the solution to a problem will be obvious. But in reality, human evil has no explanation. If that were not so, there would be no sin. Certainly there exist problems that do admit explanations, but any such explanations must end where the irrational disobedience of the transcendental precepts begins.

Finally, a reified and an understandable evil has to look, feel, and smell like something. What we affirm is real by judgment, and what we understand by insight must have some locatable data for us to experience. So the emblems of evil easily take over our imaginations. People imagine they can "see" the Devil, "smell" malice, "feel" the forces of evil in particular situations.

Then, in the name of goodness, some lofty-minded people deem certain individuals, certain nations, certain economic institutions as evil, plain and simple. From that point, sabotage, torture, murder, or even genocide become virtues for those brave souls carrying out this mad apostolate.

If evil is ontologically a vacuum but psychologically a massive force, what emblem could possibly suffice? Should there not be a symbolic representation of the ontological "missing factor" in evil? I suggest that we return to the notion of the Devil—but with a careful proviso. Among the more astute insights of Christian wisdom there is the principle that the Devil is a Teller of Lies. This suggests two things.

First, in any temptation, we suffer some illusion or other. That is, our perception of other people, of ourselves, or of the comforts of life is off the mark. We must humbly admit that this Liar has already told false stories that we have taken as true. That is, we are already biased in the ways we view the world and appreciate what we think are its values. But we saw above that we cannot rely on reason alone to reveal what is truly worthwhile; we must also rely on the value judgments that flow from transcendent love—in other words, on faith. We should turn to the fictions, the emblems, and the histories that reveal divine Mystery. We can turn to them with some good measure of confidence because we do have the gift of faith, the heart's eye that sees from a higher viewpoint than that of the Liar's false stories. So our faith is not exactly opposed to a "Devil" but rather opposed to the lies about reality that plague us. Besides that, as long as we suffer a contracted perception of reality as we wait for faith to do its work, we also rely on the gift of hope to give us the affective anchor that keeps us from jumping to rash conclusions about the truth.

Second, considered as a Teller of Lies, the Devil can do nothing but work with the truth. The Devil can neither force any external act nor prevent any interior act of attention, intelligence, reason, responsibility, or love. It is very important to keep this in mind, because the Liar's first story usually goes, "I have more power than you do." Once we believe that some evil power can force us to disobey our own love of truth and goodness, we are sunk. So when we are assailed by temptation, besides relying on the power of faith to supplant the Liar's false stories with true ones, we should follow the ancient practical advice, "Don't listen, because in what you hear there will be a lie."

If we take seriously the notion of the Teller of Lies as the antagonist in emblems of evil, then we will see that the Devil is a storyteller too. Within the dramatic pattern of experience, therefore, the human struggle for authenticity will mean choosing between several possible stories. Every significant event in our lives can be told in at least two different stories, as a story of Chaos or of Cosmos, of Despair or Hope, of Sin or Grace, and which story we choose depends on how accustomed we are to recognizing the movements of faith, charity, and hope within ourselves. This takes time to learn, both in each person's life and in the lifetime of a culture as it enlarges its deposit of wisdom. And unfortunately it is usually by our mistakes that we learn to discern the spirits. Ignatius of Loyola has said that we can tell the Devils by their trails.[3] That is, we learn to discriminate true stories from false ones only after we have already believed the false ones for a time.

Whenever we talk philosophically about evil, the question naturally arises whether "the Devil" really exists. Is the Teller of Lies more than "just an emblem"? Many have asked this question, and I believe we now have the heuristic structures for a satisfactory answer. When we are in the dramatic pattern of experience, it serves us well to think of evil emblematically, for the reasons given above. The whole orientation of the dramatic pattern is towards dignifying our living, and stories maintain our vision of ourselves through the power of affectivity and image. But once we ask whether there really is a Devil, we move from the dramatic pattern into the intellectual pattern, where understanding and truth are the proper goals. We saw above that the world of our experience does have an overall design; Lonergan named it 'emergent probability'. Within that world design we should distinguish between problems that are intrinsic to a world of emergent probability — and therefore intelligible — and problems that occur because of disobedience within — and therefore unintelligible.

So in all the human sciences, whether psychology, sociology, cultural anthropology, political science, or economics, we should expect two radically different kinds of problems, the kind with explanations and the kind without. The problems that admit explanations will also admit solutions that are intelligibly connected with the situations as they stand. But the problems that are rooted in sin, that is, in disobedience to the transcendental precepts, will admit solutions only from faith, charity, and hope. These solutions will not be logical deductions. They will be loving and healing initiatives that involve self-sacrifice and creativity. But they will be recognized for their ingenuity by all who know what self-transcendence means.

So all we can say is that we do not know whether "the Devil" really exists. In the intellectual pattern of experience, where we aim at grasping intelligibility in data, we see no need to posit a personal being intent on our downfall. Instead, we envision a dialectic of obedience and disobedience within. We do understand that the emblem of a Teller of Lies stands ontologically *between* categorials and transcendentals. And we look to emblems of Tellers of Truth to illuminate the false stories we have already accepted.

What possible emblem of true stories do we have to test the false ones against? Above all, we Christians have the Paschal Mystery, that is, the story of the man to whom we owe absolute faith, charity, and hope being abducted, tortured, pierced with a lance, and left to die without the comfort of friends. But this man who himself had absolute faith in God, absolute charity even toward his enemies, and absolute hope that sin's bondage would be broken within history, was raised up by God and given the name to which every knee shall bend. The story of his life is history—the kind of history that leaves the sincere hearer trembling in wonder over the limitless authority and the equally limitless kindness of this man. The story of his Resurrection and Ascension is an emblem, but the kind that holds out for our imaginations a vivid picture of the secure power of faith, charity, and hope over the darkness of evil and of the actual freedom Jesus now enjoys as Lord of Heaven and Earth.

Some readers may be uneasy with the suggestion that we regard the stories of Jesus' resurrection appearances as emblems and not as history. We do not mean to imply that nothing happened to Jesus in history after his death. Something surely happened to his body; all early accounts mention an empty tomb. Yet the Resurrection which the first Christians proclaimed was regarded as the Father's work, not the work of Jesus. As the Father's work, it must escape all human attempts to put it into ready-made categories. As a real event that saves humanity, it can be known *as salvific* only through faith, charity, and hope, not through the categories generated from normal attention, intelligence, reason, and responsibility. That is why the accounts of the resurrection appearances differ so widely from one another.

Furthermore, to regard the stories as emblems in no way diminishes their truth value. We in the West think of ourselves as so enlightened by the Enlightenment that we keep ourselves at arm's length

166

from emblems, myths, and symbols. For example, once we recognized that the Genesis story of creation is a 'myth', or that the Devil is a 'symbol', we have tended to look elsewhere for explanations of creation and sin. But the distinction between history and emblem is not based on the difference between truth and falsehood. Rather it is founded on the distinction between understanding a situation as unique and understanding it as universal. The Fall of Adam and Eve and the seductions of the Tempter are stories written to illumine our present universal condition of being free in principle but slaves in fact. Likewise, no one expects to repeat the unique life of Jesus in its detail, and yet we do hope to repeat the universal pattern of his Paschal Mystery. To really live that out, we need to return to the myths, emblems, and symbols, not with the undifferentiated approach of a child, but with the profounder approach of an adult who knows how necessary emblems are for keeping contact with Mystery.

Now evil and redemption can appear not only in histories and in stories that are emblems but also in those myths that are fictional in content but emblematic in purpose: the plays of Shakespeare, the *Divine Comedy* of Dante, the Greek plays, Eliot's *The Waste Land*, operas, and so on. They too deal with the recurring patterns of how people confront evil. One of the masters of literary criticism, Northrup Frye, classifies such myths into four basic plots.[4] And his classification is ingenious inasmuch as it looks at what pressures the stories lay on the desires and dreads within the reader's soul—which, of course, is right up our alley. If we examine these four kinds of plots, we can discern four distinct ways in which hearing a story can be a 'mystery' for the hearer, that is, can be an event which raises the issues of malice and liberation.

First, in the comic or lyric plot, human desire feels itself overcoming the forces of human dread. Its happy characters are blessed with luck and with the delightful surprises of springtime, where the dread of winter is melting away. Second, in the romantic plot, desire has mastered dread, and it does so not by luck but by the courage and strength of the story's characters. Romantic stories are summertime stories. Third, in the tragic plot, dread begins to mount over the forces of desire as otherwise strong characters are trammeled by their own situations and by the growing forces of determinism. It is autumn, or more significantly, Fall. And fourth, in the ironic or satiric plot, dread

167

reigns supreme over desire as all hope seems lost. Winter has set in and characters can only wait for something like spring's comic surprises.

While these plots are most clearly found in fiction, they are also found in emblems and even in histories. To take a few examples from Scripture, the story of Philip visiting the eunuch in the carriage is comic; it begins with a lucky meeting and ends on an upbeat, full of hope in future developments. The Book of Revelation is romantic; it portrays human desires as fulfilled and all dread as banished. The story of the Rich Young Man is tragic; he comes on the scene with strength, but his own history proves to be his weakness. We do not know his future, but it does not look very promising for him. Ecclesiastes ("Vanity of vanity; all is vanity!") is irony; dread reigns over desire; nothing can be counted on as absolute.

Any plot can tell a mystery. In different ways, each plot can serve to jar the reader into awareness of the insecurity of life and the inner tug towards transcendent love. The comic or lyric plot is founded on luck, a sudden appearance of salvation not coming from human strength but from the mysterious blessings of nature—surely a reminder that we cannot redeem ourselves by dint of our own effort. Even the more happy romantic plots render the reader happy only during the storytelling. He or she must return to the business of living, knowing very well that the story is not one's own. In tragedies, the reader recognizes the all-too-familiar experience of being caught up and crushed by one's past. And ironies seem to play our tired, endless song exactly as we feel it.

And even though the major plots can attune us to the mysteries of everyday life, it is important to see that most stories do not directly help us discern how to act. The dialectic of desire and dread that underlies all plots is not a dialectic between good and evil. Desire and dread are morally neutral. We can desire evil as well as good; we can dread holiness as well as malice. So meaningful stories do not necessarily give moral clarity. Often they merely recall the pulls and counter-pulls of the soul and leave us wondering which is which.

It is only when people in a certain culture perceive moral clarity in stories that they canonize those stories. They say, "These stories can be counted on to represent a view of how desire and dread ought to work in human souls." And thus they produce their Bible and their list of canonized saints. All cultures canonize some of their literature, art, and biographies with a view to passing some moral judgment on their worth. Outside of these canonical stories, however, the spiritually integrated man or woman must listen to all stories—fiction, emblem, or history—with a critical ear. The people who tell the stories, after all, may or may not be converted. That is, they may fail in intellectual conversion and think of the real as little more than the palpable. Or they may fail in moral conversion and confuse the truly good with the merely satisfying. Or they may fail in religious conversion and hate the soul's transcendent ascent towards divine Mystery.

On the other hand, in practically all cases of really profound stories told by truly wise men or women, their contemporaries were so immersed in their traditional values that they failed to see new greatness among them. In other words, while a culture regularly criticizes its own literature, great literature has the power to criticize its own culture. Thus we should maintain a dialectical attitude not only towards the inner stories that make up our personal temptations. We should also listen to all fiction, emblems and histories with an ear that discerns the threefold conversion.

4. Is History a Story?

Up to this point, our reflections on stories in terms of desire and dread have been about stories within history. The question naturally arises whether all of history itself is a story with a plot. One does not have to read Northrup Frye to wonder what a large-scale depiction of the human struggle between desire and dread should look like. Where did humanity come from and where is it going? Why do all nations that rise also fall? Is all history just irony? Or can we really look forward to a time within history when every tear will be wiped away? Will the story of history, in other words, prove to be romantic? Between these extremes we find some philosophers proclaiming that what is going on in the global community is a progressive integration, while others think it is a slow disintegration. That is, some think history itself is comic and others think it is tragic. Surely there are stories of redemption within history, but will all of history coalesce into one romantic epic of redemption?

We Christians tend to regard history as a comic plot for the time being—the good we desire is winning over the evil we dread—and eventually as a romantic plot where the desired good triumphs once and for all. This is a dangerous view. It shares with all gnosticisms an overemphasis on a pre-ordained plot and a forgetfulness of the dialectic of desire and dread writhing within every person. The untamed inner tension between the mundane and the transcendent becomes tranquilized by some explanation that points outward: "We are restless because . . . " – as if our restlessness originated at some point in past history and just carries on like a vestigial organ in the body that might just as well be cut out.[5] Such explanations of our disquiet usually name some element of humanity as The Enemy and preach a redemption through rejecting the element and embracing some redeeming secret.

So, for example, many of us have been taught to treat sexual desire as a permanent threat to the romantic plot of God's plan. Similarly, the medieval world thought of monarchy as the only redemption of anarchy[6] and took the Ptolemaic hierarchies in the sky as its cosmological emblem of order. Only recently have Christians begun to regard their sexual experiences and their social pluralisms not as emblems of evil in themselves but merely as the stages whereupon a more fundamental struggle for order takes place. But even these recent developments have not clearly enough acknowledged the often painful transcendental precepts as the hearty core of all that is sound and worthy.

A Christian theology of history cannot be a story, not even a simple collection of stories. It will contain stories, but the form of the whole is larger than story. We do not know what that form is, of course, and that is the most obvious feature of human existence in history – having to live in an order larger than any we know. We are in the middle of this 'history' and its outcome is not yet determined.

On this issue, we humans are divided, because the tension of having to live within an order whose ultimate shape escapes us brings every adult to the brink of decision wherein he or she must decide whether to act as though there really is such an overarching order to human history. Some will choose to obey merely the order at hand, spending their lives in reaction to the known demands that surround them, and suppressing their wonder about larger issues. Others will choose to believe in an ultimate order, in a real and concrete integration of all history in which the merely happenstance and the unfortunate blind alleys will reveal their hidden meanings. But to choose this path is to live in hope. It is *hope* that enables them to live in history without reducing history to a mirror of one of its stories.

If a theology of history must look beyond story-plots for its order, it should equally look beyond geometric images. Even the famous linear or progressive view of history, which Judeo-Christianity regards as a liberation from the Hellenistic cyclic view, is a naive and dangerous alliance between living history and dead geometry. In the linear view, the key events in history are laid along a time line. Civilizations rise and fall, but progress-minded historians record the events for no other reason than that the great achievements may not be lost and that old errors may not be repeated. Prosperity and great cultural foundations are the simple consequences of hard work and human commitment, and the only consequences worth thinking about. (Even most pessimists today adhere to the linear view in the sense that they measure events solely in terms of their outcomes.)

But what happened to those people who paid the costs? In most actual cases, our great cultural foundations also depended upon slavery, mass robbery, institutionalized lying, and rivers of blood. I think of the underpaid Romanians who made the shirts I wear, the Native Americans from whom was stolen the land I stand on, the American soldiers in Viet Nam who died to keep alive the myth of American moral superiority. The linear view has no answer to the questions these people pose. The significance of their lives lies blasted on charred and bloody soil, soil which the progressivist regards as just so much fertilizer.

An equally dangerous alternative to the linear view of history for Christians is what we might call the transcendent view. In this view, all human events are regarded as linked straight up to divinity. Men and women are portrayed as searching for meaning, as being drawn towards an interior conversion that liberates their minds and hearts from illusion and compulsion. The question here is not "What have we produced?" but "Are we obedient within?" This view is able to provide a partial answer to those men and women who paid the costs for the comforts of others, but such an answer is barely accessible to historians. Indeed, the answer to the question, "Are we obedient within?" can be reached only by those who pose it for themselves.

But even this more spiritual view of history is much too bound to its geometric image of the vertical line, in spite of the fact that St.

John the Evangelist and St. Augustine can be counted among its proponents. It ignores the reality of social and cultural progress within history. It inhibits the further question, "What difference will it make to your loved ones if you are obedient within?" We can just imagine how delighted the Children of Darkness must be to hear that the Children of Light can be so easily "ripped off' because they profess no interest in the future.

We are forced to the conclusion that history itself, considered as a single story, should not be thought of as ultimately comic or romantic, let alone tragic or ironic. Nor should we imagine history simply in geometric terms as either a recurring circle of rise and fall, or as a horizontal line of progress, or as a vertical line of transcendence. Whatever we think about history's ultimate shape, we should be aware that most of our understanding is analogical. That is, we think of historical process in the commonsense terms of myths, narratives, gods above and humans below, or else in the even more simplistic terms borrowed from geometry.

The question whether history itself must be a single story or must be some kind of line needs to be transposed from the realm of common sense to the realm of theory. And once we do that, we leave the dramatic pattern of experience and enter the intellectual pattern. The question then becomes not "What *must* history be?" but rather "What in fact is the nature of historical process?" It is a question for understanding, not imagination, a question about the intelligibility immanent to all historical process, not about certitude, predictions, dramatizations, or geometric projections.

But even the realm of theory is highly subject to bias and to the false consciousness it engenders. So we need to ground all theoretical positions in a dialectical method rooted in a verifiable analysis of the processes of the soul. So let us conclude this chapter on storytelling by setting all the stories within history against the background of a structural explanation of all historical process that takes its categories directly from the soul's inner workings.

5. The History of Evil and Redemption

It is the nature of explanations that they pivot on an image. Insights spring from playing with imaginal representations. But as we have tried

172

to stress in chapter 2, we should not confuse the insight or understanding with the image it needs. Nor is the image the real source of our explanations; the insight is. We have talked about three oversimplified emblems of history: the cyclic, repetitive view; the vertical, 'transcendent' view; and the horizontal, 'progressive' view. Each of these three has displayed remarkable staying power in its own time. The reason, we may guess, is that each image corresponds to a form of intrinsic intelligibility that is easily found within our world, and so there is projected onto history the kinds of laws found in nature.

Thus the cyclic view of history expects certain patterns to repeat themselves regularly, on the underlying suspicion that the laws of history must necessarily be like the laws that govern planetary cycles. It is commonly held that this is the 'Hellenistic' view of time, but a similar expectation of cycles unconnected to planetary motion can also be found in Vico and Toynbee. In its simplified form, the cyclic view is an expectation of classical intelligibility, that is, of an insight into a single law that governs events that recur regularly.

In contrast, the 'transcendent' view tends to expect that there is no intelligible order governing history considered as a whole. So it amounts to an expectation of statistical intelligibility at best. Individual events get their meanings strictly from how well participants pursue transcendent values within themselves. Thus we have John the Evangelist and Karl Barth.

Then there is the 'progressive' view of history. In its raw form it expects that although history does not repeat itself, at least it is moving inexorably towards a pre-ordained goal according to some genetic law, as if history, like a flower, is just the blossoming of some fixed seminal potentialities. In this category we can list Luke the Evangelist, Joachim of Fiore, Voltaire, and Karl Marx. We can also find a variant of this genetic view of history in the kinds of questions reporters are fond of putting to government officials: "What will you do if the other party does such-and-such?" They act as if history could be adequately understood on the model of a chess game, where there are only a limited number of legitimate moves possible and that some really brilliant think-tank could anticipate all of them. But, God knows, in real history, very few moves are perfectly legitimate. The possibilities latent in human hearts outdistance the reach of reason, whether because of evil or of love. And it is not only presidents and prime ministers who are expected to know "if they do this, then we'll do that." Every one of us, when entangled in the normal disagreements with people we love, spends great chunks of time imagining what our response will be to every possible accusation coming our way. Only gradually do we learn from experience that arguments never go as we plan.

All three of these views have the merit of expecting that some order governs the course of history. But the classical and genetic views lean towards the assumption that where there is order there also lies inevitability, while the statistical view rejects this determinism only at the cost of overlooking order within historical development. We have suggested that each of these views has its strengths because they each draw from a model of intelligibility found within history. However, there is a fourth kind of intelligibility found within history that can be discovered within any sequence of human events and yet does not determine beforehand what the outcomes must be. Philosophers of history first sensed its importance in Hegel, and now can find it clearly delineated in Lonergan. Lonergan calls this intelligibility 'dialectical'. It will help if we briefly see it in the perspective of his account of the other three kinds of intelligibility.[7]

In classical intelligibility, we understand change by grasping the single law that governs recurring events. In statistical intelligibility we understand random events by grasping that there is no direct insight available, because the relevant events are related only because they occur at the same time and in the same place. In genetic intelligibility, we understand growth processes by grasping the single law that causes, say, an organism to move through successive stages of development. Finally, in 'dialectical' intelligibility, we understand a growth process (or a breakdown) by grasping that there is no single law at work. Instead there are at least two principles of change, and they modify each other as they interact.

Let me give an example of dialectical intelligibility drawn from everyday life. We all argue. One of the main reasons why arguments become so complicated is that there are always two distinct values at stake.[8] On the one hand, there is the substance of the opinion we hold or the path we intend to pursue. On the other, there is the relationship we hope to maintain with the person we are arguing with. Hard bargainers tend to stress the substance while soft bargainers stress the relationship. These two values, substance and relationship, are principles of change within each person arguing. But how these values balance in their hearts is highly determined by the history of all the arguments previously won or lost. In other words, these principles of change have themselves changed because of the particular sequence of arguments in which they have been at work. If, for instance, a hard-bargaining husband tends to get his way with his soft-bargaining wife, then his own appreciation of their relationship tends to diminish while hers grows and grows. Had each spouse been married to someone else, their present appreciation of substantive issues and of their interpersonal relationship would surely have taken on different proportions.

This is just one of many possible examples of the kind of intelligibility we can expect to find in the growth or decline of communities of any size. The principles or sources of change can themselves be changed; this is 'dialectical' intelligibility. But among the many possible principles of the dialectic, we can also see that there is a *normative* dialectic going on within all human relationships. On the one hand we have, as a principle of change, human authenticity, that is, obedience to the transcendental precepts. On the other hand we have inauthenticity, or disobedience of the transcendental precepts. As we saw earlier, obedience within is the principle of all human progress. Were all the world attentive, intelligent, reasonable, and responsible, the human order would grow more and more coherent and meaningful. But people are also inattentive, unintelligent, unreasonable, and irresponsible. This disobedience within is the principle of all human decline. So a fundamental normative dialectic in human affairs exists between authenticity and inauthenticity. The more authenticity has the upper hand in a community, the more refined it becomes and the more power it wields over inauthenticity. On the other hand, inauthenticity can gain the upper hand, with the opposite effect. This much should be clear from our more detailed analysis in chapter 3. When we moved to chapter 4, we considered a further principle of change, namely, transcendent love. What inauthenticity threatens to destroy, transcendent love, with its first-fruits of faith, charity, and hope, promises to heal.

Another way of looking at the same processes is to distinguish between the creative mode of development, constituted by the present mixture of authenticity and inauthenticity that marks a given historical community, and a healing mode of development, constituted by the power of transcendent love. Let us look at these two modes of historical development more closely.[9]

The creative movement is the true origin of all invention—technological, economic, political, social, and cultural. It consists in the successful functioning of the first four transcendental precepts. Only when people obey these internal precepts do they attend to their situations, ask how things work and why things fail, determine what is reality and what is just illusion, and discern true value from mere comfort and commit themselves to doing what needs to be done.

Where a community is obedient within, unexpected disorders tend to be met with apt responses, and situations tend to improve. This development is not automatic; it is under that combination of classical and statistical laws we examined in chapter 2 called 'emergent probability'. As a community grows, it can recognize the need for theoretical work in physics, chemistry, biology, psychology, sociology, and theology. Furthermore, as these theoretical disciplines grow, scientists can recognize the need for a philosophy that finds a common ground in the processes of knowing, acting, and loving that actually go on in the soul. This common ground not only can provide a framework for cooperation among the sciences, it can also articulate how humans fail and what our remedies ought to look like.

In other words, norms exist for guiding the creative movement, and these norms can be spelled out by examining what goes on in the soul when we think, act, and love. As it must be evident, such is the purpose of the Lonergan enterprise and such is the purpose of this book. The enterprise aims at understanding the many differentiations within the creative process. But it also articulates the further differentiations within history's other mode of development, the healing movement.

As the creative movement begins from attention and moves "upward" by successive integrations to intelligence, to reason, and to responsible action, so the healing movement begins from being in love and integrates "downward," healing the biases endemic to common sense and forgiving the outright refusals to obey the soul's ascent to divine Mystery. As we saw in chapter 4, being in love produces faith, charity, and hope. By faith, we see values where mere weighing pros and cons does not reveal them. By charity we recognize the presence of absolute value in other persons and are moved to enhance their lives. By hope we sustain obedience to the transcendental precepts even when by all accounts the odds seem overwhelmingly against us. Such obedience to transcendent love and to its other-worldly virtues renders us more effectively responsible, more likely to be realistic, less blinded in our intelligence, and less obtuse about the issues that beg our attention.

Now for most Christian history we have stressed the healing movement. We have a good track record for being a community that forgives, that refuses to buckle under secularist pressures, and that puts its trust in God. But we have not done as well with the creative movement. We have not promoted the development of the theological-philosophical system that could give a Christian foundation to a social theory, an economic theory, or a theory of ethics that meets the more empirical issues of our times. Our attitude has been mainly reactionary, not creative. One of the major reasons for this is that those Christian intellectual giants, Sts. Augustine and Thomas Aquinas, each thought that a science of history was practically impossible. Science, they thought, dealt with what does not change. But history changes. So theological reflection had no place in the pursuit of historical progress. It was only when a full-blown empirical method for understanding change began to touch theology that we recognized intelligibility in historical process itself, that we learned to understand the exact difference between progress and decline, and that we turned our faces resolutely towards working the redemption of our real situations.

So the actual, ongoing history of evil and redemption is an intelligible sequence of events. But by 'intelligible' we mean a dialectical intelligibility which understands each real situation as a cumulative product of both authenticity and unauthenticity. And by 'event' we mean not the visible behavior but the recondite and complex interactions between people as they obey or disobey the dynamism of their souls.

Therefore, when we listen to the stories people claim are true or significant, we should listen for the presence or absence of conversion. To accomplish that, of course, requires an interior spiritual integration that knows the meaning of 'real', of 'good', and of 'God'.

In our concluding chapter we will see how a dialectical attitude is the fundamental attitude for anyone interested in overcoming what we called the "split soul" and achieving the "spiritual integration" of a world torn apart by a thousand false gods.

Discussion Questions: CHAPTER FIVE

Question 1

Does the Devil really exist? Or is it just a myth? If it's just a myth, then why has belief in the Devil held on for so many years in so many religions? On the other hand, if the Devil really does exist, how has our culture managed to eliminate wide-scale belief in it? Is it possible to affirm the existence of a personal Devil and yet not deal with this reality in spiritual direction? On the other hand, is it possible to deny the existence of a personal Devil and yet refer to a "Devil" metaphorically in spiritual direction?

Question 2

Discuss the following story (Mk 1:23-28):

"In the synagogue just then there was a man possessed by an unclean spirit, and it shouted, 'What do you want with us, Jesus of Nazareth? Have you come to destroy us? I know who you are: the Holy One of God.' But Jesus said sharply, 'Be quiet! Come out of him!' And the unclean spirit threw the man into convulsions and with a loud cry went out of him. The people were so astonished that they started asking each other what it all meant. 'Here is a teaching that is new' they said 'and with authority behind it: he gives orders even to unclean spirits and they obey him.' And his reputation rapidly spread everywhere, through all the surrounding Galilean countryside."

What elements of mystery would this story convey if it were (a) complete fiction; (b) an emblem; (c) a history.

Which kind of story do you think it is?

Question 3

By this point, you may be thinking, "All these distinctions have me confused and suspicious. I don't like the idea of finding divine truth in mere 'emblems'. It's just too relativistic for me. I want a truth that I can count on, something more certain and stable. Besides, I would expect that God would give us a story that is simply 'true', without demanding that we make all the qualifications coming from literary criticism."

Whether or not these are your thoughts, try to respond to this objection. What is 'truth' and in what sense is the Gospel the 'true' word of God?

Question 4

Any view that calls history 'dialectical' is going to run into opposition. The first will come from people rightly nervous about Marxist dialectical materialism. The second will come from philosophers rightly nervous about a Manichaean conception of history as a struggle between the powers of good and the powers of evil.

In what sense is Lonergan's 'dialectic of history' neither Marxist nor Manichaean?

Question 5

The Christian mission today is usually expressed as the creation of community. In our times of breakdown of relations between nations and nationalities, between wives and husbands, between labor and management, between economists and environmentalists, we feel a longing for community more than ever. The "Quest for Community" has become an emblem for one of the major goals of the 20th century.

On the other hand, modern science is committed to progressive improvements in technology and economics. Sociologists, economists, and politicians consider themselves as the changers of the social order. And indeed we have changed, so much so that few people really expect that the harmony and stability of community will ever be achieved. Not only do we approve of most of the technical advances made so far; we approve of a commitment to ongoing and continuous improvements from now on. And this means continual change. 'Progress', therefore, has become another major emblem for a major goal of the 20th century.

Discuss how these two emblems pull in different directions. Then, given the material we discussed about the true nature of history, suggest an emblem that would contain the best of Community and the best of Progress, while reconciling their antithetical elements.

Notes to Chapter Five

1. This definition of 'mysteries' has been provoked by, but is not identical to, Quentin Quesnell's definition in his "Beliefs and Authenticity," in Matthew L. Lamb, ed., *Creativity and Method: Essays in Honor of Bernard Lonergan* (Milwaukee: Marquette University Press, 1981), pp. 173-183.

2. *Mystery and Manners*, ed. Sally and Robert Fitzgerald (New York: Farrar, Straus & Giroux, 1957), p. 96.

3. "When the enemy of our human nature has been detected and recognized by the trail of evil marking his course and by the wicked end to which he leads us, it will be profitable for one who has been tempted to review immediately the whole course of the temptation." *Spiritual Exercises of St. Ignatius*, trans. Louis J. Puhl (Chicago: Loyola University, 1959), para. 334, p. 148.

4. Northrup Frye, *Anatomy of Criticism* (Princeton: Princeton University Press, 1957), pp. 158-239.

5. These reflections on gnosticism and the more authentic alternative of living in the tension between the mundane and the transcendent have been inspired by the works of Eric Voegelin. In particular, see *Order and History IV: The Ecumenic Age* (Baton Rouge, La.: Louisiana State University Press, 1974), p. 9.

6. For an analysis of the danger of regarding monarchy as the only alternative to anarchy, see Matthew L. Lamb, "Christianity Within the Political Dialectics of Community and Empire," *Method: Journal of Lonergan Studies* 1/1 (Spring 1983), 1-30, esp. 11.

7. For a summary view of these four kinds of anticipated intelligibility, see Lonergan's *Insight* (New York: Philosophical Library, 1957), p. 485.

8. See Roger Fisher and William Ury, *Getting to Yes: Negotiating Agreement Without Giving In* (Boston: Houghton Mifflin, 1981).

9. See Lonergan's "Healing and Creating in History," *A Third Collection: Papers by Bernard J.F. Lonergan, S.J.*, ed. F.E. Crowe (New York: Paulist Press, 1985), pp. 100-09.

CHAPTER SIX

Spiritual Integration

Our concluding question must be: So what? In our first chapter we began by looking at what we called the split soul and how the roots of social order and disorder are located in the soul. Then we spoke briefly of the materialist and the idealist reactions to the problems of order. From there we saw that we needed to spell out for ourselves exactly what goes on in our souls when we think, act, love, and tell stories. So we spent the next four chapters working out this self-understanding in detail.

But so what? How will this self-understanding bring about a spiritual integration in the social order? We can formulate a general answer to that question by recalling four lessons that emerged from our study. This will enable us to give a more precise definition of spiritual integration.

1. *Spiritual Integration Defined*

First, we have seen that our common sense is not adequate to meet the problems of the world. Common sense thinks that its own short-range and piecemeal kinds of insights are the best kind. It spontaneously neglects taking the long-range historical perspective. It belittles rigorous theoretical analyses. It disregards philosophy. So the first step in a spiritual integration is a commitment to an intellectual life, be it in science, in historiography, literary criticism, philosophy, theology, or what have you.

Second, we have seen that even within an intellectual life the empirical sciences and historical scholarship seldom deal adequately with psychological and social problems. In most cases they neither give sound enough analyses nor provide sufficiently effective policies for halting the spiral of decline. The reason for this is that they have not articulated the dynamics of consciousness as well as they have articulated what goes on in the world of sense. That is, they have not sufficiently recognized that values and meanings constitute human realities just as surely as atomic particles constitute physical realities. Because they have generally failed to study the origin, development, and breakdown of values and meanings, they regard all human problems as fundamentally intelligible. They have not taken seriously the difference between authenticity and unauthenticity. This is why the therapies and solutions they propose usually just add to the complexity of situations rather than expose the biases and supplant the incoherent ideas that have made situations intolerable. Therefore a second step is to reflect on the methods of science and historiography to see if they deal adequately with authenticity and unauthenticity.

Third, we have seen that transcendent love has a redemptive role to play in the social order. Whether or not that love is called religious, it recognizes values where biased minds fail to see them. It impels a person to act on behalf of others, even at painful costs to oneself. And it integrates a person's affective life in such a way that he or she is enabled to withstand the debilitating psychological undertow of a decadent culture. In other words, transcendent love gives faith, charity, and hope. These work to heal an otherwise biased consciousness and free it to create the social structures that will be effective in reacting to crises and in meeting the needs of all people. A solid spiritual integration does not merely acknowledge this healing movement of transcendent love. It also works to enhance it within scientific and philosophic spheres. It raises the categories we call faith, charity, and hope to the level of explanatory terms in the human sciences and historiography.

Fourth, we have seen that stories can bear redemptive power, and that the best stories touch each person's inner sense of the struggle between authenticity and unauthenticity. The fundamental lesson here is that history itself is an unfinished story. We have no guarantee of its outcome. So we are left with the challenge to live out the struggle in our own times and places. We are called to live with a dialectical attitude not only regarding the world of common sense but also in whatever theoretical or scholarly specialty our work demands of us.

Notice how we have moved through five realms of meaning. The limitations of common sense require the higher viewpoint of the realm of theory. The realm of theory, in turn, needs the higher viewpoint of the realm of method, that is, of philosophic interiority or generalized empirical method. Within the realm of method we can understand the realm of religious transcendence and see how it possesses the power to heal the world of its ills. Finally, the question of redemption raises the need to examine the realm of historical and literary scholarship in order to listen to and tell the stories that touch the transcendent in ordinary living.[1]

We can now define what 'spiritual integration' is. It is the capacity to move through these realms of meaning intelligently. That is, the kind of authenticity needed today is the kind by which a person has a basic understanding of these different realms of meaning and can move from one to another as the situation demands. The spiritually integrated person overcomes the division of the split soul because he or she understands the aims and techniques of both commonsense practicality and theoretical analysis. But beyond healing that split, spiritual integration allows a person to ground all the workings of the mind and all the practical decisions of a responsible life in the love of divine Mystery.

Notice that spiritual integration is not primarily a commitment to some theory about human nature. It does not insist that you memorize metaphysical categories. Obviously, we have had to define many categories in our discussion here, but only to help you perform the inner experiments that lead to your own understanding of how you in fact know, act, love, and tell stories. How we name the processes we discover in ourselves is not of the utmost importance. What counts is the actual discovery, understanding, and verification of our understanding of the processes. Only then do we expand upon that inner achievement by developing language that is intelligible to others across the widest possible variety of fields.

So spiritual integration is primarily a commitment to using one's head and heart not only about the realities of the outer world, but particularly about the head and heart themselves. It is a habit of soul, not a body of knowledge. It regards the data of consciousness as the testing-ground for any theory about how we use our capacities for transcending ourselves. In this sense, spiritual integration is by no means complete. It will develop and grow as any empirical science does, by the self-correcting process of trial and error.

Does this approach seem too intellectual for the average person? Even if it is not primarily a framework of categories, does it not ask too much of most men and women who love God and neighbor?

I insist that the answer is no. The so-called "average person" today is already somewhat familiar with the realms of common sense, theory, religious experience, and historiography. But being familiar with is still a long way from explicit understanding. The one thing lacking is the further insight into exactly how these realms differ from and relate to one another. Without such insight, a person has no clear grasp of the limits and procedures proper to each realm, and so the person will easily slip over a border, smuggling the methods of one realm into another without realizing it. With such insight, he or she will move through these realms of meaning much more intelligently and be more able to cooperate with God's redemption of a world shrouded in darkness.

Spiritual integration, as we have seen, is also a dialectical habit of mind. It is relatively suspicious of consciousness, and yet it is committed to cooperating with transcendent love and its first-fruits of faith, charity, and hope. It is ready for a battle, and yet it is ready to love. Fortunately, the notion of a dialectical attitude is not completely foreign to Western thought, so we are not trying to inaugurate an enterprise that nobody has ever heard of. We can use the building blocks that others have already assembled, even though, as we shall see, these others have built their houses on sand. They need the solid underpinning that Lonergan's generalized empirical method promises to give.

After everything we have said about taking the long-range view and regarding all historical situations as partly coherent and partly incoherent, we should now review how various elements of the dialectical attitude have already entered our intellectual history and separate the coherent core from the incoherent accretions.

2. History of the Dialectical Attitude

We live in an age when truths, certitudes, dogmas, and authoritarian monarchs are no longer accepted, even in the Church. Yet this is not because people reject truth or authority. As we saw in chapter 1, the reason is that the way in which ordinary people use their minds has been revolutionized by the emergence of empirical method. It may be true that the Enlightenment was a deliberate rejection of Christianity as an apt set of ideas and an apt political order upon which to build a decent future. But the Christian ideas and political entities which were dumped needed to be dumped, not because they were Christian but because they were corrupt. With the emergence of empirical method, thinkers rejected pronouncements from higher-ups and turned their attention to verifiable hypotheses to discover the nature of everything from plants to planets. Before this revolution Christians put their trust in certitudes. After it, they slowly began to see the value of asking how things work. So the emphasis shifted from reliance on judgments reached through beliefs to reliance on progressive understanding reached through checking things out. This revolution changed not only the content of people's thoughts but the very manner in which people think.

This fundamental shift in how people use their minds was accompanied and facilitated by a growing accessibility to education for all, and by the experience of regular progress in medicine, astronomy, physics, chemistry, and psychology, through the goods and services they provided. Still, all this "progress" has yet to be accompanied by an equally empirical philosophical and theological achievement. As we have tried to demonstrate in previous chapters, a generalized empirical method needs to be employed to understand how spiritual experience works. Only by attending to the data of consciousness will empirical method, with its proud mastery of the data of sense, reach the full range of its capability. Only then will it be possible to unify the sciences so that they each respect their own limits and yet intelligently collaborate with one another on improving the future of humankind.

To some extent, a turn to subjective consciousness has arisen within empirically oriented academies. Three nineteenth-century movements stand out.[2] One is the recognition by Wilhelm Dilthey and others that historians cannot get direct access to people's experience. They can only deal with various understandings of expressions of those subjective experiences. A second movement is the emergence of Freudian psychology and the discovery of the unconscious as a proper field of investigation with its own surprising and elusive processes. A third movement is the emergence of Marxist analysis of consciousness as being rooted in economic processes.

All three movements have one thing in common. They are suspicious of consciousness. They recognize that the 'facts' in the human sphere are quite unlike 'facts' in nature. In physics, for example, one might estimate the energy required to move an automobile from point A to point B. And physicists easily agree. But in criminal law, that same automobile may be considered by a prosecutor to have been "stolen" and by a defendant to have been "borrowed." Here agreement is seldom reached. Human facts are, as we have seen, *facta*, that is, constructed. And the people who do the constructing are full of biases, ambitions, fears, and covetousness. So a Dilthey will regard historical accounts as representing not "what happened" but, more modestly, "what people think happened." Likewise a Freud will regard a client's story as possibly a mask for a deeper, more fearful perception. And a Marx will take an employee's account of a work situation as evidence for an oppressive economic superstructure of which the employee has no knowledge at all.

Faced with these anomalies, the empirical attitude also becomes a dialectical attitude because the aim is not only to understand how things may have gone wrong but how to set them right. In the concrete, this means reversing deep-seated commitments and long-standing habits in great numbers of people, and this will certainly present enormous problems. How one initiates such a change when it is bound to meet with opposition is not within the ken of good will alone. It means not only unmasking bias but promoting development on a foundation that very few people are familiar with.

But these and many other unforeseen problems in promoting a dialectical attitude lie in the future. Unfortunately, the dialectical revolution which Dilthey, Freud, and Marx might have ignited has already been doused. Each of the schools of thought and practice which they began has lost control of its own dialectical method. The story of that loss of control is rather long and complicated, but at root the same problem can be discerned in each. They did not sufficiently clarify how human beings think, decide, and love. In particular, they did not fully articulate the role of bias in the human drama. As a result they failed to recognize four practically unlimited resources for making this world a better place: (1) how the structure of consciousness has creative norms for finding what is intelligible, realistic, and worthwhile; (2) that these norms can be formulated and taught; (3) that these norms can be counted on to generate specific values and goals for any community; and (4) that where the creative norms are suppressed through bias or the absence of conversion, they can still be healed through transcendent love with its fruits of faith, charity, and hope.

As if these failures in method were not failure enough, the practitioners of historiography, psychology, and economics have, in large measure, sold themselves into slavery to nationalistic and hedonistic masters. Few German historians attempted to criticize the aims of the Third Reich, just as few British historians tried to spell out the evils of colonization which ultimately contributed to the breakup of the British Empire. Similarly, there are hardly any psychologists today who carry the Freudian suspicion of consciousness to the point of suggesting that a client may have done something malicious or stupid. They are content to help clients find what they please, without any question that what a client pleases might only harden him or her in bias and unconversion. And among economists, we find only men and women intent on making more efficient the capitalist or socialist system, rather than ever questioning the end towards which these systems head. They are "managers" in the strict and lifeless sense of the term, specialists in managing to achieve whatever goals somebody else wants badly enough to pay them for. Thus, the suspicion of consciousness, which we take to be a healthy start, has unfortunately degenerated into mere expertise in manipulating consciousness for the sake of money and position. We must begin again on a firmer footing.

3. The Dialectical Attitude Today

The dialectical attitude begins from the recognition that bias belongs to the very structure of our consciousness. Any one of us can recognize this about ourselves. We avoid certain kinds of insights, and consequently we carry into practice ideas which are not entirely coherent. In short, we recognize that we are not completely authentic; we are also unauthentic; we suppress the work of the transcendental precepts within us. From that recognition, a number of strategic precepts follow.

First, we ought to be suspicious of situations. Situations have histories, and the histories comprise a series of oversights as well as insights, of inept as well as appropriate actions. Situations, therefore, are combinations of routines that are intelligible and routines that are not. We should approach situations ready to distinguish, somewhat like the mathematician, between the rational and irrational, or between the integral elements and the surds. We must not accept, a priori, a situation as a mere given, as if being realistic meant believing that everything that exists exists legitimately.

Secondly, we ought also to be suspicious of *reports* of situations. Not only are the people who make up a situation's history biased: the people who talk about it are too. The reporter, the narrator, or the historian is a human being prone to personal neurosis, to self-comfort, to uncritical acceptance of his or her group's commitments, and to the myth that good common sense is all we need. Their biases show up not only in what they report but also in what they avoid reporting. So our second strategic precept prompts us to be alert for the slanted view.

Third, we ought to be careful not to rush to the conclusion that it is the other person, not ourselves, that is causing the problem in the situation or is slanting the report of it. As we have seen, the intractability of bias lies in its apparent coherence for the person who holds it. Like the blind spot in our eyes caused by the area of the retina where the nerves head for the brain, a bias cannot be "seen." We can only report that we do not see anything in that particular area. Therefore, we ought to be content with the initial recognition that differences exist among the people in a situation or in the reports of a situation, and the incoherence may possibly lie in ourselves as well as in others.

This brings us to our fourth strategic precept for a dialectical attitude. Once we acknowledge that differences exist, we should keep in mind that there are different kinds of possible differences, because not all differences between people call for the same kind of strategies. For example, two people or two groups may be at different stages of development along a common line, such as a young novice and an old monk in the same religious order. Here the strategy involves lots of mutual respect. Another kind of difference arises from the fact that different people have had different questions and interests. An old Benedictine and an old Franciscan have grown along different, but complementary, lines of development because their respective communities have had different purposes. Here the strategy calls for a readiness for dialog and mutual education. Such was Thomas Merton's attitude towards Eastern mysticism. Finally, there is the kind of difference that can be overcome only by an intellectual, moral, or religious conversion. Here is where the dialectical attitude is meant to do its most important work. A theist and an atheist regard the tension in the soul in completely opposite ways—as gift and as curse, respectively. A morally good person and a hedonist mean completely different things by the word *good*—as truly worthwhile and as merely satisfying, respectively. A critical realist has a completely different criterion for saying something exists than the materialist or the idealist does—verification, picturability, and coherence, respectively.

Our fifth strategic precept regards this dialectical kind of difference. Like the developmental and complementary kinds of differences, the dialectical kind requires some amount of mutual respect and mutual education. But when the converted and the unconverted sufficiently uncover their presuppositions to one another, there is no logical argument for talking the other person into conversion or unconversion. The most effective strategy is to uncover one's own basic positions on the tension in the soul, the meaning of *good*, or the nature of knowing—depending on which conversion is at stake—and hope that the transcendental precepts at work in the unconverted will be attracted to the basic position of the converted. How one does this concretely can vary widely. Religious conversion is often best revealed when a person tells the story of how his or her conversion happened. Moral conversion is usually shown better in deeds than in words. Intellectual conversion needs words, particularly the explanatory categories that are needed to account for what knowing, deciding, and loving involve. The reason a strategy of uncovering basic positions is so effective is that it not only promises to attract a person who is searching, but it casts light on a possible incomplete conversion in the person who uncovers it. So both parties stand equally indictable under the finger of conversion.

This dialectical attitude has several distinguishing features. For one, it is humble. When a person begins to live out these strategies, it is not only the shortcomings of others that are exposed; his or her own shortcomings stand bare for all to see as well. This double exposure accounts for the effectiveness of the dialectical attitude in principle. Unfortunately, it also accounts for the failure of the dialectical attitude in practice. In principle, were everyone to engage in ongoing dialog, were everyone to pursue discussions to their end, were everyone to commit themselves to a pursuit of the truth which disregarded personal reputation, then the assumptions which lie behind ideologies and biases would come to light rather quickly. People would accept criticism as readily as they give it. But in practice, no one enjoys being wrong, let alone being told so in public. So we find several alternate strategies employed, the ancient strategies by which people become dogmatic, or rhetorical, or just silent. So further counter-strategies will be needed to engage the fearful in friendly dialog. And there are no tricks or shortcuts to this which do not involve acknowledging one's own shortcomings.

The time has come for this humility to be raised from the level of private religious piety to the level of public political virtue. The self-loss which mystics praise and all great world religions preach must now be understood as a strategy for a revolution. It is the loss of concern and fear for one's reputation while one is engaged in dialog, disagreement, and debate. Indeed, all the old spiritual doctrines about mortification, self-effacement, and abandonment to the will of God can now be understood empirically. We no longer have to accept them as mysterious practices that somehow make us better persons. We can now understand how they make us better—because we put being attentive above being smug, being intelligent above being narrow-minded, being reasonable above being a dreamer, being responsible above being hedonistic, and being in love above being stiff-necked and hard of heart. The authenticity that results from obedience to the transcendental precepts—the "Be-attitudes" as we have called them—changes ourselves and our world for the better in intelligible and verifiable ways.

Another distinguishing feature of the dialectical attitude is that it is courageous. Perhaps the saddest legacy in Christianity is the fear of making a mistake in public. A great many good-willed ministers, bishops, priests, nuns, brothers, and lay persons have spent thousands of dollars getting a "Christian" education. They understand a great deal about psychology, about science, about politics, about history, about theology. Yet it seems as though everything they learned has merely rendered them catatonic. They are prepared to react but not prepared to try; prepared to defend and to survive, but not much motivated to enhance the lives of others. It is a strange vice, this defensiveness. We sincerely want to protect our loved ones, and so we count ourselves virtuous. But we have not understood that consciousness is by nature expansive and creative and that human problems are surprisingly malleable under the force of will and imagination. Granted, we Christians have always been taught to forgive others' mistakes. But the mistakes and the malice we have become so practiced in forgiving have been mostly the kind that come from obvious self-centeredness. We are less ready to forgive someone who risks our money and time on a creative project that falls flat.

The nuclear peril provides an excellent example of how uncourageous our Christian morality has been. The realization that we can blast ourselves to smithereens demands that we make conscious choices and form deliberate policies regarding the future of the human race. Having to make choices and set policies only recently has fallen within the purview of ethical thought.[3] Most moralists have talked about what should not be done or in what special circumstances certain immoral actions might be tolerated. The list of things we ought not do is long and concrete. But what we ought to do positively is left to human imagination and creativity. It demands inventiveness, risk, daring, and an active compassion. Many of us grew up with a three-part view of the moral world. We had the idea that there are extraordinarily virtuous things that a few are called to do, that there are extraordinarily malicious things that a few others feel compelled to do, and that there are a zillion things left in the middle, in the grey area of moral life— things that have no particular moral weight and really do not count very much because they seem to be just harmless human desires. The time has come to disabuse ourselves of this notion. Everything counts. But it takes an actively responsible person to realize it. It takes a healthy soul who will not only stick with the long-range view and live with unanswered questions but will try great things anyway.

Besides being humble and courageous, the dialectical attitude is compassionate. That is, it is concerned about the experience of suffering of every human person. In one sense it seems unnecessary to point this out. We have stressed that the value of the human soul is, next to the value of divine Mystery, the highest value we know. We have recognized the value of the entire human community, not merely this group or that, as the ultimate object of the good we try to do. We have dreamed of a social order where the intelligence of every man, woman, and child is given free rein and freedom of expression. But in another sense, our stress on an 'intellectual' conversion can portray the dialectical attitude as merely the privilege, or the plaything, of the elite. And elite groups tend to ignore the experience of the masses. For their part, these ordinary people who work hard for a living, particularly the people who are victims of social injustice, have neither the time nor the education to engage in social criticism.

We must admit that generalized empirical method, like any reflective technique, can remain stuck in the head. But the point of religious and moral conversion is that it impels even ivory-tower thinkers to effective action for the sake of others. Indeed, that effectiveness is multiplied a hundredfold when it originates in intellectual conversion and undergoes refinement through the dialectical attitude. So intellectual conversion ought to expand our moral and religious conversion by leading us to experience the agony and oppression which so many souls of infinite worth suffer.

And where do we begin to experience oppression? By working on a soup line? No. We begin by realizing that we ourselves are enslaved by the same commonsense symbols of ourselves that the most abject in the world are. I am a Nigger, or a chick, or a Yankee, or a Whitey, or a Wop. I inspire condescension, fear, or contempt in the hearts of millions of others. And do I even realize it? Like all problems which seem to have no solution, it is no longer considered a problem, just a fact. Well, intellectual conversion can begin where this 'fact' is unmasked as the absurd and violating symbol which it is. John Howard Griffin (author of *Black Like Me*) comes to mind as a person who broke, at least for himself, the symbol of being a Black, and thereby learned the value of each person beyond our enslaving symbols.

Once we are able to recognize our own self-symbols and reject the false shame they bring, then we will be free in a very practical sense. We will listen for self-transcendence in others and resist the stereotyping that blocks decent communication. Then we will have the inner freedom to walk with other victims of this world where we can. We are apt to learn something about the sturdiness of their faith, charity, and hope in the face of heavier crosses than we have ever borne ourselves. And we can entice them along the road to freedom by helping them break their own enslaving symbols.

4. A Christian Theory of Power

Will the Christian churches soon manifest the humility, the courage, and the compassion demanded by the dialectical attitude? There is one enormous political obstacle standing in the way. The Church has steadfastly refused to admit that it is interested in power.

Too often religiously committed men and women have shied away from thinking about power because it easily connotes ruthless political oppression. Yet all churches are interested in effecting change in a suffering world as well as in meeting their own internal goals. It does no good to disclaim power on the one hand and to strive mightily to wield it on the other. Likewise it is two-faced to preach that the Church should not be interested in politics while the Church itself is a set of political institutions structured to make social changes in a political world. If we are going to take the dialectical attitude seriously in our churches, then we not only have to admit our interest in power but also to formulate the dialectical attitude as a positive theory of power used and promulgated by the Church.

The starting point is to think of power as simply the ability to achieve aims. In other words, conceive power as morally neutral. Next, we must begin to draw the distinctions between legitimate and illegitimate uses of power.[4] Here we can only appeal in summary form to all we have said about the causes of social progress and decline. Briefly, power is legitimate when it flows from attentiveness, intelligence, reason, responsibility, and love. In other words, authenticity makes power legitimate. It may not render power free of error, particularly in the short run, but it will correct past errors and reduce future errors in the long run.

Conversely, inauthenticity makes power illegitimate. As we have seen, illegitimate uses of power come in relatively few varieties, in spite of their many manifestations in our ragged history. There are the four biases of the mind: neurosis, egoism, group bias, and commonsense shortsightedness. There is the presence or absence of three kinds of conversion: religious, moral, and intellectual. And there is the ability or inability to move intelligently between six realms of meaning: common sense, theory, method, religious transcendence, scholarship, and arts and letters. The upshot of our analysis of inauthenticity was that a dialectical attitude is needed to deal with sin and redemption in our empirically minded world.

Notice that we are not basing this theory of power on an expectation that it must be deployed monarchically or democratically or hierarchically or anarchically or in any other way of organizing community. We are beginning from our threefold experience of (1) how we are creative, (2) how our creativity is suppressed, and (3) how our creativity is healed. We reached this understanding of our experience and tested

it through the further experiences of the three conversions, with intellectual conversion — the chief topic of this book — casting light on how
all the processes of the soul's experiences are structured. In other
words, the starting point of this 'theory' does not lie in the realm of
theory at all. It lies in the realm of method. So the theory of power
we need begins from the praxis of self-appropriation by which the soul
orders itself.

From this base in the self-experiments proposed by generalized
empirical method, we turn to questions that belong properly to the
realm of theory. Here we can only raise a few of the more salient questions. But we know at least that the answers to these questions ought
to facilitate our exercise of the humility, the courage, and the compassion which the dialectical attitude demands.

1.   A Dialectical Theory of Communications:
How Can We Learn to Argue Creatively?

Very few people know how to do this. We seem to employ the
same clumsy approach in all kinds of disagreements — domestic quar-
rels, political arguments, discussions in school faculties or parish councils, and conferences with superiors who criticize our performance.
Most of us act as though what counts most is winning, or at least not
losing. We wield our wits and tongues as if we really expected the other
party suddenly to see the wisdom of our words and sheepishly to acknowledge how right we are and how wrong they have been. But it
never happens. No one ever changes clothes, *investments*, in public.
Yet we keep falling into exasperating arguments that go nowhere.
A theory of creative arguing would probably stress acknowledging
common interests before pushing one's own solution. It would suggest understanding others' statements — and letting them know we
understand — before expressing our disagreements. It would give guidelines on how to deal with strongly expressed feelings, our own and
those of others. My bet is that it would find excellent examples in the
Dialogs of Plato.

2.   A Dialectical Philosophy of Education:
How Can We Teach Dialectical Method in School?

In our discussion of Cosmos and Chaos in chapter 3, we noted
how easily we rank fidelity to transcendental achievements above obe-

dience to the transcendental precepts. As a result, we adhere to traditional values without understanding. At best we then accept the finest portions of our tradition without the savvy necessary to apply its wisdom to the present situation. At worst we mindlessly cling to our tradition's worst mistakes.

This tension shows up poignantly in schools. How can we disseminate knowledge and still encourage questioning? Should a student's goal in education be to know as much as possible or should it be to learn how to learn? In all branches of education, from elementary to graduate school, from vocational schools to liberal arts colleges, students are given two messages. One is to learn the stuff, to memorize the dates and formulas, to be prepared to use what they know. The other is to see why things work the way they do, to understand why history unfolded as it did, to sharpen their abilities to meet new challenges.

A dialectical philosophy of education ought to present past achievements not as carved in eternal stone but as the fruits of living inquisitiveness. It ought to teach a person to read textbooks not only for information on a certain topic but also as evidence of bias in their authors. It ought to emphasize the clarification of values, but it should go further and be ready to criticize any commitments that reveal bias.

3. A Dialectical Theory of the Magisterium, The Teaching Role of the Church:

Dialectics does not work by force but by attraction. Therefore, the Church will not promote the dialectical attitude in the secular social order unless it first practices it in its own ecclesiastical and educational institutions.

One of the chief obstacles standing in the way of even the smallest steps towards reform in this area is the practice of guaranteeing a lifetime position of authority to members of the hierarchy and to professors in church-related universities. The magisterium of the Church is not a group of people who hold titles. Nor is it even a list of correct teachings. Our intellectual conversion should enable us to see that the magisterium is basically a process, dialectical in nature, which is shared in by many people in many different ways, not all of whom hold an office. No doubt, there have to be positions of authority and recognizable roles and contracts which guarantee employment for reasonable

195

periods of time. But people can run out of ideas. They can gradually become identified with one specific interest group. So the performance of authorities needs regular review. Or, if the weight of some moral opinion on, say, sexuality or medical practice or nuclear war shifts away from what has been taught in the past, there is no need to guarantee office-holders who teach the older opinions that they will never have to share the podium with other voices. There is no loss of dignity when people admit they have been wrong. Indeed, they can scrutinize why they were wrong and make that public too. Such a practice would promote honesty and the exposure of presuppositions and hidden commitments. The time and energy people spend on trying to save face could be diverted towards the humble, courageous, and compassionate work of occasionally doing an about-face.

How can we begin this reform in our churches and schools? First, we should seriously review the practice of guaranteeing lifelong tenure for bishops and university professors. We can appeal to the lessons of history and to the gains which a dialectical attitude makes possible. But we must also institute a fair system of due process and periodic review in which a person's job is neither constantly in jeopardy on the one hand nor permanently guaranteed on the other. Indeed, the more open a person in authority is to new questions, the more likely he or she will remain in office.

In the same vein, we should create forums for open dialog between the authorities in our churches and schools and the people these authorities are appointed to serve. It is true that dissent and confusion should not be preached at the pulpit, but mutual criticism is always going on in the Church. This is how the actual magisterium — conceived as the process of communal learning — has always worked in the past. So why not provide the means whereby the criticisms can be dealt with responsibly?

4. A Dialectical Christology: How Did Jesus Use Power?

It will be very important to retrieve, as far as possible, some understanding of how Jesus exercised power. If we do not admit that he did, we will never admit that the Church does. We must be careful, however, not to expect a simple transition from Scriptural exegesis to doctrinal pronouncements. Anyone making such pronouncements based on Scripture is also basing them on their own intellectual conversion or lack of it. We must also be careful not to expect to find agreement in Scripture. In Matthew, for example, Jesus is presented as the teacher whose words guide the Church; whereas in Luke Jesus pours out his charismatic Spirit to guide the Church. We will never unearth some ecclesiological flowchart of authority in the mind of Jesus. But we can unearth some features of authority that Jesus both exercised and taught. For one, he seems not so much to *possess* the power to teach and heal as to *receive* it. He always pointed to the Father as the one on whom he depended for everything. For another, he did not exercise his received power unilaterally.[5] He quickly invested his disciples, even Judas, with both charism and juridical authority.

The central question here is whether the way in which Jesus exercised power can be regarded as power in the fully empirical sense. That is, can it enable a community to achieve worthy social and political goals? Can we institutionalize the ways in which Jesus both received and shared power so that the Lord is recognized even in the structures of the Church? Jesus has always been the model of individual Christian behavior; can he also model how the entire People of God depend on God for their functional unity?

I believe we should begin to answer this question by understanding the complementary roles of both the Holy Spirit and Christ Jesus in salvation history.[6] Obviously there are sound theological reasons for starting here: it is both by God's Word and Spirit that we are saved. But there are sound anthropological reasons too: human order is achieved through outer terms of meaning (the Word) mediated to consciousness through inner acts of meaning (the Spirit). And we have already examined in great detail how the anthropological elements of consciousness can achieve the authenticity necessary for legitimate power. A dialectical Christology will name Christ Jesus as an outer term of consciousness, will name the Spirit as the inner transcendent love that integrates acts of consciousness, and then spell out the dialectical attitude in properly Christian terms.

If we can work out theories like the above, then the odds will increase that intelligent solutions to problems will surface and that many positive results will follow. Intelligent solutions to problems will more likely surface because the fear of being wrong, or of being fired, will be lessened. The solutions will more likely be combined with other, complementary solutions because attention will be fixed on the intrin-

197

sic merit of the solution, not on what authority proposed it. Even where solutions do not meet the needs of a situation, the person who proposed them will soon find out why and will grow in understanding of the nature of the problem.

Not only will everyday problems and psychological or social theories be tested. The very procedures of the dialectical attitude will come under scrutiny too. Better methods of dialog will be proposed, improved guidelines on how to run meetings will emerge, strategic precepts on how to criticize authorities will come to light. Gradually the Church will practice the humility, the courage, and the compassion which it so easily preaches. It will provide a model for imitation by every kind of human community, ranging from individual families to the entire family of nations. In the long run, the community called Church will become the light unto the world it is called to be.

5. Hope for the Future

While writing these closing reflections, I have been gazing out the window of my room in the Jesuit residence of the University of Detroit. Across the street stands Gesu Elementary School, where the I.H.M. Sisters endured me for eight years. Now, as I watch the children burst through the doorways every afternoon, it strikes me quite forcibly that the power we need for the future lies in the fragile heads and hearts of children such as these.

Consider this with me. Children ask questions continually. The dialectical attitude is already at work in the youngest of them. The quick learners are not afraid to admit their ignorance. They seem curious about practically everything, and when the answers we adults give them do not satisfy, they present us with yet another question.

But somewhere along the line the familiar fear about being ignorant or not being sure has intervened. Perhaps it comes from us adults who want to hide our own ignorance, and so we tell children to stop pestering us with questions. Perhaps it comes from the pride of children which makes them resentful that another child may know more. Whatever the reason, children quickly learn the lesson that if you want the respect of others, you must establish a reputation for being good at something. Subtly the emphasis in early education shifts from being intelligent to being merely knowledgeable. The knower gets the gold stars and the questioner wonders why. Further on, even the knower is left in the wings as the practical-minded doer takes over the limelight. In other words, children learn the game of illegitimate power, and they learn it by default.

I suppose, like many people who try to read the signs of the times, I seem pessimistic about the present generation. By finding hope in children, perhaps I despair of my elders and peers. But the scope of the spiritual integration which generalized empirical method envisions will have to be as large as the problems it promises to meet. That means, I believe, the large-scale reformation of educational techniques and the fundamental changes in the authority structures of our churches which the dialectical attitude demands. Yet I myself have been taught this by my elders and I work towards it with my peers. What counts is not a person's age but a person's authenticity. I hope this introduction to generalized empirical method and spirituality will inspire you to join this very old enterprise of trying to live authentically in a relatively new and terrifying world.

Notes to Chapter Six

1. We have not mentioned the realm of art and music here because we have not treated it above. Yet it too is an important realm because of its role in refining feelings and consolidating moral conversion.

2. Here I am following the analysis worked out by Matthew L. Lamb. See "Christianity Within the Political Dialectics of Community and Empire," *Method: Journal of Lonergan Studies* 1/1 (Spring 1983), pp. 1-30, esp. 2-9.

3. Jonathan Schell enlarges on this point, made originally by Pope John Paul II at Hiroshima, in his article, "The Abolition, I: Defining the Great Predicament," *The New Yorker*, Jan. 2, 1984, p. 36.

4. See Bernard Lonergan, "Dialectic of Authority," in F.E. Crowe, ed., *A Third Collection: Papers by Bernard J.F. Lonergan, S.J.* (New York: Paulist Press, 1985), pp. 5-12.

5. See Bernard Loomer, "Two Kinds of Power," *Criterion* 10/1 (Winter 1976), pp. 12-29.

6. See my "Trinity in History," *Theological Studies* 45/1 (March 1984), pp. 139-152.

Appendix

Responses to Questions

CHAPTER TWO: *Knowing*

Response to Question 1

We have to distinguish here between how understanding and judgment function in theological statements. It is by our judgment that we believe that God causes absolutely everything and sustains the existence of everything. But that does not say a thing about *how* God does this. To ask "how?" is to ask a question for understanding, not for judgment.

Augustine is not saying that God does not create and sustain everything. He simply says that his explanation of how God does this was false. He realized that he was depending on a mere picture to imagine God as physically permeating the universe the way light permeates the air on the surface of the earth.

We have come quite a way in understanding the different ways in which God is present anyway. God is present through the world-design, a design which Lonergan has articulated in part as 'emergent probability'. God is also present through the dynamism of transcendent love operating in every human being. God is also present through the person of Jesus of Nazareth, eliciting from us a faith, a charity, and a hope that belong only to one whose existence and goodness are absolutely unconditioned. God is also present as the "where-unto" of consciousness.

Augustine eventually anticipated much of this in his great search for God in his *De Trinitate*. There he rejects an invisible but physical/local presence of God. Rather he finds God in the manner in which our self-images, our minds, and our wills work together to welcome God's Word in Christ Jesus.

Response to Question 2

I have taken these excerpts from William J. O'Malley's excellent article, "Carl Sagan's Gospel of Scientism" (*America*, Feb. 7, 1981, pp. 95–98). He makes the observation, correctly, I believe, that Sagan mixes up description with explanation where he says that physical reality "arose," "sensed," "has had to practice," "has come up with," "permits." Sagan himself does not seem to realize that he fails to explain evolution within a total world-design. He slips into description without realizing that description covers over questions for explanation and that such questions for explanation will raise the question of an intelligent source of the universe.

The result is that Sagan himself presents a dogmatism in scientific disguise, as is exemplified in the last two quotations.

Response to Question 3

First, notice the criteria each position uses for determining whether something may be real. For the idealist (the first passage), the criteria are cogency, coherence, and understanding. The position has great appeal to intelligence, though not to judgment and verification. It appeals, in other words, to the second level of consciousness, not the third. Besides, by its uncritical comparison of ontology to talking, it also appeals to the underlying idealist hope that everything must have a common structure. As a hope, that is certainly legitimate. But it is a tricky business to know where a comparison to talking moves from mere metaphor to basic ontology.

For the materialist (the second passage), the criteria are visibility, palpability, the human sensorium, and immediate experience. That is, it counts on the first level of consciousness for the sense of the real. This position has great appeal to our imaginations. But it also appeals to an uncritical acceptance of the idea that knowing works like looking.

202

For the critical realist (the third passage), the criterion is judgment on the correctness of an explanation of data. Verification is a process quite unlike intelligence or understanding taken by itself. It is quite unlike imagination or experience taken by itself. It is a combination of operations at all three levels of consciousness, culminating in a judgment on the third. As Lonergan points out, science has no basis for saying that only the physical can be real and that the chemical, the biological, the psychic, and human insight are nothing but our names for what "in reality" are just organizations of physical events. To address the question of what can be real, Lonergan directs his readers to this fundamental question: "Do I or do I not perform such activities as experiencing, understanding, and judging? Yes or no?" Obviously a No answer is radically inconsistent because one's negation is itself contradicted by the performance of making the negation. Once a Yes answer is admitted, Lonergan leads the reader on to link the real with the verified. As a result, human insight, commitment, love, and so on, are known to be just as real as atoms, and there opens up the possibility of divine realities as well.

Response to Question 4

This is a trick question. It sounds as though it has to do with our faith. In fact, it is an example of a common mistake in thinking about anything at all. It starts off not in data, but in sheer hypothesis: "What if . . . ?" The data here are imaginary, not real. Should such a real situation like this arise, there would also be a wealth of other factors to contend with—the trustworthiness of the archeologist, the strength of our own faith at the time, our interest or lack of it, and the amount of theological education each of us brings to the question. And in the concrete, these factors make a big difference.

Let me give a parallel example from my own experience. Not long ago, I got into a discussion over the question, "What would you do if celibacy became optional for you as a priest?" The question seemed very relevant, and our discussion lasted a long time. But it didn't get anywhere significant. The problem was that the question is not as relevant as it first sounded. The reason is that all hypothetical situations are just hypothetical; all the data are dreamed up, no matter how probable they might seem. Hypothetical questions can alert us to possibilities and can prompt a general readiness, but they seldom commit us to specific responses.

To all such "What if?" questions, there are only two adequately intelligent responses. One is to add a dozen more ifs to make it concrete. "If they found the bones of Jesus, and if I was convinced by the evidence, and if I had enough money, and if I could let go of a number of other commitments I had, and if I was interested in trying to understand what it all meant for me, I might consider buying the books theologians would write on the subject and studying them for a year." But such a response just shows how unanswerable the question is regarding specifics. The other response is more accurate, though overly general: "When it actually happens, I will tell you exactly what I will do—I will be as attentive, intelligent, reasonable, responsible, and loving as I can."

Response to Question 5

Remember what the purpose of the notions of both emergent probability and God's providence are.

Emergent probability has the limited purpose of giving insight into the intelligibility intrinsic to the world. It is meant to appeal rather strictly to the second level of consciousness, that is, to insight. It aims to give a background understanding of all the reality we have data on so that a theology of grace and sin can be built upon a properly empirical approach to the world. It is a needed schema for anyone working in the realm of theory.

Divine Providence, on the other hand, has the wider purpose of acknowledging *that* God has dominion over all creation. So it appeals to the third level of consciousness, that is, to judgment. It does not ask how God's dominion works, only whether it is present everywhere. It is a necessary dogma for anyone trying to live religiously in the realm of common sense.

Still, there is a workable connection between the two notions. Emergent probability gives the background structure not only of all creation, but of everything in creation, including human consciousness. Anyone trying to translate the notions of sin and grace into terms consistent with a verifiable model of consciousness will need to see how

204

the emergence of transcendent love, of faith, of charity, and of hope are under probability and yet, once they emerge, do give us a real and immediate union with God in our history.

From there we can understand the old theological notions of sin and grace in terms of scientifically generated categories—much as Aquinas did in his day using Aristotelian categories to attain a systematic understanding of the same sin and grace. We will do this in chapter 4.

CHAPTER THREE: *Acting*

Response to Question 1

If we were to map Marx's view of the human good onto Lonergan's structure of the human good, it might look something like this:

Two Meanings of Good	*Individual Operations*	*Community Dimension*
Particular Goods	Desires, Needs	Cooperation
Good of Order	Habits, Skills	Institution, setup

Marx would see the "Institution, setup" as the origin of both "Habits, Skills" and "Desires, Needs", as if the public order were the sole source of personal conscious events. Notice that "Insight" is completely missing.

It is quite true, as Marx says, that our desires and our skills are conditioned by economic and social forces. And it is also true that we are largely unaware of the extent of this conditioning. But we can become aware of it through insight. Marx himself had such an insight and concluded that capitalist forms of conditioning ought to be eliminated. There is even some truth in this. But what Marx did not elaborate upon was that his own capacity for insight was precisely what enabled him to get out from under the false consciousness engendered by industrial capitalism.

In other words, Marx failed to notice in his own performance that economic forces do not completely determine consciousness but that insight has the capacity to break the conditioning element in any social order. We may be *conditioned* by socio-economic structures, but we are not *determined* by them. Socio-economic structures originate with insight, depend on insight to keep functioning, and only through insight undergo reformation.

Besides failing to see the role of insight in creating and critiquing socio-economic orders, Marx also failed to differentiate between an order that is merely efficient and an order that enhances human living. He knew the meaning of particular goods, and he knew the meaning of structural good, or the good of order. But he did not raise to the level of theory the further distinction between true values and mere satisfactions. He allows no systematic place for the question whether particular goods or any given socio-economic setups are truly worthwhile. In the chart, the entire level of "True Value, Value Judgments, Commitments, Moral Conversion, Cultural Order, and Personal Relations" is missing.

Now this does not mean that Marx did not sense the worthlessness of industrial capitalism. Nor can we say that he measured the value of a social system merely by how efficiently or coherently it produced the particular goods people want. Paradoxically, Marx himself depended on his own moral conversion to pass socio-economic value judgments. He was in fact a powerful cultural force, deeply committed to the spiritual well-being of his people. In his early days, he longed for the time when personal relations between people could be a cause for celebration. But he did not attend to how his own strong feelings and dedication were, much like his insight, resources to be found in all people. So, by default of an in-depth analysis of himself, he settled on the idea that the deployment of materials shapes human consciousness more than anything else.

Response to Question 2

In practically all sticky situations, the problem does not lie with a single person or a small clique. Situations are circles of events, schemes of recurrence, in which A causes B, then B causes C, and so on, until Z causes A and keeps the circle going.

In the case of our beleaguered teacher, the principal is not the problem. Unilateral power is not merely something exercised by one person. It is an entire system in which decision-making lies with the few and is also accepted by the many. Each of the teachers, in other words, has different reasons for acquiescing: fear of conflict, fear of losing a job, hope for a promotion, a feeling of security in the present setup, and so on. And the principal himself certainly has his own reasons for dominating everyone else; for example, fear that he will lose prestige, hope for a promotion, or lack of skill in negotiating and cooperating.

Until these underlying fears, hopes, and skills become known, no one will understand what is going on. That is, no one will see the circle of mutually reinforcing events that keep the principal a tyrant and the teachers his slaves. So the first thing to realize is that everyone is part of the problem and that no one understands it completely. If the means are available for bringing everyone to see that, then the next step would be to communicate to each other each one's personal fears about the school, about one's skills, one's job, one's future, and so on. Once these are out on the table, the real problem is more easily recognized and adequate solutions can be pursued by all parties in cooperation.

Without such a systems approach, we slip too easily into the more naive adversarial view of human situations. "It's either them or us!" "They are the oppressors and we are the oppressed!" The trouble with this interpretation is that no one sees the nature of the problem, and everyone thinks in terms of revolt. And revolt usually does little more than star different actors with the same unacknowleged hopes and fears, playing the same roles, in the same tragic play.

Response to Question 3

We saw that the human good is normally a flow of concrete, particular goods, but always under two major conditions. First, there is a set of operative insights that govern the flow and shape the habits and skills of everyone involved. Second, there are the moral commitments, or lack of them, in the people who desire both the particular goods and the setup that keeps them flowing.

But to understand the whole situation, we first have to determine what the particular goods are, then what the actual setup is that keeps them flowing, and finally what underlying value commitments are at work in the participants. In the case of our friend the teacher, we should not presume that since it is a school it must have education as its highest value. We can determine that only by examining the particular goods and the setup first.

So, we ask, what are the particular goods desired by people in the school? To determine them, we have to look at concrete instances of what specific people want. Information on science? A hamburger for lunch? Quiet in the study hall? Winning this football game? One practical way of ascertaining the actual particular goods which people desire in a specific situation is to ask questions like these: When did you last feel proud to be a part of this school? When did you feel a deep sense of accomplishment? When have you felt ashamed of a student or of yourself? What photographs would represent the most typical scenes in this school? Be careful not to filter out those needs which you would rather not see operative; you are trying to see what actually is, not what ought to be.

Next we look at what setups keep these particular "goods" recurring regularly: What are the library hours? How easy is it to order books in the bookstore? In what ways do we maintain the school spirit, such as it is? What are the operative lines of communication? What management style keeps certain things recurring (things that we are proud of and things that we are not)? What material and technical resources do we depend on? What skills are needed on the part of the faculty here? (This can range from pedagogical technique, to baby-sitting, to being magician and entertainer.) Again, be careful not to overlook the routines you wish were different; analyze why things actually flow the way they do, not the way you would like them to.

Only now can we evaluate the school, because it is only after answering questions such as these that we see the school as it really is.

When a faculty is in such a position to evaluate, they realize that in praising or blaming things in the school, they also reveal their own basic value commitments. Normally we could expect that everyone has at least one common interest: the education of students. But not everyone actually ranks that interest above other interests that may be closer to their own speciality.

The advantage of discussing this together is that it enables the English teacher to see the value of sports, and the gym coach to pay equal respect to the English department. In other words, people see their departmental interests within the context of actual interests of other people, and they see a common interest underneath them all. From this base in common and interlocking interests, a discussion can follow of how best to meet them. To start with the written manifesto of the school's ideals is to start with mere possibilities, not the data on reality. To start from an analysis of the way "we" or "they" *want* to do things only makes the atmosphere more adversarial. The key is to start with common interests first, and then discuss ways to collaborate on meeting those interests.

Response to Question 4

Any reply to this question must have many facets. So allow me to offer a few brief remarks on some of the major issues as I see them.

First of all, we must insist that the overriding justification for the work spent on understanding our feelings is that it helps us to distinguish those feelings which respond to mere satisfaction and those which respond to true value. This is a moral obligation which underlies all other moral obligations because objective value is what human well-being is all about. It applies equally to community leaders and to its members. Anybody who acts as if "good" means only "good for me" literally does not know the difference between good and evil.

Furthermore, the task of understanding one's own feelings is more than merely a psychological need. It is also theologically demanded. Even though feelings are within us, they are no less a part of the universe which God moves us to understand and to take dominion of. A community that becomes aware of this theological exigence in emotional life will more likely find its kinship with one another on this deeper level of life's mystery. There is the constant danger that a community may define itself merely by socio-economic class feeling, or by some common project or, what is worse, by a common hatred for some other group.

Besides these fundamental reasons for attending to feelings, there are some practical dynamics to notice as well. The less dominated ministers are by unmonitored feelings, the more free they will be to go where the objective needs are, rather than be driven by subjective needs. For example, a gay minister ought to be able to minister beyond the gay community, in spite of his or her own needs.

Also, when it is evident to a community that a minister regards the effort to understand feelings as a lifetime obligation, the more humble and available he or she will appear to a community. It makes a world of difference to see a minister admit personal struggles with the same interior enemies that other people struggle with. It takes the focus of ministry off merely social or psychological values and places it on the mystery of life, where it belongs.

On a wider level, attention to feelings can play an important critical function in a community's self-definition. As a community takes shape and develops, a need arises for symbols around which it rallies. All the rituals, songs, slogans, dress codes, and standards of style play a powerful role in shaping the feelings of a community. This is largely their purpose. But if a community is going to be able to criticize its own symbols, it needs to be aware of exactly what feelings it wants to incite, and what feelings it actually does incite.

A final remark is in order here about the nature of the question. Notice that it springs out of an overdrawn distinction between the individual and the community. This is common in common sense. By being merely descriptive and focussing on imaginable 'things' it ends up unable to rejoin what it has presumed to be separate. In contrast, our systems/process approach sees 'things' as event-conditioned. From the explanatory viewpoint, the individual and the community mutually condition one another in every case. They form a system in which the private feelings of individuals have public functions, just as public functions condition private feelings.

Response to Question 5

It will help if we exclude from "personal relations" the meanings that belong to the first and second levels of the structure of the human good.

On the first level, there are relations among persons that arise because of common desires. These have only an instinctual basis and last as long as the passing desires last. For example, people rushing together to get out of a rainshower, boaters waving to each other as they pass, or a person shouting "look out" to a stranger stepping into the path of an oncoming taxi. We could call these 'instinctual relations'.

On the second level there are relations among persons that arise because of common insights and judgments. For example, people working side-by-side on an assembly line, the millions of drivers who obey traffic lights, and practically anybody working at a profession inasmuch as his or her work links up to the work of others in some rational fashion. We could call these 'intelligent relations'.

Then there are the relations properly called 'personal'. They are more than mere instinctual relations and more than mere intelligent relations because they depend on one central act: the persons relate to each other because they see value in one another. Personal relations are constituted by a value judgment on one another as persons. In other words, people appreciate each other, prescinding from any instinctual and intelligent relations among them.

It is not always obvious that a given group is bound together by personal relations. To demonstrate what such a relation is, let me draw a picture of a person in whom it is missing, although at first glance it doesn't appear so.

Ruth is an alcoholic. She is friendly, outgoing, gracious, intelligent, and a hard worker. At home she does not always meet her responsibilities, but she seems to show true compunction about the effects that her drinking has had on her relationships. So people appreciate Ruth, although they feel sorry for her.

On the surface, it appears that Ruth does have 'personal relations'. But in fact they are almost non-existent. Ruth is more preoccupied with making sure she will get her next drink than she is about the well-being of others. She has almost no sense of the value of simply being with a friend because, whenever she slows down, her mind returns to its favorite watering hole. When she is with friends, her affability and gregariousness are efforts—to her they feel like efforts—simply to maintain herself among others. Even her compunction functions more to maintain access to the bottle than it does to mend broken relationships. These 'social virtues' are highly developed 'intelligent relations' and nothing more.

This may be an extreme example, but to greater or less degrees, we all have our addictions—if not to drink, then to drugs, or sexual pleasure, or power, or the elimination of conflict, or excitement, or change, or stability, and so on. These easily block the development of personal relations because they often *look like* personal relations, even to the person nursing whatever it is he or she loves so much.

The more one realizes the value of other persons *as persons*, then the better sense one has of what 'culture' should be about. The communal dimension of human 'good' is about whatever is the highest value to humans. It is not necessarily about ballet or architecture or the arts. Where these do not enhance our appreciation of the human person, they become part of 'intelligent relations' rather than 'personal relations'. That is, they are likely meant to maintain some institution or setup without much ethical reflection on how well it reveals the beauty and worth of human beings.

CHAPTER FOUR: *Loving*

Response to Question 1

As we have presented George, he is not religiously converted. That is, he has no memory of any experience of being in love with the transcendent. If he ever had such an experience, he was unable to name it when it happened. It is clear to him that in this text Jesus believes in God, that Jesus is a good person, and that he at least made a claim to rising again after being destroyed. Such is George's understanding.

But he does not understand correctly. He cannot verify 'zeal' within himself. He can only think of it as anger, or as a righteous indignation that any person would have when crucial values are threatened. George never experienced zeal, never experienced being driven by values that originate in transcendent love. Or, if he has, he doesn't know it. Further, he cannot verify John's passion for writing down such an account. He imagines that it is simply normal self-concern operating in an author caught up with an idea. He has no remembered experience of being inspired by a love that is not his own.

George has not considered the possibility that the historical event reported here might be more than a 'human' event, that it has divine sources, that it was caused through divine initiative. He has never wondered about the continuation of divine initiatives within himself. Even if he were the most moral of persons, he has not necessarily set his heart on any good higher than the happiness of humans. Blind to God, he neither listens within nor sees without. For him, human love is both the most important source and the most worthwhile product of human enterprises. He wonders what the religious person "sees" in religion; he wonders what the religious person "wants" in the world; he admits he has no idea. He can think very highly of the example which Jesus gives here, but he brackets out Jesus' own interpretation of it. He considers it meaningless in the modern world to talk of "rising again."

Notice, then, how religious conversion is a principle for verifying one's understanding in theology. It ought to be effective, not only in the theologian's living, but in a theologian's theology as well. George is not so different from many scriptural exegetes. Without an interior understanding of an interior experience, they will not understand the fundamental meaning of this text.

Response to Question 2

The Israelites' dedication to Yahweh was neither a primitive work-for-your-reward morality nor a sophisticated explanation for suffering in the world. Somehow they were able to simultaneously stand in awe at divine transcendence beyond the world and yet recognize God as intimately involved in their own history as well. We can only conjecture about what historical factors helped maintain this balance, and surely that story is full of failures in this religious vision. But we can make a plausible case for what factors in consciousness make such a dedication possible.

Also, making such a case will help us personally to discover the core of our faith in God underneath the shell of our stories of an afterlife. In each of us, our longing to see the face of God is not totally translatable into mere waiting until this life is over. Such a reduction of our hearts' ache has been too often foisted on us in the past, with the unfortunate result that we cared little for our brothers and sisters in this world. We overlooked the face of God in God's own people.

Although most of us grew up surrounded by stories of God, and although even the great religious experiences that engendered profound traditions were expressed in stories about an anthropomorphized God, those stories and symbols still had to make sense of some inner experience. The inner experience that forms the core of all profound responses to the transcendent is precisely the experience of being *drawn* to something beyond ourselves, to something we cannot conceptualize very well, to something that eludes even the best of our stories and symbols. Even as our spiritual ancestors retold these stories and refined these symbols, they did not consult other stories and symbols to measure their worth. They looked instead to the transcendent tug in consciousness to see if their clumsy objectifications were effective enough to elicit a similar response in others.

As we tried to show in this chapter, this transcendent pull in consciousness has immediate fruits in faith, charity, and hope. That is, it enables a person to see value where it was otherwise unnoticed. It moves a person to be kind to the neighbor. And it strengthens a person's emotional stamina to endure seemingly overwhelming odds. So far, there is no obvious need to deduce that another life must follow this one. Consciousness sets its own norms for acting. If there is any "reward," it lies first in the austere pleasure of obeying one's own heart.

Even within the limits of the world as we know it, we find that love works like this. We are moved to love someone else come hell or high water. We commit ourselves not to succeed in loving effectively but merely to loving as best we can.

Also, we need to be aware of what exactly we do believe in when we say we believe in an "afterlife." We are not saying we merely fall asleep at death and wake up somewhere else, for we truly die, body and soul. Nor are we saying that beyond this life there is time and space as we know it; perhaps we have no alternative but to imagine time and space, but only God knows what reality is like for those who have died. As Christians, all we know is that what God did with Jesus, so God will do to us, whatever that is. Our faith here is on the level of judgment: is it true or not that the Christian will not be separated from Christ? Yes or no? We are not putting our faith in the story of how an afterlife is arranged; that would set our faith on the trembling ground of mere insight and imagination.

So even we must get along without an assurance of an "afterlife" in some sense. "We are already the children of God but what we are to be in the future has not yet been revealed; all we know is, that when it is revealed we shall be like him because we shall see him as he really is" (1 Jn 3:2).

Response to Question 3

We can briefly put the answer in three ways: (1) From the point of view of theory, God is unchanging; but from the point of view of common sense, God changes. Or (2) in the intellectual pattern of experience, we should not conceive God as changing, but in the dramatic pattern of experience we ought to imagine God as changing. Finally (3) our faith needs an unchanging God, while our hope needs a changing God. Let me spell this out in more detail.

As we saw in this chapter, the meaning of the term *God* is derived from our felt orientation to the transcendent. The term refers to the end-point of that orientation. And by the term *transcendent* we mean (a) the intelligibility that makes all the familiar things we know work the way they do. We mean (b) the reality which does not need any prior conditions in order to exist and which itself is the necessary condition behind everything that does exist. We mean (c) the moral 'person' whose good will produces everything we regard as truly good. And we mean (d) the 'Mystery', the where-unto of the longing we feel which goes beyond every concrete thing we know.

If this 'Mystery' also underwent real change, then it would cease to be an ultimate ground of the transcendent in our world. This is because every change we know of depends on conditions outside itself in order to be coherent, in order to happen, and in order to be of any value. In other words, it needs an outside ground in intelligibility, reality, and goodness in order to undergo change. But the precise meaning of *God*, the where-unto of our transcendent orientation, is that of a reality which is its own ground. So, within the intellectual pattern of experience, we cannot say that God "changes" in the sense that we do.

On the other hand, in Christ Jesus we see the constantly changing ministrations of God upon us. And we experience God's Spirit not as something static within us but precisely as something moving. So we need to talk concretely about God as on the move so that we can make divine mercy meaningful within the dramatic pattern of experience.

Within the fifth level of consciousness itself we find a similar disjunction. By our faith we cling to truths and values which do not ultimately depend on our feelings or our imagination or our understanding. They depend on our affirmation, our judgment, our assent to their reality. We do not need to imagine God as "changing" in order to affirm that God redeems us through some mediation of the eternal Word and the eternal Spirit. But in order to consolidate our feelings, in order to give vivid images to our imagination—in other words, in order to sustain our hope—we need to visualize God as "sending," visualize the eternal Word as suffering on the cross, and visualize the unbounded Spirit as making strategic moves in the hearts of people.

I see no great difficulty, therefore, in talking at times as though God does not change and at times as though God does change. It is only necessary to know in which realm of meaning one is speaking, or in which pattern of experience, or for the sake of which theological virtue.

Response to Question 4

The reason why faith always demands justice can be found in the nature of faith itself.

Faith, the "eyes of the heart" (Eph. 1:18), sees value where reason would not otherwise see it. In its central movement, faith appreciates the absolute value of a divine "other." It does so not only during a mystic's prayer, but also when, because we are in love, we appreciate the intelligibility, the beauty, or the goodness of concrete things in the world.

Thus the natural response of a person in love with God is not to try to return that love. Rather it is to cooperate with that love as it works in the heart. It means seeing as God sees, appreciating as God appreciates, giving as God gives. St. John says, "Surely, if God has so loved us, then surely we ought to love. . . ." Does he say "love God," as if divine love demands a return? No, he says "we ought to love *one another*." Likewise St. Paul hardly ever mentions our love for God. His entire stress is on God's love for us in Christ Jesus and our subsequent love for one another which ought to be the fruit of God's love for us.

Why is religious love not tit for tat? One reason is that even on the human level, we have a natural aversion to measuring whether we have adequately returned love and whether others have sufficiently returned our love. And it is our experience that when we fall in love with a certain person, we very soon find ourselves more benevolent and kind to others as well.

But there is a more profound reason on the theological level why we do not "return" God's love in the ordinary sense. God's love for us is a double gift. We are not only given God's Word as a concrete object of our love, but we are also given the very love with which we love. No human can do that for another human. Still less could anyone return that to God. The only appropriate response to the gift of *being in love*—which is a gift of God's own self to us within us—is to direct our love *with* God to everything that God loves.

Thus faith always leads to charity. And that charity has to be as concrete and actively involved in the world as God's perfect Word was when he walked the roads of Palestine.

Response to Question 5

A spiritual director has two tasks: one is psychological and the other is theological. The psychological task is to determine just what Tim's experience is. He needs to acknowledge the possibly suppressed feelings and hopes associated with his religious experience and to understand how these function in his life. He needs to relate this experience to other known experiences in his life with a view to finding any pattern that may be emerging.

The theological task is first of all to determine whether the experience is consistent with transcendent love in Tim's life as he knows it. This is a matter of "tasting" to see if it has the flavor of other religious experience, "harmonizing" with the melody, so to speak, to see if harmonies can be made. Then Tim must be helped to act responsibly with what he finds. If the experience seems consistent with the movements of God's Spirit in his life, then he should plan to cooperate with the movement in practical terms; if inconsistent, then to ignore it.

On rare occasions a person can experience the movement of God's love so purely that no testing at all is needed. The "taste" is so right, and the "harmony" so beautiful that questions do not arise at all. It is as if our entire capacity to ask questions were suddenly put at rest because, for a brief time, we welcome the One in whom all answers will be found. Here the director does no "testing" at all. The only task is to help Tim carry the movement into practice.

So the director should be aware of some psychology in order to help a directee understand *what* this or that experience entailed. But once the breadth of that experience is revealed, then both parties face the task of testing where the divine mystery is moving.

Once that is determined, of course, the director ought not to let the directee off the hook. The movements of transcendent love always have reference to this world. So the question of what fruits religious experience brings forth does arise. But not simply as a test of whether the experience came from God. Rather, the ultimate purpose of getting spiritual direction is that we might cooperate with God's action in the world. Love-inspired action binds us far more intimately with the end-point of our transcendent love than merely experiencing inner movements does.

CHAPTER FIVE: *Storytelling*

Response to Question 1

Before answering the question whether the Devil exists, we should answer the question whether the Devil is a completely evil person. And to answer this question we must distinguish whether we are taking the word *person* as an experiential term or as an explanatory term.

As an experiential term, *person* is used only to indicate something distinct from other "persons." We do not necessarily mean a person in the explanatory sense of a distinct center of consciousness—the sense in which human beings are persons. Thus, the "persons" of the Trinity are thus described not because they have distinct centers of consciousness (the explanatory meaning of "person") but because they are distinct and conscious. In fact God cannot have three distinct centers of consciousness. Each "person" of the Trinity is not a person in exactly the same sense that human beings are.

In the same fashion, the Devil can be referred to as a "person" as long as we avoid projecting all aspects of human personality on it indiscriminately. The chief difference is that human persons are self-transcendent. We *become* persons through self-transcendence. Whatever this "thing" is that we call a Devil, it is not acting anything like a real person when it does what the Devil's business is reported to be, that is, evil.

This explanation, deriving from the realm of philosophic interiority and expressed in the realm of theory, leaves a kind of symbolic blank in the realm of common sense. There appears to be a need to posit a "Devil" for the simple reason that we do not create the temptations that assail us. Instead, we experience a source other than themselves for the evil we are tempted to do. So we need a symbol for this source which can instill a healthy fear in us, a kind of symbol for felt expectations born of despair, presumption, and false hopes. We need to objectify this source in art, music, and language. From that point of view, I believe it is possible to use the metaphor of a Devil—partly in order to scare ourselves, and partly to avoid regarding our own persons as the ultimate source of the temptations we experience.

The one danger of such a metaphor is that it can project intelligence and reason and self-transcendence on precisely what lacks it. It makes evil a power in the exact same sense that God is a power. I have suggested in chapter 5 that the metaphor of a "Teller of Lies" might work well. Perhaps another practical strategy is to treat evil as terrifying because it *is* unintelligible. Use the metaphor of Darkness. Encourage people to walk in the light at all times. Warn them that the "force" of Darkness, once it has touched you, will never be comprehended by you. Even to study books on Devil worship and so on is flirting with Darkness.

Notice how this solution is an attempt to mediate between the realms of common sense and theory. It does so by turning to the operations of the subject by which one becomes a real person. It is a solution derived from the realm of interiority. This is a good example of how philosophic interiority can mediate between the realms of common sense and theory.

Response to Question 2

If the story were complete fiction, then the elements of mystery would lie more in how these particular people, with their particular hopes and fears, respond to the transcendent in the exorcism event performed by Jesus. The focus would be on how their inner experience itself is part of the mystery rather than on the outer phenomenon of an exorcism. The people were astonished. They began asking each other what it all meant. They were full of wonder. They were amazed at a teaching that was new—presumably: 'The time has come. The Kingdom of Heaven is close at hand. Repent and believe the Good News' (Mk 1:15). And they were also astonished at the authority behind Jesus' words. In other words, the emphasis would not be so much on Jesus' miraculous power to drive out an unclean spirit as on how Jesus spoke with authority and how the people spread his reputation around.

Hearers of this story would be moved to reflect not on the historical actuality of Jesus but on how people tend to react in situations where a wonderworker appears among faithful Jews. They might well deepen their sensibilities towards people with charismatic authority. They might see the world as far more mysterious than rational reflection would lead one to believe.

If, on the other hand, the story were presented as historiography, then the elements of mystery would appear elsewhere. By historiography I mean an accurate report of the facts plus a plausible explanation of the event within a larger series of events. The transcendent appears in historiography not in the inner consciousness of individuals but more in the developments which took place in our own past and perhaps still bear their effects on us today.

Hearers of this story who take it as good historiography might discover the transcendent in how the authority of our ancestor, Jesus, was a major cause in his being executed and yet grew all the stronger in his disciples. That does seem to be the case with Jesus, and it is difficult to explain why it often happens that the disciples of a defeated Messianic figure grow stronger thereafter.

Finally, if the story is told as an emblem, then the elements of mystery show up in yet another place. An emblem is a story of an actual event whose significance lies in the fact that it seems to happen again and again in the lives of people all through history. In this sense, an emblem is a history that does repeat itself. The transcendent appears in regular and unexplainable reappearance of mythic dramas, as though the stage directions remained the same and only the actors were different. Yet the actors in each performance are profoundly changed when they enact the drama.

Those who hear the story as an emblem perceive a direct connection to their own personal present. They feel the present authority of Jesus to drive out unclean spirits in their own lives. But even more, if they understand Mark's purpose in this pericope, they acknowledge the total authority of Jesus over absolutely everything in their own lives and in the lives of others.

So, is this story fiction, emblem, or history? Or is it some combination of several story-forms?

Few hear it as sheer fiction. It is difficult to deny the historical actuality of Jesus, and it is practically impossible to regard Mark as a fiction writer.

Many hear the story as history. That is, they take pride in the fact that this Jesus, who started Christianity and inspired the institutions to which they belong, was indeed a miracle-worker and a person of tremendous personal authority. They justifiably marvel at the fact that God entered history and astonished everyone in the person of Jesus. In this perspective, the story is like most of the Bible. It relates the string of events in which God stooped down and saved the humble and downtrodden.

Still, there is also something to be said for hearing the story as an emblem. Mark, as it happens, is not only narrating events which he believes to be actual, he is also arranging his materials in such a way as to encourage and support his audience, an audience which included Christians who were liable to be martyred in Rome. He is also setting the story within a theology of history that sees Satan as ruling the world before the coming of Christ. So the story takes on meaning as an interpretation of the hearer's own experience. Life in Christ is a struggle unto death between God and Satan. Anyone who dies in the struggle overcomes Satan in a manner exactly like Christ himself. And victory is assured because Christ has defeated Satan and has begun a brand-new epoch on the face of the earth.

Perhaps we could say that Mark wrote the narrative as a history, in continuity with the biblical tradition of proclaiming the deeds of God in history, but he was well aware of its emblematic value as well.

Response to Question 3

There are two meanings to the word *truth* which we often get confused. First there is the 'truth' reached by our judgment when we assent to some proposition as referring correctly to reality. For example, "It is true that she decided to get married."

Then there is the 'truth' which stands as an ideal we are always striving towards. "He walks in the truth." This is not a set of certitudes. Rather it is the attitude of utter honesty which a man or woman embraces for the purpose of being as fully human as possible. This is a much older meaning of the word. In Lonergan's terms, it amounts to obeying the transcendental precepts, Be attentive, Be intelligent, Be reasonable, Be responsible, Be in love. To have this attitude of 'truth' is to be authentic.

Notice that in the first definition, although it is our inner judgment which reaches a truth, it is to something other than our inner processes themselves to which our judgment refers. Like the pearl of great price, such a truth may be so valuable for our living that we sell everything we have to make this truth our own. Still, we never would have noticed the pearl in the first place unless we were already possessed of 'truth' in the second sense. That is, unless we were already obedient to the inner drive towards all that is more intelligible, more fully real, more appreciable and lovable, we would have been deaf, mute, and blind to any such 'truth' in the first sense.

Thus it is that the Gospels present many 'truths' in the first sense, but they depend on the prior, inner attitude of 'truth' in the reader's heart searching for all that is transcendent. Furthermore, the Gospels also present many such searchers; Nicodemus, the Woman at the Well, Matthew the tax-collector, Zachaeus in the tree, the Rich Young Man, the Prodigal Son, and so on. If you want the 'truth' of these stories, there is no need to verify that they 'really happened'. What counts, what obviously counted in the mind of the Scriptural writers, is that those who walk in the 'truth' welcome the Gospel.

It is quite natural for Christians today to think that nothing more is necessary than to welcome Jesus into our lives. And that means obeying the 'truths' of the Gospel and of the Church which authoritatively interprets that Gospel. It is natural because we have never been taught about inner space, never explored the movements that take us beyond ourselves. We are forgetful of the inner drive to wonder, even while we wonder about all kinds of things. We stand in awe as we gaze up at the stars, but only the profounder people also stand in awe at awe itself.

However, if any 'truth' (in the first sense) is primary in Christianity, it is that God gave the divine self in *two* gifts, not one—not only the gift of the eternal Word in our history but the gift of the eternal Spirit in our hearts as well.

So it is quite appropriate that God work through emblems because they point more readily than accurate histories to the inner work of the Spirit. This is not to deny the absolute worth of certitudes and factual accounts within the Gospel narratives. But in order to live out those certitudes, we depend on first walking the path of 'truth', which means living in the Spirit of God, in every aspect of our lives.

Response to Question 4

The full-blown theory of dialectical materialism was not worked out by Marx, but by his disciple, Frederick Engels. It can be briefly summarized like this: The world of nature and the world of history are both essentially contentious. In nature, the evolution of the cell, the transformations of matter and energy, and the evolution of biological species occur because of struggles between opposites. Likewise new social forms appear in history because of struggles between the oppressed and oppressors, just as molecules appear from atoms because of struggles between electrons and protons. All matter evolves by a fundamental dialectical process, and all reality, including social reality, is a manifestation of it.

Dialectical materialism has been criticized on many fronts, so we need not attempt that here. We only want to contrast it with Lonergan's view of the dialectical nature of history.

For Marx/Engels, the poles of the dialectic are social classes, some classes being dominant, some subservient. For Lonergan, the poles of the dialectic are authenticity and inauthenticity—where people obey the transcendental precepts, social progress results; where they disobey them, social decline results.

Furthermore, the Marxist dialectic is ultimately determinist, although Marx and Engels believed that a revolutionary "praxis" was necessary to accelerate the evolutionary process towards its inevitable end. Lonergan, on the other hand, sees the dialectic of authenticity and inauthenticity as open; there is no telling ahead of time what history must eventually be. The only "praxis" that will promote human liberation is obedience within.

Finally, the Marxist view of history considers the human person to have been good-willed, but unenlightened; so all that was needed for a permanent liberation was the correct view of history. Lonergan follows the classical Christian belief that the human person is not always good-willed, not always enlightened, so that both a healing of sin and an enlightenment of mind is needed, and will continue to be needed because of the biases to which human consciousness is permanently prone by nature (neurosis, egoism, group-centeredness, and suspicion of the long-range view).

Let us now compare this view to the Manichaean. By the way, although few people talk about "Manichaeanism" nowadays, many people view the struggle for moral living to be such a warfare between the powers of good and the powers of evil. And evidence abounds in our history that "God" is not very strong against "Evil." The forces of evil easily take on the same emblematic character as the forces of good.

224

Were we talking about history only from the point of view of emblems, then such terms as "forces of evil" would indeed be useful because they incite the affectivity and rouse the imagination. But Lonergan's dialectical view of history is not emblematic. It is meant to ground both speculative history and critical historiography. That is, it articulates an intelligibility intrinsic to historical process and it gives historians a question-raising structure for investigating historical periods.

On this showing, the "forces of evil" have no metaphysical reality in themselves. Basic evil is a *failure* in what ought to be, a deliberate suppression of attention, or intelligence, or reason, or responsibility, or love. From such basic "failures" there follow the absurd situations that resist further attention, intelligence, reason, responsibility, and love, even when these are not suppressed. Such is the nature of "structural evil."

Finally, we should add that both basic evil and the structural evil which results from it are to be distinguished from the "evils" inherent in a world of emergent probability. In other words, there are accidents and blind alleys in both nature and history that do not result from deliberate suppression of transcendental precepts; they are an intelligible component of the ongoing process of learning and of reacting to the unforeseen.

Response to Question 5

To understand Progress and Community as *emblems*, a bit of *history* might be helpful here.

Hegel, with his view that history is being guided by a Cunning of Reason *above* history, set the stage for the rising hope that somehow things are taking care of themselves, in spite of how badly we humans do. But Auguste Comte may be called the father of the modern ideal of Progress because he raised it to the level of science, understood in its modern, empirical sense. 'Automatic progress' became the hope of those who thought modern science, once it understood the "laws" of history, could cooperate with it much more effectively. Marx, far more aware of the dialectical workings among human institutions, also expected a kind of automatic progress, but one precipitated by social revolution rather than by scientific guidance. Spencer too, the originator of what we call "social Darwinism," expected automatic progress, but more along the lines of "survival of the fittest."

We must realize that what these thinkers actually said and what commonsense understanding heard are two different things. Commonsense expections are always emblematic, never historical. So the average devotee of the achievements of science now had confidence that such a hope was also founded in the thoughts of philosophers. Optimism reigned around the turn of the century, until, of course, two world wars made most people think again.

As these hopes were being shaken, another movement was taking place among novelists, dramatists, social scientists, philosophers, and theologians. They began to realize that the small, local community which mediated between the individual and society at large was becoming functionally irrelevant. Family ties and clan loyalties were breaking down as the "intermediate community" began to disappear from the face of the earth. In the West, bureaucracy gained the power and family units became isolated from one another as the need to find work split up ethnic groups. In the East, oligarchies wielded the power and the clan expanded into "the masses" who were perhaps affectively bonded but politically impotent. It was a significant loss of a valuable reality: a middle-level social body which was both affectively strong and capable of wielding political and technological power.

So, as the guardians of our cultural riches decried the loss of community, commonsense understanding again perceived Community emblematically. That is, not as a sociologically precise analysis or a properly historical critique, but as an amorphous symbol of nearly everything we lost in the good old days.

As we have suggested, the *emblems* of Progress and Community are antithetical. But this is largely because they each connote ideals far more imaginary than a solid understanding of human nature warrants. So we turn to philosophic interiority, as Lonergan has done, to ground a more realistic emblem of human hopes.

Community is the achievement of common meaning; that is, of common experience, common understanding, common judgment, common responsibility, and common love. These refer to activities that go on at the five levels of consciousness of all humans. Notice that they do not say "common sights, common concepts, common truths, common behavior, and common care-taking." These are static notions, too

226

easily disconnected from their roots in self-transcendence, while community is a changing reality, and essentially a matter of inner obedience. So we should avoid any emblem of community which does not involve the struggle for authenticity and self-transcendence.

Progress can be defined heuristically as whatever results from authenticity. That is, where people obey the transcendental precepts within, there will result (in the long run), increasing intelligibility in the social order, growing awareness of what we know and what we need to learn, more effective mastery over the problems of nature and human bias that keep recurring, and above all that, holding it together, the garment of love.

So community and progress are the same thing, in principle, provided we keep in mind that being a person in community means struggling against bias and depending on the faith, charity, and hope that flow from transcendent love.

What emblem might represent our hopes? There are many possible ones, and only history will test them adequately. I suggest that at least the Christian churches speak of history as a *Dialogue* between God and humanity. Or, when speaking to the secular world, to speak of the Dialogue each person has with the longing of his or her heart, which is the same thing as transcendent love. Such an emblem has the advantage of being easily verifiable: doesn't everyone hold inner dialogue with themselves? It also has the capacity for representing the most profound Christian doctrines of God's Covenant and of the workings of God's "Word" and "Spirit" in our history.

Bibliography

The following is a short listing of Lonergan's five main works. *Insight* and *Method in Theology* give his cognitional theory, epistemology, metaphysics, and method. (*Understanding and Being* gives a shorter and somewhat easier entrance into the material found in *Insight*.) The three "Collections" contain most of his published articles and range across a variety of fields.

Insight: A Study of Human Understanding. San Francisco: Harper and Row Publishers, 1958 (1957). (*Understanding and Being: An Introduction and Companion to 'Insight'*. Elizabeth A. Morelli and Mark D. Morelli [eds.].Toronto: Edwin Mellen Press, 1980. [This is a transcript of ten lectures Lonergan gave on *Insight*.])

Method in Theology. London: Darton, Longman and Todd, 1972.

Collection: Papers by Bernard Lonergan, SJ. Frederick E. Crowe (ed.). Montreal: Palm Publishers, 1967.
Contents:
"Finality, Love, Marriage" (1943)
"On God and Secondary Causes" (1946)
"The Natural Desire to See God" (1949)
"Theology and Understanding" (1954)
"Isomorphism of Thomist and Scientific Thought" (1955)
"Insight: Preface to a Discussion" (1958)
"Christ as Subject: A Reply" (1959)
"Openness and Religious Experience" (1960)
"Metaphysics as Horizon" (1963)
"Cognitional Structure" (1964)
"Existenz and Aggiornamento" (1964)
"Dimensions of Meaning" (1965)

A Second Collection: Papers by Bernard Lonergan, SJ. W.F.J. Ryan and B.J. Tyrrell (eds.). London: Darton, Longman and Todd, 1974.
Contents:
"The Transition from a Classicist World View to Historical Mindedness" (1966)

"The Dehellenization of Dogma" (1967)
"Theories of Inquiry: Responses to a Symposium" (1967)
"The Future of Thomism" (1968)
"Theology in Its New Context" (1968)
"The Subject" (1968)
"Belief: Today's Issue" (1968)
"The Natural Knowledge of God" (1968)
"The Absence of God in Modern Culture" (1969)
"Theology and Man's Future" (1969)
"The Future of Christianity" (1969)
"Philosophy and Theology" (1970)
"An Interview with Fr. Bernard Lonergan, SJ" (1971)
"Revolution in Catholic Theology" (1972)
"The Origins of Christian Realism" (1972)
"Insight Revisited" (1972)

A Third Collection: Papers by Bernard Lonergan, SJ. Frederick E. Crowe, (ed.). New York: Paulist Press, 1985.

Contents:
"Dialectic of Authority" (1974)
"Method: Trend and Variations" (1974)
"Mission and the Spirit" (1974)
"Aquinas Today: Tradition and Innovation" (1978)
"Prolegomena to the Study of the Emerging Religious Consciousness of Our Time" (1980)
"Christology Today: Methodological Reflections" " (1976)
"Healing and Creating in History" (1980)
"Religious Experience" (1976)
"Religious Knowledge" (1976)
"Ongoing Genesis of Methods" (1976)
"Natural Right and Historical Mindedness" (1977)
"Theology and Praxis" (1977)
"A Post-Hegelian Philosophy of Religion" (1980)
"Pope John's Intention" (1981)
"Unity and Plurality: The Coherence of Christian Truth" (1981)

For an entertaining book of dialogues between Bernard Lonergan and various interviewers, see *Caring About Meaning: Patterns in the Life of Bernard Lonergan.* Montreal: Thomas More Institute Papers, 1982.

I recommend a short, simplified book on prayer which I have written from these perspectives: *We Cannot Find Words: Foundations of Prayer* (New Jersey: Dimension Books, 1981). I must also recommend William Johnston, *The Inner Eye of Love* (San Francisco: Harper and Row, 1978), and Robert Doran, "Jungian Psychology and Christian Spirituality: I" in *Review for Religious* 38 (1979/4), 497–510.

To keep up with the latest in Lonergan studies, see *Method: Journal of Lonergan Studies.* Los Angeles: Loyola Marymount University.